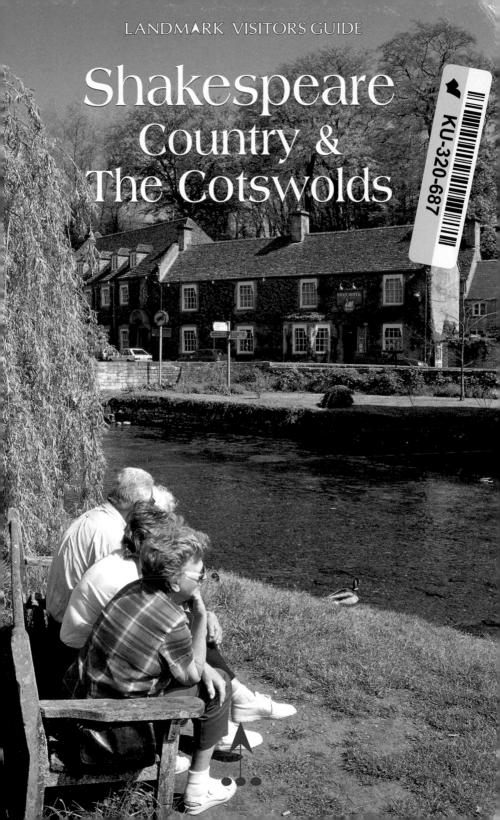

Shakespeare
Country &
The Cotswolds

KU-320-687

CONTENTS

THE SOUTHWOLDS 158

THE SOUTHWOLDS
AROUND BATH 174

FACTFILE

• FEATURE BOXES •

• MAPS •

Introduction

The Cotswolds and Shakespeare. There could hardly be a better definition of England. On the one hand, an area whose villages of stone, grouped around a green or beside a clear stream, lie in the folds of green and rolling countryside. On the other hand, the playright whose work has defined literature in the English language for centuries —the most famous writer in the world and, many would argue, the greatest of all writers.

This book explores Shakespeare's Warwickshire, seeking out the places he lived in and knew — lovely half-timbered cottages, some thatched, in the best tradition of Englishness. It also visits Warwick itself, one of England's finest towns and home of a castle which ranks with the best in the country. Warwick Castle was visited by many of the kings whose lives Shakespeare explored in some of the best of his plays.

The book then takes the visitor the few kilometres southwards to the Cotswolds, historically one of England's most important areas, and certainly its most distinctive. Here the cottages of Warwickshire are replaced by houses of Cotswold stone, roofed by the same stone split to form a rugged tile. The Cotswold trade provided the wealth for the area's grand houses and for its fine churches but, ironically, it was the trade's collapse that lead to the survival of the villages and towns, leaving them trapped many hundreds of years ago. This lack of development brought problems for the village and townsfolk, but for today's visitor it brings only delight — a single step into a Cotswold village can be a step of several centuries back in time.

THE COTSWOLDS

Maps of the area east of the River Severn often show the uplands as the Cotswold Hills. This is not strictly true, as there are no hills. The true name is The Cotswolds, which not only drops the offending word, but also accurately describes the area, the word wold being old English for 'an upland common'.

The Cotswolds are, geologically, a limestone mass, but not the Carboniferous Limestone which dissolves so easily in water, forming the gorges and caves of the nearby Mendips. Cotswold limestone is Oolitic, which means 'egg-stone' in Greek, and is representative of the stone: a fish roe-like mass of small granules. Since such limestones are laid down beneath sea, there is also a large number of fossils in the rock. This, together with the relative softness of the rock, allows the fossils to be easily extracted, and makes the exposures of the rock happy hunting grounds for the fossil-hunter. The most accessible areas are Cleeve Hill, on the side of the A46, and Leckhampton Hill.

The limestone mass has been split by river valleys, the water cutting the valleys rather than dissolving them, and this gives the appearance of hills; as does the collection of 'outliers' to the west of the main rock mass. The geography of the area is typically limestone — the scarp slope, or escarpment, produced by erosion on one side (here, the west) and a long shallow slope, the dip, on the other. The formation of a scarp slope by erosion frequently leaves behind outliers which are lumps of harder, less easily weathered, rock. The most striking is Bredon Hill, but other smaller masses are Churchdown and Robinswood Hill near Gloucester. Further south, the effect can be seen quite strikingly near Dursley, where, to the north, Cam Peak and Cam Long Down are 'recently' created outliers, while to the south Stinchcombe Hill has been narrowed to only a few metres at a point some 800m back from the main scarp slope.

The rock, at least the so-called 'freestone', has long been a source of considerable wealth for the area. When newly quarried, it is soft and can be cut readily with a saw, but on exposure to the air it hardens. It therefore has great advantages as a building stone, and was extensively used in the Middle Ages, for example in St Paul's Cathedral. As the stone split easily it produced roof tiles. The splitting was mainly produced by natural causes, the stone being stored wet by laying wet sacks over it. When the winter frosts came, it was exposed and the water froze in the cracks. Thawing later caused the rock to shatter, and as the cracks were usually even and parallel, slates were formed. They were very thick, however, and a roof required the support of huge oak beams; trade rapidly diminished when Welsh slates became readily available in the nineteenth century. Today the production of Cotswold building stone is on a much reduced scale. But its variety of colour, from golden-brown to pale grey, still makes it attractive where price is not the dominant factor.

But if 'wold' is easily defined, the derivation of 'Cot' is more difficult. Some authorities believe it may derive from the word for a sheep enclosure, and that is certainly appropriate in view of the medieval usage of the wolds. Others dispute this, pointing out that in earlier times the name was used only for a very tiny portion of what is now the Cotswolds. They contend that the name derives from Cod, pronounced 'code', a Saxon leader who farmed around the headwaters of the Windrush some 1,200 or more years ago. The name Cotswold would then be 'Cod's high land', and nearby Cutsdean would derive its name from the same root. If the latter derivation is correct, it explains why the name was at first applied only to the area around the source of the Windrush, reaching the Stroud valley by the late nineteenth century, and extending to cover the geologically and geographically similar areas south to Bath only in very recent times. It would also appeal to the romantic, for the Windrush is the most essentially Cotswold of all the rivers that split the wolds.

By the time of Cod, if we accept the fact of his existence, the area was already steeped in history. The earliest inhabitants were early Stone Age hunters following the animals in the forests that grew here after the last Ice Age. These early forests of pine and birch gave way later to oak, elm and beech. The beeches, now such a spectacular feature of the central area of the region, were crucially important to Neolithic, or New Stone Age, man, the first to settle in the area, for it was on the beech mast that the Neolithic farmer's pigs fed. The farmers also cleared the forest and cultivated the fertile wold soil, and it was they who left the first permanent memorial to man's involvement in the area — the long barrows. Such is the importance of the area's barrows — over 100 of them — that they form a specific class — the Severn-Cotswold group. Perhaps the most interesting feature of the barrows, which are actually burial chambers, is that although they are basically chambers of stone slabs, covered with earth,

Introduction

they usually have a doorway flanked by horns of dry-stone walling. There is a noticeable continuity, over 4,000-5,000 years, between this work and modern stone-walling.

The defensive advantages of the area, with its many promontories, were realised by the Iron Age people. They built a great number of hillforts along the Cotswold edge. One of the best, in terms of remains, is at Little Sodbury, although the extensive excavations at Crickley Hill have made it the best understood. The biggest is at Minchinhampton, on the edge of the Stroud valley. Here the remnants of the Iron Age tribesmen, fleeing north from the invading Romans, made a last stand, and were annihilated. It is easy to regard the coming of Rome as the march of civilisation over a few pagan savages, but the Birdlip mirror, now in Gloucester Museum, shows that the Iron Age tribes of the Cotswolds included skilled craftsmen, and were undoubtedly highly civilised.

The fine remains at Cirencester and Bath, and at the villas at Chedworth and Woodchester, show how much the Romans liked the area. Bath was, of course, tailor-made for a people whose social life revolved around bathing, but the main reason for the area's importance was, again, strategic. The high wold-land was easily defended, particularly on its western (the most vulnerable) flank, and many important highways were built across it — the Foss Way, Ermin Street, Akeman Street and others. Its importance was later recognised by the Saxons, reaching the Cotswolds around AD600, after a decisive battle at Dyrham. Gloucester and Winchcombe now became very important, standing

on the Mercia-Wessex border, and the Cotswolds were the high level route between these two strong, and occasionally hostile, kingdoms. Such was the area's importance, in fact, that Gloucester could well have become the capital of England, had not the Normans arrived and transferred central power to London and the south-east.

The number and wealth of the abbeys and churches show the continued importance of the area, but 200 years later that importance increased, again for a geographical reason. On the wolds a local breed of sheep — known as the Cotswold Lion — fared very well, producing a 28lb-fleece. The rivers, in their steep valleys, provided power for mills, and large deposits of fuller's earth (used to clean the wool) fulfilled the basic needs of cloth-making.

At first the important item was the fleece itself, which was exported raw to continental Europe. There its full importance was realised, the Duke of Burgundy instituting the Order of the Golden Fleece. Soon however, Edward III 'began to grow sensible of the great gain the Netherlands got by our English wool'. 'Golden Fleece' was indeed a true description — the fleece was English, the gold was Europe's. So Flemish weavers were brought to England to start a woollen industry. In a few years it dominated the English economy, being by far the largest single item. The Cotswolds produced more than half the cloth; every other worker in the area was involved in the industry in some way. The area had over 500,000 sheep and the shepherds were very important. They received a bowl of whey daily in summer, the ewes' milk on Sundays,

Holy Trinity Chapel from across the River Avon

Above: Warwick Castle

Right: Castle Combe

Below: Shakespeare's Birthplace, Stratford

a lamb at weaning, and a fleece at shearing.

The shepherds were important, but it was the merchants who were rich, some almost beyond our comprehension, even lending money to the king, as they had more of it than the Exchequer. They built fine houses, but their chief method of spending was the endowment of churches — the wool churches. All over the Cotswolds fine buildings were erected and stocked with treasures, and then with the tombs of the merchants themselves. No visit to the area is complete without a pilgrimage to the churches of Cirencester, Northleach and Chipping Campden. But many others are minor treasure houses, and the inquisitive visitor will be well rewarded. The merchants knew where the prime source of their income was — one merchant's house being inscribed:

I praise God and ever shall
It is the sheep hath paid for it all

The Government was well aware of this wealth: the Lord Chancellor still sits on a woolsack in the House of Lords.

The trade lasted several centuries, but when it ended the devastation was appalling. Whole families starved to death; others survived long enough to move out of the area; the poverty was awful. Ironically it was this poverty that made the Cotswolds a tourist area. The lack of development in the towns and villages after the seventeenth and eighteenth centuries meant that they were not modernised in any way, and rows of beautiful, old buildings can still be seen in, for example, Chipping Campden High Street.

Lately the region has been designated an Area of Outstanding Natural Beauty, shortened to AONB for the remainder of this book, and it is that area which forms the basis of this section of the book, though certain places outside the 'official' area are included where they are of significant interest.

The visitor to the Cotswolds need never be short of something to do. In good weather he or she may follow rivers, explore villages and visit viewpoints, and if it rains, the interest of all members of the family may be kept by visits to buildings and museums. Neither is it all food for the mind, as a tourist information sheet 'Eating out in the Cotswolds' mentions some excellent restaurants.

The Cotswolds are about people and buildings, and differ in that respect from other tourist areas, notably the mountainous National Parks. Many of the walks described in this book are centred around villages. A newcomer to the area, more used to the empty silence of the hills, will find that these suggested walks, like the Cotswolds themselves, are most rewarding.

Walking in the Cotswolds

T he walks suggested in the text are not intended to be field-by-field guides, but general indications of worthwhile excursions so that walkers can devise their own detailed route. It is assumed that the relevant 1:50,000 series OS maps are used.

In addition the interested visitor would find it worthwhile to obtain the Gloucestershire Ramblers' Association's maps on the public rights-of-way in the county; they cover the greater part of the Cotswold area. It must be recognised that there is little common land in the area, and that the walks follow rights-of-way across private farm land. The Cotswolds are not mountainous, but may still spring the odd surprise on the walkers, so it is wise to be prepared.

Selected Walks

In addition to the walks covered in the text, at the end of most chapters the author has included his personal selection of walks in that particular area. These are a small number of relatively short – half day or long half day – walks that explore the range of scenery and features offered by each chapter. The walks are classified as moderate (short and/or level); moderate/strenuous (longer and/or with section(s) of uphill walking); or strenuous (long and/or significant section(s) of uphill walking). No times are given for the walks as these are dependent upon the walkers, stops for picnics and sightseeing, etc.

The Cotswolds is not a wild area in which specialised equipment is required. Nonetheless some of the routes, particularly the high wold walks, are weather-swept, and it is advisable to be prepared for wet and windy weather. The recommended maps are all from the Ordnance Survey 1:50,000 Landranger Series.

Scenic Car Drives

These routes seek country lanes rather than main roads so as to make the most of the scenery. Particular sites of interest on route are noted.

Short Cycle Rides

These routes are about 15 miles in length and seek level ground unless climbs are unavoidable. The routes have been chosen to pass refreshment stops at regular intervals.

Shakespeare Country

W arwickshire claims (quite rightly) to be Shakespeare's country, but to cover the whole country would be to cast the net too wide. Strictly, Shakespeare Country means Stratford-upon-Avon, as none of the sites associated with the great man lie more than a few Kilometres from the town. Having said that, few visitors to Stratford will miss the opportunity of visiting Warwick, a fine town with one of the most complete medieval castles in England; the romantic ruins of Kenilworth; or some of the interesting visitor sites along the way.

WILLIAM SHAKESPEARE, PLAYWRIGHT AND POET

William Shakespeare was born on 23 April 1564. That 23 April is St George's Day, the festival day of England's patron saint, seems too good to be true, and it seems almost churlish to note that the birthday is actually a guess - albeit a very good guess. All that is known with certainty is that the baptism register of Holy Trinity Church, Stratford, records that on 26 April, Gulielmus, filius Johannes Shakspere – William, son of John Shakespeare – was baptised.

John Shakespeare was a glover and seller of skins from Snitterfield, a village a short distance to the north of Stratford, who had moved to Stratford. The earliest record of John is in 1552 when he was fined for making a dung heap in the street. The incident shows that John was a Stratford householder, and therefore that he was already prosperous. What it does not necessarily show was that John was a man of few manners. Mid-sixteenth century England had no sewage or refuse disposal systems, and the offence was less significant than it implies. By 1557 John Shakespeare was a prominent member of the town and already holding the minor, but presumably very agreeable, office of ale taster. In that year he married **Mary Arden**, one of eight children of Robert Arden, a prosperous farmer from Wilmcote, to the north-west of Stratford. The couple set up home in Henley Street, Stratford, in a substantial house that is an indication of just how prosperous John Shakespeare was. In 1561, John was appointed Chamberlain of Stratford, a post he also held in 1562. In 1565 he was made an Alderman of the town, and in 1568 he was appointed Bailiff (an office that is now equivalent to Mayor).

William was the third child, but first son, of this prosperous couple. John and Mary were to have five more children, though only six of their eight offspring lived past infancy. Of William's childhood nothing is known, though it is assumed that because of his father's wealth and position in the town he would have attended the Grammar School. The school's educational grounding can also be detected in his writing.

William next appears in the historical record in late 1582 when he married **Anne Hathaway** of Shottery, then a small village to the west of Stratford, but now almost a suburb of the town. At the time William was 18, while Anne was 26. She was the daughter of Richard Hathaway who, like William's grandfather Arden, was a prosperous farmer. She was also pregnant, and on 26 May 1583 she gave birth to a daughter, Susanna. Two years later, Anne gave birth to twins, Hamnet, a boy and Judith, a girl. Shortly after this William left Stratford for London. It is now agreed by scholars that William left in about 1587, though there is no record of him in London (or anywhere else for that matter) until 1592. There is a local legend that William left Stratford in a hurry to avoid prosecution for poaching a deer from the park of Sir Thomas

Lucy at Charlecote, to the east of Stratford, but it is more likely that the move was for more pressing domestic reasons. William had a wife and three children to support, all of them living in the Henley Street house, and his father's financial position was declining, though the cause of this is not known with certainty. It is suggested that Shakespeare's enthusiasm for public office at the expense of his own business interests led to the decline. If that is the case, William certainly learnt from his father's experience, putting his own financial security first at all times in his subsequent career, though it is also likely that William was a shrewder businessman than his father.

The years immediately before Shakespeare's departure had seen an upsurge in public enthusiasm for the theatre, with companies of actors touring the country and putting on plays in places such as Stratford. It is known that in 1587 five such companies visited the town, and it has been suggested that William joined one of these, determined to try his hand at acting and writing.

The London of the 1590s was, artistically, a remarkable place. The Spanish Armada had recently been defeated and Elizabethan England was at its most optimistic. It was also a rich place and, as with Renaissance Florence, there were patrons seeking artists to sponsor. But unlike Florence, the patrons sought writers rather than painters and sculptors. Johnson, Bacon, Spenser and, perhaps finest of all, Marlowe were already working in London when Shakespeare arrived. But he was not overawed: secure in his abilities, William began to write. Historians now agree that Henry VI (all parts),

Richard III and Titus Andronicus were all produced in the period before 1592. In 1593 he wrote Venus and Adonis and in 1594 The Rape of Lucrece, these long poems gaining him immediate recognition and the sponsorship of **Henry Wriothesley, the Earl of Southampton.**

Southampton's sponsorship and the success of the acting company to which Shakespeare belonged (called Lord Strange's Men until the death of Strange in 1594, then called the Lord Chamberlain's Men until James I acceded to the throne in 1603 after the death of Elizabeth I: the company was then called the King's Men) gave him financial security. Henry VI was first performed in March 1592 at the Rose Theatre. Later plays were performed there, and at the other London theatres until, in 1598, Shakespeare bought a 10% share in the Globe Theatre. Although William's artistic life was blossoming and he was becoming wealthy, there was also tragedy. In 1596 his son Hamnet died. In that year he wrote King John, and in Scene IV (Constance's speech, from line 93) is all the sadness of a grieving father.

It is clear that, despite his success in London, William remained a Stratford man, returning often to see his parents, Anne and the children. In 1596 he acquired a coat-of-arms from the college of Heralds, a gift, it seems, for his father who had tried but failed to do the same in 1576. Then, in 1597 he bought **New Place**, a substantial Stratford house. Over the next ten years he divided his time between Stratford and London, his purchases of land in both towns implying that his writing had made him wealthy. It had also bought him fame: with the death of Marlowe in

1593 (killed in a drunken brawl) he was recognised as the foremost writer of his age. In 1601 his father died, followed by his mother in 1608, just a year after his daughter Susanna had married Dr John Hall. Soon after, in 1610, Shakespeare returned to Stratford for good, living at New Place. By then his best writing was completed. He wrote The Tempest in 1611 and his last work, Henry VIII, was written in 1612, though most experts now agree that Shakespeare's input to this last play was limited, the major hand being that of John Fletcher. Ironically, it was during a production of the play (at first called All is True) in June 1613 that a cannon shot (part of the dramatic effects) ignited the thatched roof of the Globe. The theatre burned to the ground.

In early 1616, William made his will, leaving his fortune to Susanna and her husband. There is no mention of his wife Anne, though it seems implicit that she should be cared for by Dr Hall and Susanna. History records almost nothing of Anne and, though William remained loyal to her, he is known to have been unfaithful many times. At the end he, too, leaves her out of the historical record. Nothing more is heard of her until her death in 1623.

In April 1616 Ben Johnson and Michael Drayton visited Shakespeare at New Place. There was a 'merry meeting' after which William 'died of a feavour there contracted'. He died on St George's Day, his 52nd birthday, the register of Holy Trinity Church recording the burial, on 25 April, of Will Shakspere gent.

Susanna Shakespeare and Dr John Hall had a daughter, Elizabeth, in 1608. Though she married twice, Elizabeth died childless. Judith Shakespeare had an unhappy marriage to Thomas Quincy. They had three sons, all of whom died relatively young, and childless. William's line therefore ended with Elizabeth when she died in 1670.

Over the years there have been many attempts to prove that William Shakespeare did not write the works attributed to him. Some even suggested that his lack of education and knowledge of historical events meant that he could not have written them. A variety of other names were put forward as the 'real' Shakespeare. In 1909 Dr Orville Owen of Detroit even built a coffer dam in the River Wye near Chepstow to find clues he had deduced lay buried there which proved, he claimed, that Francis Bacon had written the works. He went home empty handed. In one sense it does not matter who wrote the plays: the wonder of the vocabulary and imagery now stand independent of their author. But the better evidence points to the Stratford glover's son.

SHAKESPEARE'S STRATFORD

Below the major sites associated with William Shakespeare are listed. They are also mentioned in the following section on Stratford, but are gathered together here for the convenience of those whose visit is a pilgrimage to the writer.

BIRTHPLACE

John Shakespeare's house in **Henley Street** was built in the late fifteenth or early sixteenth century, that is about 100 years before William's birth. It is a beautiful timber-framed house, the space between the oak beams being filled with wattle and daub. In Shakespeare's time the house would have been part of a continuous run of housing, but the buildings on either side were demolished in 1857 to reduce the risk of fire damage to the birthplace. A year later the house was restored to the form indicated in a drawing of 1769. The house is furnished in period style, in a fashion appropriate to John Shakespeare's standing in the community. The part of the house that formed John's offices is now a museum. As with the rest of the house, the room in which William was born has period, not original, furniture.

Visitors to the house enter through the **Shakespeare Centre**, built in 1964 to commemorate the 400th anniversary of William's birth, and extended in 1981. The Centre has an exhibition on the writer, and a library and archive for the use of students from all nations.

The exit from the Birthplace site is through another house in Henley Street, now converted to a gift shop.

Opposite the Centre is **Shakespeare Bookshop** where the plays and poems are available as texts, videos or audios, together with study notes, criticisms, biographies and books on Tudor history.

NEW PLACE/NASH'S HOUSE

In 1540 Sir Hugh Clopton, a local man who had moved to London and become a rich merchant (and Lord Mayor), built a house across from the Guildhall and Guild Chapel which he had already paid to have refurbished. Clopton had to demolish an existing building, so his new house was called **New Place**. It was this house that Shakespeare bought in 1597 and where he died in 1616. The house was left to Dr John Hall and his wife Susanna, Shakespeare's eldest daughter. Following their deaths the house had many owners, passing eventually to Rev Francis Gastrell in the mid-eighteenth century. By then Shakespeare's reputation was such that the house attracted many visitors, much to Gastrell's annoyance. So many came to sit under Shakespeare's mulberry tree – where, reputedly, the poet had sat – that in 1756 Gastrell cut it down. The bitter confrontations which followed this vandalism culminated, in 1759, in Gastrell's demolition of the house. Such was the outrage at this that Gastrell was forced to leave Stratford.

Now all that remains of the house are the foundations and two wells, and contemporary drawings which suggest a splendid half-timbered building. The grounds are a recreation of a period Elizabethan garden. They are reached through Nash's House, the home of Thomas Nash and his wife, Elizabeth, daughter of John and Susanna Hall and grand-daughter of Shakespeare. Nash's House is furnished in period style and houses a museum of local history.

HALL'S CROFT

John Hall was born in 1575, the son of a Bedfordshire doctor. He studied at Queens' College, Cambridge, becoming a qualified physician in 1597. After spending several years abroad he settled in Stratford in 1600. He married Shakespeare's daughter Susanna in 1607. Their only daughter, Elizabeth, was born in 1608. The couple lived at Hall's Croft until 1616 when, following Shakespeare's death, they moved to

New Place, Stratford

New Place where, it is assumed, they cared for Anne, Shakespeare's widow, until her death in 1623. John Hall died in 1635, Susanna in 1649. All three lie beside William in Holy Trinity Church.

Hall's Croft is a beautiful half-timbered house furnished in the period style appropriate to the Halls' standing in the community. The spacious gardens include Dr Hall's herb garden where he grew the basic ingredients of his remedies. There is also an exhibition on the development of medicine during the medieval period, complete with some gruesome instruments. There is also a collection of apothecary jars and some of Dr Hall's original notes. Hall is a very interesting man, too often overlooked because of his Shakespeare connection. In his day he was renowned for his scurvy cure which was based on watercress, blackcurrants and other items rich in Vitamin C. Hall may not have understood why his potion worked, but it did. Today, we are inclined to think of scurvy as a sailor's disease, but in Shakespeare's time it effected townsfolk equally. The painting in the Croft, though of a Belgian family, gives an idea of how the Halls might have looked, and of their diet – meat and bread, very short of Vitamin C-rich foods.

Hall also made notes of his most difficult cases, probably with the intention of publishing them. They were published in 1657, some years after his death, and reveal some amazing treatments. He treated vertigo with a potion of white wine and peacock droppings, and drew out fever by placing the patient's feet in dead pigeons.

His case book includes his wife and daughter (Shakespeare's daughter and grand-daughter) but not William himself. Tantalisingly, only one of two volumes of case notes was published, the second having disappeared. Was the great man mentioned in that one?

ANNE HATHAWAY'S COTTAGE

This magnificent thatched cottage stands at Shottery, a short distance to the west of Stratford. Far from being a cottage, the building is the twelve-roomed house of a prosperous yeoman farmer, as Richard Hathaway, Anne's father, indeed was. It is estimated that Richard owned between 50 and 100 acres of land adjoining the cottage. The cottage was built in the fifteenth century with a cruck frame, with additions in sixteenth and seventeenth centuries in the traditional timber-frame/wattle and daub. The cottage is furnished in period style and includes some original pieces of furniture, one of which, the 'courting settle', a rather upright and uncomfortable wooden seat, may actually have been sat upon by Anne and William during the days before their marriage. The cottage's garden has been restored to the traditional style of Anne's time.

MARY ARDEN'S HOUSE

What was long thought to be the family home of Shakespear's mother stands at Wilmcote, to the north-west of Stratford. This superb early sixteenth century building, with a striking half-timbered frontage and delightful gabled dormer windows; was believed to reflect the prosperity of Mary's father, Robert Arden, a gentleman farmer. However recent evidence suggests that the family home was another, nearby building.

Robert Arden was buried in the churchyard at Aston Cantlow, a short distance west of Wilmcote, and it is thought likely that Mary Arden and John Shakespeare were married in the same church. Mary was youngest of Robert Arden's eight daughters, but inherited substantial property on his death.

Continuous occupation has meant that the house has been almost perfectly preserved. It is now furnished in period style. The farmhouse and its outbuildings were acquired by the Shakespeare Birthplace Trust in 1930: the Trust converted the outbuildings into a museum of Shakespeare's time, this being enlarged by the acquisition of Glebe Farm next door. **The whole now represents the Shakespeare Countryside Museum.** There is a dovecote with 657 nesting holes, a cider press and a collection of farming equipment/machinery illustrating the development of local farming. Glebe Farmhouse is furnished in early 1900s style, and has tableaux depicting life of the time. There are also tableaux illustrating the work of the blacksmith, cooper, wheelwright and other country craftsmen. The Museum also has a falconry with regular flight displays.

ROYAL SHAKESPEARE THEATRE

Following the celebrations to commemorate the 300th anniversary of Shakespeare's birth, in 1864, Charles Edward Flower, a local brewer, campaigned vigorously for the construction of a theatre at Stratford, claiming it was the only place where a memorial theatre could stand. Due almost entirely to his efforts, the first theatre was opened on 23 April 1879. A festival of Shakespeare's plays was held in the theatre annually, at first lasting a few weeks but ultimately extending for longer periods. The original theatre burnt down in 1926 and was replaced by the present buildings in 1932, a very radical design for its time. At first called the Shakespeare Memorial Theatre, it was renamed the Royal Shakespeare Theatre in 1961. Two other theatres have been constructed since, the **Other Place** in Southern Lane, a short distance to the west of the Royal, and the **Swan Theatre,** beside the Royal. The Swan, constructed in the form of a Jacobean playhouse, stages plays chiefly written by contemporaries of Shakespeare.

SHAKESPEARE MEMORIAL

In Bancroft Gardens, beside the River Avon, is Stratford's memorial to its famous son. A bronze statue of a seated Shakespeare surmounts a wide stone pillar on a square flower-bedded base, at the corners of which are bronze statues of Lady Macbeth, Prince Hal, Falstaff and Hamlet. The memorial was designed and erected by Lord Ronald Sutherland Gower in 1888.

HOLY TRINITY CHURCH

The church houses Shakespeare's grave, together with those of Anne Hathaway and his eldest daughter, Susanna, and her husband Dr John Hall. William's grave is inscribed:

Good Frend for Jesus sake forbeare
To digg the dust enclosed heare!
Blese be ye man yt spares thes stones
And curst be he yt moves my bones

Legend has it that the verse was actually penned by Shakespeare, leading to speculation that the grave contained evidence to prove that William was not (or, of course, was, depending upon the prejudice involved) the author of the plays. In reality it is more likely that William wished to avoid having his bones removed to the local charnel house when space was needed, as was the custom of the time.

The monument to Shakespeare was carved by Gerard Johnson, an Anglo-Flemish artist, within a few years of the poet's death. The bust appears to be a copy of the image on the First Folio of Shakespeare's plays published in 1623 (it is assumed that the drawing of William for the folio was made a few years before his death.) It is almost certainly a true likeness of Shakespeare, having been created while his wife Anne, his two daughters and many of his friends were still alive. But it is hardly great art: perhaps the best description was one that claimed it made Shakespeare look like a self-satisfied schoolmaster.

The church also houses the baptismal and burial records of Shakespeare, copies of these being displayed.

SHAKESPEARE'S BIRTHDAY CELEBRATIONS

Each year on, or close to, St George's Day (23 April) there is a celebration in Stratford, the highlight being a procession from the Birthplace to Holy Trinity Church, local and invited dignitaries carrying floral tributes to lay on Shakespeare's grave.

Opposite page: Ann Hathaway's Cottage, Stratford

STRATFORD-UPON-AVON

There is more to Stratford than Shakespeare, though you could be easily forgiven for finding that difficult to believe, especially when contemplating the fact that for every resident of the town, there are some 20 visitors during the year.

Although there is evidence for local settlements by the Romans (Fosse Way passes about 8km (5 miles) to the south-east) and the Saxons (the Saxon church at Wootton Wawen, to the north-west, is probably the oldest in Warwickshire) Stratford is essentially a medieval town. As a market town it was prosperous before Shakespeare's birth, the majority of its most historically interesting buildings dating from the early sixteenth century. It is fitting, therefore, to start a tour of Stratford from the medieval bridge that crosses the Avon at the eastern edge of the town.

There was probably a wooden bridge over the Avon here in the twelfth century, but in 1480, Sir Hugh Clopton (the builder of New Place, where Shakespeare died) paid for the construction of a stone bridge, a sturdy low bridge of 19 arches of which 14 still survive. During the Civil War two arches of the bridge were demolished to improve the town's defences. Apart from the major repair this required, the bridge remains as it was built over 500 years ago.

Close to the bridge's town end are the **Bancroft Gardens,** laid out on former common land, and now one of the town's most attractive features. The **Gower Memorial** stands here, and colourful narrowboats ply the canal basin and the river, taking passengers from the Bancroft quay. The canal was opened in 1816, chiefly for bringing coal to the town. At its height it served 14 wharfs, 11 of them for coal. Trade declined from the 1850s and the canal fell into disuse and disrepair. It was restored in the 1950s, re-opened by HM the Queen Mother in 1964 and is now one of Britain's most popular canals. Visitors can enjoy a narrow boat ride, but for the more energetic, skiffs are available for hire. Close to the memorial **Cox's Yard** is a refurbished timber yard with restaurant, tea rooms and pub, gift shop and art gallery. Here, too, is The Stratford Tales which explores the town's history with models and audio-visual displays.

At the southern tip of the Gardens a bridge to the right reaches an extension of the gardens and the starting point for **Grimm's Ghostly Tour of Stratford**, an acclaimed tour which promises an hour of fear for all the family as it explores the town's darker moments.

Alternatively from the tip of the gardens the old tramway bridge takes visitors across the river. The bridge was built in 1823 to take horse-drawn trams along a railway to Moreton-in-Marsh, a market town to the south, on the edge of the Cotswolds. Cross the bridge and walk along the riverbank for a good view of the Royal Shakespeare Theatre and, further on beyond the foot ferry, a wonderful view of Holy Trinity Church, its spire reflected in the water.

Cross the river using the ferry, a delightful barge that is hand-cranked across a chain slung below water between the two banks. Turn left along Southern Lane, passing Avonbank Gardens, on the left.

Within the Gardens is the **Stratford Brass Rubbing Centre** which has resin reproductions of some of England's finest memorial brasses. At the end of Southern Lane bear left to visit **Holy Trinity Church**. The church was begun in the twelfth century, but has additions in both the Decorated and Perpendicular styles of English Gothic. The elegant spire is eighteenth century, replacing an earlier wooden spire. Inside, in addition to the Shakespeare graves and memorial, is the excellent canopied tomb of Sir Hugh Clopton. Near Shakespeare's grave are copies of his baptism and burial records, and the font in which, it is believed, he was baptised. Look, too, for the fifteenth century misericords in the choir stalls.

From the church, take Old Town towards the town centre, passing Hall's Croft on the right. Turn right along Church Street. To the right is a beautiful range of half-timbered buildings. First are the Almshouses built by the town's **Guild of the Holy Cross** in the early fifteenth century. The Guild was an association of the leading members of the town - merchants, doctors, etc - founded in the mid-thirteenth century. It combined with the Guilds of Our Lady and St John the Baptist in 1403. Such associations were viewed with suspicion by Henry VIII and the Guild was suppressed and its property confiscated in 1547. However in 1553, after Henry's death, the property was restored. The Almshouses were built to house 24 old folk, and are still used by elderly Stratford residents. Note especially the chimneys: they were made very tall so that sparks from fires in the hearths at their bases could be taken well away from the original thatched roof.

Beside the Almshouses is the **Guildhall**, built in 1416. Its upper floor, the Over Hall, is the Grammar School where Shakespeare is thought to have been educated. Originally the upper floor was used by the Guild, but was taken over by the school when the Guild was suppressed and has remained part of the school ever since.

Beside the Guildhall is the **Guild Chapel**, rebuilt by Sir Hugh Clopton who added a tower and nave to an existing chapel. The chapel has some medieval wall paintings, including a Last Judgement on the chancel arch. The painting, which is poorly preserved, is partially obscured by the whitewashed arc above it. There is also a Dance of Death (in which skeletons lead figures – from the Pope to a farmer – to their doom) behind the oak panelling on the southern wall. Such paintings were executed to encourage (or warn) the congregation.

Cross Chapel Lane to reach New Place/Nash's House, continuing along Chapel Street. To the left as you cross is the **Falcon Hotel**, a fifteenth century half-timbered building. When Shakespeare lived at New Place he would have seen only two storeys, the third having been added in the seventeenth century. The hotel has had a licence for selling ale for over 500 years. Further on, to the right, is the magnificent **Shakespeare Hotel**, one of the most beautiful buildings in the town. The hotel's four northern gables existed in Shakespeare's time, the rest having been added after his death. Beside it is the Town Hall, a Palladian building built in 1767. In the next street to the right, Sheep Street, is Shrieves House, a particularly fine, late sixteenth century timber-framed house.

To the left now is **Harvard House**, rebuilt in 1586 as the home of Katherine Rogers. She married Robert Harvard of Southwark and their son, John, was the founder of Harvard University. In 1910 the house was given to the University by Edward Morris, a Chicago millionaire. It is administered for the University by the Shakespeare Birthplace Trust and houses some very rare items including the Neish Collection of pewter, with examples from Roman times through to the nineteenth century. Beside the House is the superb Garrick Inn, named for the famous actor, was built at the same time. Further on, on the corner of High Street and Bridge Street, is the house of Thomas Quincy and Judith Shakespeare.

At the roundabout, turn left along Wood Street, crossing into Greenhill Street to visit the **Teddy Bear Museum**, a collection of several hundred bears from all over the world and including some very old and very rare examples. Winnie the Pooh and Paddington are here too. The next road from the roundabout is Henley Street in which stands Shakespeare's Birthplace.

Turn right at the roundabout and walk down Bridge Street. To the right, at the bottom in Waterside, is the World of Shakespeare. Cross Bridgefoot to return to Clopton Bridge.

AN EXTENSION OF THE WALK

Two interesting sites can be reached by extending the town walk. Close to the bridge (follow the old tramway) is Europe's largest **Butterfly Farm**, when tropical butterflies are bred in a simulated rainforest. There

Right: *The Shakespeare Hotel, Stratford*

Below: *Spring in Bancroft Gardens, Stratford*

Below: *Enjoying a stroll along the banks of the River Avon in Stratford, Holy Trinity Church in the background*

Canal/Avon Lock, Stratford

are also insect colonies (stick insects, beetles, ants, bees etc), scorpions and spiders, some of the latter large enough to cause recurrent nightmares. It is a fascinating place.

Continuing along the old tramway, a walk of about 2½km (1½ miles) reaches the **Shire Horse Centre**, which has not only the horses of the name, but a pet's corner, rare breeds paddocks, an adventure playground and a giant slider. The site has a licensed restaurant and a tea garden, and there is a daily programme of events.

AROUND STRATFORD

To the east of Stratford, visitors can maintain the connection with Shakespeare by visiting **Charlecote Park**. The Lucy family have held the land here since the twelfth century, though the present mansion was built in the 1550s by Sir Thomas Lucy. Very little of that Elizabethan house remains, George Hammond Lucy almost entirely rebuilding it – but maintaining the Elizabethan style – in the nineteenth century. It is said that the plan of the house, an E, was in honour of Elizabeth I and it certainly is true that the Queen was entertained here by Sir Thomas in 1572. With its mix of red brick and grey stone, its curious semi-onion dome cupolas and tall chimneys, the mansion is a delightful building, especially when viewed from along the main drive. The house, which is elegantly furnished (mostly with the Victorian pieces of George Hammond Lucy) and has a good collection of paintings, is still occupied by the Lucy family, but is now owned by the National Trust. In addition to the house, visitors can

see the old brewery and the carriage and tack room, and enjoy a break in the Orangery coffee house/restaurant. The house stands in almost 250 acres of parkland landscaped by Capability Brown. Both house and park are the venue for a series of concerts held annually in late June.

William the Poacher

Charlecote Park is where William reputedly poached the deer that caused his hasty departure to London. The park has long been home to fallow and roe deer (and is now also home to a herd of Jacob sheep) and it is one of these that Shakespeare is said to have taken. One version of the story has him being taken before Sir Thomas Lucy, the bawling out he presumably received being the basis for the suggestion that Shakespeare caricatured Lucy as Justice Shallow in Henry IV (Part 2).

In the nearby **St Leonard's Church** are the tombs of several members of the Lucy family. That of Sir Thomas, with alabaster effigies of him and his wife, is particularly good. In the village of Hampton Lucy, to the north of the Park and named for the family, the church has beautiful stained-glass windows depicting the life of St Peter, to whom the church is dedicated.

Close to Charlecote, at **Wellesbourne Watermill** enjoy the noise and smells of a functioning stoneground flour mill. There is also a small exhibition of old craft tools and a pleasant wildflower garden. Flour milled on site can be bought, and there is a tea/lunch room in a restored nineteenth century barn.

To the south-west of the centre of Wellesbourne, on a 1939-45 wartime airfield, there is a museum housed in an original underground bunker. The museum has a collection of posters, ration books, gas masks etc, and a recreated RAF operations room. There is also a Vampire airframe.

WARWICK

Northwards from Wellesbourne along the A429 (or from Stratford along the A439) is Warwick, whose castle saw at first hand some of the events that form the basis of Shakespeare's 'King' series of plays. The town of Warwick was founded in 914 by Ethelfleda, one of the daughters of Alfred the Great, to defend the Avon valley and the local river crossing against Danes raiding from the north. The hill-top site was a perfect defensive position, the Saxon settlement being surrounded by a wall and ditch. Later the town's position on the Avon, and also on one of England's most important salt ways, running south-eastwards from Droitwich, ensured its prosperity. But in 1694, fire swept through the town razing its centre and almost completely destroying it. Just a few outlying houses remain of late seventeenth century Warwick. The centre was rebuilt in brilliant style, but by the late eighteenth century local prosperity had shifted a few kilometres east, to the spa town of Leamington. Warwick's relative stagnation meant little development or expansion: it may have been the unwelcome period for the inhabitants, but for

the visitor it means a near perfect eighteenth century town, ringed by some of the finest medieval buildings in the country.

To explore the town, start at the **Court House,** on the corner of Castle Street and Jury Street, which houses the Tourist Information Office. The House was built in 1724 and replaced a smaller building on the same site (which had been destroyed by the fire) which housed the Mayor, the town corporation and magistrates' court. The new building's style reflected the fresh wave of optimism in the town after the miseries of the fire. It is stone and four-square, a solid house, constructed to last, but its lines are softened by the Italianate Doric façade and the statue of Justice in her niche. The house is by Francis Smith, a local architect, the statue by Thomas Staynor. They provided what the corporation wanted, but at a cost well over budget, the Corporation's pride in their new building being tempered by a long series of court actions over the debt they had incurred. The Court House now houses, amongst other things, the Town Museum with changing exhibitions exploring the history of Warwick.

The **Mayor's Parlour,** with panelled walls and a decorated fireplace, is now the Tourist Information Office. In front of the fireplace is Oken's Coffer which, legend has it, was owned by Thomas Oken, a wealthy medieval merchant who was a major benefactor of the town. In it, the story maintains, he kept his silverware, cash and important documents. Above the Parlour is a splendid ballroom now used for social events, while in the old cellar kitchen is the **Warwickshire**

Yeomanry Museum with a collection of uniforms, medals and weaponry of the county's Mounted Volunteer Regiment, covering the period from 1764 to the present.

Just around the corner from the Court House, in Castle Street, is **Oken's House**, a beautiful late fifteenth century half-timbered house which, along with several other fine buildings nearby, escaped the fire of 1694. As the name implies, the house once belonged to Thomas Oken: indeed, needed only a ditch and rampart to complete, but there was a wall on either side of West Gate (sections of which still exist). The Gate is topped by a chapel, originally (like the Gate) eleventh century, but rebuilt around 1400.

Lord Leycester Hospital, beside the Gate, is the highlight of Warwick, a magnificent group of buildings erected in the fourteenth century by the town's Guild of St George. When, in 1545, the Guild realised they would be dissolved by Henry VIII, its members gave the buildings to the newly formed Corporation. The Corporation gave the buildings to Robert Dudley, Earl of Leicester, in 1571 to house the hospital he was endowing. Dudley, the favourite of Elizabeth I, founded the hospital (an almshouse rather than a hospital in today's sense) for 12 'brethren' and their wives, the brethren being old or disabled soldiers who had fought for him. There was also a master who looked after the buildings and the interests of the occupants. Today the buildings are still occupied by old soldiers. The occupied parts of the hospital are obviously not open to the public, but other parts are: the galleried courtyard, the Great Hall (where James I once dined), the Guildhall (where the early Guild met)

and the candle-lit chapel can all be viewed. There is also a fascinating museum exploring the history of the Queen's Own Hussars. The Master's Garden, in which an arch of the original chapel above West Gate has been erected, can also be visited.

From the hospital, turn left along Brook Street, then left again to reach the Market Place, dominated by the arcaded **Market Hall** which, together with some nearby timber-framed buildings, escaped the fire of 1694. The Hall was built in 1670, when the arcades would have been open. The upper floor, of the Hall has been the magistrates court and the town hall on occasions, but is now occupied by the **Warwickshire Museum** with exhibitions on the county's history, geology and wildlife. The museum includes the Warwick Bear, the symbol of the county, and the Sheldon Tapestry, a stitched map of the county.

Cross the Market Place beyond the Hall to reach Abbotsford, a fine early eighteenth century house, now a part of the County Offices. **Abbotsford** is linked to the newer Shire Hall by a glass 'bridge'. Go under this and bear right along Barrack Street, then turn right along Northgate, passing the old town jail to reach the original Shire Hall, a splendid red sandstone building. The jail, on the site of an even older jail, incorporates a seventeenth century dungeon. The rings in the wall by the jail were for ropes to restrain crowds at public executions. Continue along Northgate Street to reach **St Mary's Church**, its tower arched across the pavement.

The first church on the site was Norman, erected in 1123. This was rebuilt in the fourteenth century, but a further rebuild was necessary when

Warwick Castle

the fire of 1694 destroyed the tower, nave, aisles and transepts. The new church cost £12,000, Queen Anne donating £1,000, the town finding the rest. The town asked Sir Christopher Wren to design the new church, paying him a £10 fee (and £1 for his man), but then accepting another design by Sir William Wilson. The church tower dominates the Warwick skyline, and the church is imposing, but the real treasures are inside. In the chancel is the tomb of Thomas Beauchamp, Earl of Warwick, who died of Black Death in 1368. He captained the English army at the Battles of Crecy and Poitiers and is shown in a recumbent alabaster effigy, together with his wife whose hand he holds. The tomb chest is ringed by small mourners, a strangely exuberant crowd given the reason for their presence.

THE BEAUCHAMP CHAPEL

Good though the tomb of Sir Thomas Beauchamp is, it is overshadowed by another in the Beauchamp chapel. The chapel is itself a masterpiece. It was built in the fifteenth century and (obviously) survived the fire. It is thought to be one of the two finest examples of architecture of that period in Britain (the other being Henry VII's chapel in Westminster Abbey).

The chapel's centrepiece is the **tomb of Richard Beauchamp**, Earl of Warwick, who died in 1439. Beauchamp played a part in the events that led to the execution of Joan of Arc, and is portrayed in George Bernard Shaw's St Joan. In the chapel Beauchamp's gilded copper effigy lies on a table tomb, protected by gilded hoops. It is said

that, in his quest for the perfect memorial, Beauchamp left instructions that a surgeon should be employed to advise the sculptor on the form of the hands. The effigy is dressed in the best representation of fifteenth century armour to be found in Britain, and Richard's eyes gaze up at the portraits of God and the Virgin Mary on the chapel's roof, his hands, which had been clasped in prayer, opening in awe at the wondrous sight. The chapel also contains the tomb of Robert Dudley, Earl of Leicester, who died in 1588, and his wife, an ornate, (even ostentatious) tomb with painted effigies. The chapel also houses the tomb of Dudley's son, who died at the age of 3.

Finally in the church, in the south aisle there is a memorial to the poet **Walter Savage Landor**, below an eighteenth century clock, while on the wall of the south aisle are two shelves holding symbolic loaves, a reminder of when 32 loaves were distributed each week to Warwick's poor, thanks to a benefaction of three rich townspeople.

From the church, walk down Church Street and turn left along Jury Street. At the end is **East Gate,** built in the early fifteenth century and topped by a delightful chapel to St Peter. The chapel has been a school since about 1700 and is now part of Kings High School. Opposite the Gate, to the right, are the late sixteenth century Oken Almshouses. Go past East Gate and along Smith Street, lined with elegant houses. The first of these is the late seventeenth century Landor House where Walter Savage Landor was born. Further on is **St John's House**, a beautiful Jacobean mansion named for the Hospital of St John, founded in

1175, that once stood on the site. The House is now a museum, with a Victorian parlour, kitchen and school, each authentically furnished. There is also the Museum of the Royal Warwickshire Regiment, with a display of uniforms and medals. The House's delightful gardens are also open to visitors.

From St John's House, go back towards the town, bearing left along St Nicholas' Church Street where there are some very pretty houses, to reach a roundabout. Ahead is Mill Street with some beautiful late sixteenth century houses along with some from the seventeenth and nineteenth centuries. Another section of medieval Warwick which escaped the fire can now be seen by turning left to reach the Avon, passing St Nicholas' Church and the beautiful St Nicholas Park to the left. Now cross the bridge, an elegant, single-arched bridge built in 1789, and turn right into Bridge End. In this section of the old town there are also beautiful views of the castle.

WARWICK CASTLE

The first castle at Warwick was built in William the Conqueror's time, and the motte (mound) of this motte-and-bailey still exists within the present walls. Over subsequent centuries the castle was enlarged and rebuilt of stone. Most of what now exists dates from a huge rebuilding in the fourteenth and fifteenth centuries. Of this work, the finest piece is the 45m (147ft) Caesar's Tower, though the domestic buildings that run from it tend to hide the brilliance of its design. The 39m (128ft), twelve-sided **Guy's Tower** is also a brilliant piece of military engineering, and more easily seen because of the relatively low rampart

walls on each side. Close to Guy's Tower is the heavily fortified **Gatehouse** and **Barbican**, the castle's main entrance when it was at its peak as a military fortress. On the other side of Guy's Tower are the smaller **Clarence** and **Bear Towers** which were to have formed part of a new fortified gatehouse, begun by Richard III in 1478. With Richard's death at Bosworth, work stopped and was never restarted.

The domestic buildings, so impressive when viewed from beyond the Avon, were added in the seventeenth and eighteenth centuries as the castle changed from war engine to stately home. The initiator of this work was Sir Fulke Greville, who had been granted the castle in 1604. Sir Fulke was murdered by one of his servants and buried in the chapel he had built in the castle. **The Ghost Tower**, at the other end of the domestic range from Caesar's Tower, is so-called because Sir Fulke's ghost is supposed to emanate from a portrait of him which hangs in the tower.

Within the domestic range are not only the chapel, but a series of magnificent rooms with phenomenal collections. **The State Dining Room**, where Victoria and Albert (amongst other royals) dined is exquisitely furnished, as are the several drawing and bedrooms. The furnishings include some excellent portraits, early seventeenth century Delft tapestries and elegant furniture. The **Great Hall**, arguably the finest of all, with its arched ceiling, has a remarkable collection of arms and armour, including a knight on an armoured horse. There is a shield reputedly carried by Bonnie Prince Charlie, and the armour worn by Robert Greville at the battle of Lichfield

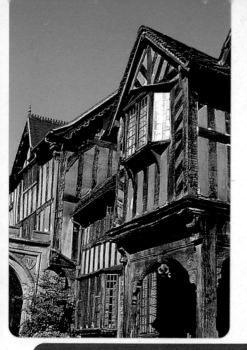

during the Civil War. The armour did not save Greville from being killed by a sniper's bullet. Also from the Civil War era is a death mask of Oliver Cromwell, a fascinating (if macabre) item. Equally interesting is the castle's dungeon, above which there is another collection of arms, together with a collection of torture equipment. The details of the use of some of these latter items makes the visitor wince.

The south-western end of the domestic range is furnished in Victorian period style, and has waxwork models illustrating a weekend party which took place in 1898. Guests included the Prince of Wales (the future Edward VII), his son the Duke of York (the future George V), the young Winston Churchill and his mother. The superb quality of the models is a tribute to the Tussaud Group which now owns the castle.

Caesar's Tower also has a superb

exhibition, again with waxwork models, illustrating the preparations for the battle of Barnet in 1471 where Richard Neville, Earl of Warwick, was killed. Neville is better known as the Kingmaker, after a speech in Shakespeare's Henry VI (Part 3) in which he is referred to as a 'putter up and plucker down of Kings'. Of the many owners of the castle and title, Neville is the most historically important. During the Wars of the Roses he was at first a Yorkist, capturing Henry VI when he commanded the Yorkist army at St Albans in 1455, and setting Edward IV on the throne. However, when the young King married and his power waned as a consequence, Neville imprisoned Edward at Warwick Castle. He therefore held both the Yorkist and Lancastrian Kings captive simultaneously.

Unable to rule England successfully through either King, Neville went to France, changed to the Lancastrian side and returned to England with an army. He restored Henry VI to the throne and chased Edward out of the country. Edward returned in 1471 and his army met that of Neville at Barnet on Easter Sunday. Neville's army was defeated, with over 3,000 of its 12,000 men killed, the deaths including the Earl himself.

The grounds of Warwick Castle are as magnificent as the buildings. The **Victoria Rose Garden** has 'old-fashioned' types of roses while the Peacock Garden has several of the birds, together with formal beds around a central fountain. The nearby **Conservatory** has many exotic plants and the Warwick Vase, a reproduction of a Roman vase which is now in the Burrell Collection, in Glasgow. From the **Peacock Garden**, visitors can wander across the Pageant Field, once used by medieval knights and now once again the scene of jousting. Jousts are held at various times of the year; full programmes of events, which also include craft displays, concerts and firework displays are published annually. Visitors can also stroll beside the River Avon or cross on to River Island for a breathtaking view of the castle's domestic range.

TWO SHORT DETOURS

From Warwick, two short detours are worthwhile. One, northwards, is to another castle, this one an evocative ruin. But first we head westwards along the A4177 to visit the **'Stairway to Heaven'**, the flight of 21 locks at Hatton which lift boats up (or down) a 44^1/$_2$m (146 ft) step on the Grand Union Canal. The view towards Warwick from the top of the locks is superb, while the

sight of the boat and barge folk sweating their way through the flight is enough to bring joy to the heart of any idle man. Just beyond the flight, a turn left along the B4439, and another turn left soon after, visits the **Hatton Country World**, Britain's largest craft centre. Here, too, are antique shops and much else besides, including rare farm breeds, a pets' corner, regular falconry displays and daily farming demonstrations.

KENILWORTH

The castle is at Kenilworth, about 8km (5 miles) north of Warwick. Kenilworth is one of the largest castle ruins in England. It is also one of its finest and one of the most romantic, particularly when the morning or evening sun lights up its red sandstone. When Nathaniel Hawthorne came here the ruins were clothed in greenery, prompting his observation that 'without the ivy and shrubbery (it) would not be a pleasant object'. The stripping of the greenery may have made it less picturesque, but it has certainly not detracted from its beauty.

The first castle on the site was built by Geoffrey de Clinton, Chamberlain to Henry I, in about 1120. That castle would have been a simple motte-and-bailey, but the monks of the Augustinian Priory to the east, were granted leave to fish in the castle's pool so even at this early stage there must have been the beginnings of the lake that formed so vital a part of the castle's defences in later years. The castle was taken over by Henry II and completed in stone by King John. So significant a war engine was it that, at the time of the signing of Magna Carta,

Kenilworth was one of the four castles the barons demanded from King John as an insurance against his future actions.

Henry III gave the castle to Simon de Montfort in 1253. After his death at the battle of Evesham in 1265, de Montfort's supporters held the castle against a siege by the King. It proved a formidable target, the lake preventing the possibility of undermining the walls and making barges necessary for a frontal attack. After considering this option the King decided against it. Finally, after a siege of over five months, shortage of food forced the castle's defenders to surrender, though they received safe passage in exchange for the castle.

Henry V came here to recuperate after the battle of Agincourt. He extended the lake around the castle and created a pleasance (a summerhouse and garden) at its western end, reached by boat from the castle. But it was Robert Dudley, Earl of Leicester, the favourite of Elizabeth I who carried out the next major works. The need for a purely defensive castle had passed, so Leicester softened the castle's lines by making larger windows. He added the stable block that is still such a picturesque part of the site and built a domestic block as a guest house. It was here that Elizabeth I stayed during several trips to visit the Earl. Perhaps most symbolic of the new usage, Leicester planted a formal garden to the north of the castle. This has been reconstructed from a plan of the original drawn up about 100 years after Leicester's death.

At the time of the Civil War the castle was again in the hands of the Crown, but Charles I withdrew his troops and it was quickly occupied by a Parliamentarian force. At the end of the War, Parliament, fearful of the castle's potential, ordered it to be demolished. The lake was drained by rupturing the dam that retained it. Today's visitor arriving from the car park to the south of the ruins, crosses the causeway that once carried Elizabeth I across the lake and which had also been used as a tiltyard for her entertainment. Just how formidable a defence was the lake can be judged by looking out from the causeway. The castle had only been partially destroyed before the Restoration put an end to the vandalism. Time and weather then took its toll on the buildings. Deterioration was halted when the site passed to the government in 1937, though the ruins had already been protected by the fame it received after the publication of Sir Walter Scott's novel in 1821. The novel, Kenilworth, centres on a visit Queen Elizabeth made to the castle in 1575. The castle is now administered by English Heritage.

ABBEY FIELDS

To the east of the castle are **Abbey Fields,** with the scant remains of the Augustinian Priory founded in 1122 by Geoffrey de Clinton. The best of the excavated finds can be seen in the Abbey Barn. Of the town beyond the fields, the best parts are the church which, despite Victorian restoration, retains an excellent Norman doorway, claimed by many to be the best in the country, and Little Virginia, a very good group of cottages at the eastern end of the High Street. Legend has it that the name derives from the site having been the first place to have been planted with the potatoes Raleigh brought back from Virginia.

Kenilworth ruins

The Cotswolds are home to the largest collection of antique dealers outside London, dealers with a reputation for being 'less stuffy' than their counterparts in the capital. Many are members of the Cotswold Antique Dealers' Association (CADA) which produces a leaflet listing all its members. This is available from Barcheston Manor, Shipston-on-Stour CV36 5AY. Tel: 01608 661268.

There are dealers spread throughout the area (and in Shakespeare country), but the leading centres are at:

Bath
A network of dealers forming the Bath and Bradford-on-Avon Antique Dealers Association. An Antiques Fair is held in March each year, and guided tours of the dealers are available. A free brochure on the dealers is available from 3/4 Piccadilly, London Road, Bath BA1 6BL. Tel: 01225 442215. At 5/10 Bartlett Street there is an Antiques Centre with over 60 dealers. ☎ 01225 466689.

Broadway
There are four members of the British Antique Dealers' Association (BADA) in the town, specialising in paintings, seventeenth and eighteenth century furniture, as well as having more general collections.

Burford
There are six members of the Cotswold Antique Dealers' Association (CADA) in the town, specialising in sporting antiques, eighteenth and nineteenth century furniture and carpets, as well as more general collections.

Cheltenham
The Montpellier/Suffolk Road area has large number of dealers, many of them members of the (BADA.). The Antiques Market at 54 Suffolk Road (Tel: 01242 529812) has 20 dealers. Cheltenham is also the home of the area's two major antiques fairs. On the last Sunday in the month the Cotswold Antiques Fair is held at the Racecourse, while on the second Sunday of each month the Cheltenham Spa Antiques Fair is held at the Pittville Pump Rooms.

Cirencester
There are several members of the CADA, and other dealers, specialising in furniture, silver, glass and books.

Gloucester
In Gloucester Docks there is a nationally-famous antiques centre with almost 70 shops covering four floors of an old warehouse. The centre is open daily and has a licensed restaurant.

Stow-on-the-Wold
One of the Cotswolds' leading centres, the town has 12 members of the CADA (4 of BADA), their specialities covering the entire range of antiques.

Warwick
The Hatton Country World centre has 25 antique dealers, and there are also several excellent dealers in the town.

In addition to the above, there are excellent dealers at Moreton-in-Marsh, Tetbury and Winchcombe. At Toddington, near Winchcombe, a CADA dealer specialises in architectural and garden antiques.

KENILWORTH

Abbey Barn
Abbey Fields
☎ 01926 852595 for information
Open: Under negotiation at the time of writing. Will probably be April to September, alternate Sundays 2-5pm, but please check.

Kenilworth Castle (English Heritage)
☎ 01926 852078
Open: April to September daily 10am-6pm; October daily 10am-5pm; November to March daily 10am-4pm. Closed 24-26 December.

STRATFORD-UPON-AVON

Shakepeare's Birthplace and Anne Hathaway's Cottage
☎ 01789 204016
Open: Mid-March to mid-October, Monday-Saturday 9am-5pm, Sunday 9.30am-5pm; Mid-October to mid-March, Monday-Saturday 9.30am-4pm, Sunday 10am-4pm. Closed 23-26 December.

New Place/Nash's House, Hall's Croft and Mary Arden's House
☎ 01789 204016
Open: Mid-March to mid-October, Monday-Saturday 9.30am-5pm, Sunday 10am-5pm;Mid-October to mid-March, Monday-Saturday 10am-4pm, Sunday 10.30am-4pm. Closed 23-26 December.
The above five properties are owned by the Shakespeare Birthplace Trust. Combined tickets for some, or all, are available. The Guide Friday bus makes regular trips between the five properties as well as visiting many other Stratford sites. The buses operate between April and October, daily starting between 9.30am and 10am and running every 15 or 20 minutes until 4.30pm or 5pm. For information, ☎ 01789 294466

Holy Trinity Church
Old Town
☎ 01789 266316
Open: March to October Monday-Saturday 8.30am -6pm, Sunday 2-5pm; November to February Monday-Saturday 9am -4pm, Sunday 2-5pm.
There is a charge to view the graves of Shakespeare and his family.

Brass Rubbing Centre
Royal Shakespeare Theatre Summer-house
Avonbank Gardens
☎ 01789 297671
Open: May to September daily 10am-6pm; October to April daily 11am-4pm.

Butterfly Farm
Tramway Walk, Swan's Nest Lane
☎ 01789 299288
Open: May to September daily 10am-6pm; October to April daily 10am-dusk. Closed Christmas Day.

Cox's Yard
Bridgefoot
☎ 01789 297671
Open: all year daily 9am-11pm, but opening times of individual sites within the yard vary.

Grimm's Ghostly Tour of Stratford
Country Artist's Fountain
Bancroft Gradens
☎ 01789 204106
Open: April to September daily at 7.30pm. No booking needed, just turn up. October to March, bookings only.

Harvard House
High Street
☎ 01789 204507
Open: Mid-May to mid-September Monday-Saturday 10am-4pm, Sunday 10.30am-4.30pm.

Shire Horse Centre

Off the A3400 (Shipton road) 2½kms (1½ miles) from the centre of Stratford.
☎ 01789 415274
Open: March to October daily 10am-5pm; November-February Saturday-Wednesday 10am-5pm.

Teddy Bear Museum

19 Greenhill Street
☎ 01789 293160
Open: March to December daily 9.30am-6pm. Closed Christmas Day and Boxing Day; January and February daily 9.30am-5pm.

WARWICK

Doll Museum

Oken's House, Castle Street
☎ 01926 412500 or 495546
Open: Easter to October Monday-Saturday 10am-5pm, Sunday 11am-5pm; November to Easter Saturday 10am-dusk.

Hatton Country World

5kms (3 miles) west of Warwick, off the A4177 and B4439
☎ 01926 843411
Open: all year daily 10am-5pm.

Lord Leycester Hospital

High Street
☎ 01926 492797
Open: May to September Tuesday-Sunday 10am-5pm; October to April Tuesday-Sunday 10am-4pm. The Master's Garden is open Easter to September, Tuesday-Sunday 10am-4.30pm.

St John's House

(Victoria Museum and Museum of the Royal Warwickshire Regiment)
☎ 01926 412132/412021
Open: all year Tuesday-Saturday and Bank Holiday Mondays 10am-5.30pm. Also open on Sundays 2.30-5pm from May to September.

St Mary's Church

Old Square
☎ 01926 403940
Open: April to October daily 10am-6pm; November to March daily 10am-4pm.

Warwick Castle

☎ 01926 406600 or 495421
Open: April to October daily 10am-6pm; November to March daily 10am-5pm. Closed Christmas Day.

Warwickshire Museum

The Market Hall, Market Place
☎ 01926 412500 or 492212
Open: all year Monday-Saturday 10am-5.30pm. Also open on Sundays 2-5pm from May to September.

Warwickshire Yeomanry Museum and Town Museum

The Court House, Jury Street
☎ 01926 492212
Open: Easter to September Friday-Sunday and Bank Holiday Mondays 10am-1pm and 2-4pm.

WELLESBOURNE

Charlecote Park (National Trust)

Nr Wellesbourne
☎ 01789 470277
Open: Easter to early November Friday-Tuesday Grounds 11am-6pm, House 12noon-5pm. Also open on Bank Holidays.

Wellesbourne Watermill

Kineton Road, Wellesbourne
☎ 01789 470237
Open: Easter to October Thursday-Sunday and Bank Holidays 10am-4.30pm. Also open Tuesday and Wednesday during school summer holidays; October and March Sunday 1-4pm.

Wartime Museum

Old Airfield, Wellesbourne
☎ 01789 293127 for information
Open: all year, Sunday 10am-4pm. Also open on occasional Bank Holidays.

The North-Western Edge

As there are no true Cotswold Hills (the name is misleading) only if visitors are approaching from the west, or, to a lesser extent from the north, ascending the limestone escarpment, is there a clear indication that they have arrived in this most beautiful of areas. So it is a good idea to begin an exploration at a point where one can, with a walk of little over 5 kms (3 miles - allow an hour), grasp the essential elements that make up the Cotswolds, their scenery and history.

The starting point is the car park of the National Trust site on **Dover's Hill,** a little way north-west of Chipping Campden. After going left out of the car park and down to the crossroads, one turns right along the road signposted for Broadway and Willersey and a little way along the road, cross to the left side to look down and back. There, nestling in a gently wooded valley, is the town of **Chipping Campden**. It is a typically Cotswold town and from this vantage point the essential 'typical Cotswold' features are apparent.

First is the stone, pale grey and cream limestone. The second feature is the church. Almost all Cotswold towns and villages are dominated by marvellous churches bequeathed by the rich wool merchants.

Again geography has played a part; the high wolds, or common land areas, together with the streams that run from them, produced the wealth of the Cotswolds in the late Middle Ages. The sheep that fed on the wolds produced the wool that formed the basis of the economy of England, and the merchants who

Woolstaplers' Hall, Chipping Campden

traded in it were incredibly rich. They vied with each other, not to build lavish buildings for themselves (although fine houses were built) but to raise and decorate churches, the 'wool' churches. The church at Chipping Campden is perhaps the finest 'wool' church in the Cotswolds.

Continuing along the road, the visitor reaches, tucked away in woodland to the right, the **Kiftsgate Stone** which is, in its way, as remarkable as the wool churches themselves. This is a 'moot' point, a place where the people of the area could gather to discuss business, hold court, or hear of important events. The 'gate' in the name is not to be taken literally; there is no gate, the word deriving from the Saxon for 'track'. But if Saxon times seem long ago, one must remember that when the name was given to this stone it was probably as ancient to the Saxons as they are to us.

Few areas in Britain can claim to have a longer and consistently more important history than the Cotswolds. From this spot the proclamation of George III was read,

The Cotswold Olympicks

There is an enjoyable half hour walk along the escarpment near Dover's Hill, the site visited briefly at the start of the chapter. On the hill a panorama dial identifies the points of interest in the Vale of Evesham below. The hill's name is from Robert Dover, a local lawyer who in the early 1600s created the Cotswold **'Olympick' Games** there. The games were famous in their day; they had the royal seal of approval and were mentioned by Shakespeare, who possibly visited them. The actual events would probably not be recognised by the current Olympic committee, who would scarcely class as a sport either shin-kicking, or singlestick fighting. Competitors in the former reputedly toughened their shins by beating them with planks of wood, while in the latter sport the object was to break your opponent's head with your staff before he did the same to you. Neither would they like the boisterous good-humour of competitors and spectators alike, which led to the eventual prohibition of the games in the mid-nineteenth century. By then the boisterousness had become riots, with vandalism in Chipping Campden.

The open land that now affords such fine views of the edge and vale is only a small part of the original games area and was bought by the National Trust in 1928. On the National Trust plaque in the car park is a portrait of a man on a white horse, in a suit with a feathered hat, probably a picture of Robert Dover himself since it is known that King James gave him a similar suit and that he opened the games on a white horse, while cannons were fired from a mock fort. In 1951 the games, though not all the original sports, were revived. They are held on the eve of **Scuttlebrook Wake**, a Chipping Campden festival which includes the crowning of the May Queen in the Market Square, on the Saturday following the Spring Holiday.

probably the last great event recorded here. At the same time as the woollen industry was declining, so were the Cotswolds. Unhappy as this decline was for those who worked in the industry, its result has been that the villages and towns are now as they were then, and so have maintained a charm that would undoubtedly have been lost if continuous prosperity had resulted in the further modernisation of old houses and the building of new.

Returning to the car park, visitors can now go across to the panorama dial from where they will enjoy not only an expansive vista over the Vale of Evesham to the Malvern Hills, but also a nearby view along the northern edge of the escarpment. Here the true geography of the Cotswolds is seen; there are no hills at all; it is only this escarpment, which rises to about 300m (1,000ft) in its more northerly reaches, but being cut by river valleys it has the appearance of hills. If the escarpment here is sudden, the dip slope behind is not, falling the same height over a distance of many kilometres towards the Upper Thames Valley. Those, therefore, who approach from the east can be deep into the Cotswolds before they realise that they have gained any height at all.

CHIPPING CAMPDEN

The first of the town walks in this book starts at Chipping Campden. Here a short walk (3/4 hour) takes in the better parts of the town itself, and also visits the picturesque and very non-Cotswold thatched cottages of Westington, reached from Sheep Street. The itinerary for any visitor to Chipping Campden must include St James' Church, not only because it is such a fine example of a 'wool' church, and so structurally perfect, but because of the wealth of its treasures and curios inside. Most noticeable perhaps is the Grevel brass, commemorating William Grevel (who died in 1401) and his wife. The brass is the largest, and one of the oldest, in Gloucestershire. Especially notable is the craftsmanship with which Grevel's wife is depicted: her dress is closed with over eighty buttons, each individually formed. Equally interesting are the life-size alabaster effigies of Sir Baptist and Lady Elizabeth Hicks in the south chapel. They lie in their coronation robes and are overlooked by two more life-size figures of their eldest daughter and her husband in funeral shrouds, hand-in-hand, arising from their tomb on judgement day. Other busts of the Hicks family adorn the walls, the whole chapel being virtually a private mausoleum.

Sir Baptist Hicks was one of the great wool merchants of his day, with immense wealth. Indeed he was so rich that he often lent vast sums to King James I. His London house commemorated this Gloucestershire village, giving its name to the area – Campden Hill Square – and his bequests raised some of the more interesting buildings in the town, including the almshouses near the church, built for £1,000 to house six poor men and six poor women, and the Market Hall in the centre of High Street.

William Grevel's house remains in High Street. It is over six hundred years old, and opposite it is one that is equally old – Woolstaplers' Hall. This was the meeting place of the staple (ie fleece) merchants.

The visitor who has started at St James' church and has then entered High Street Grevel House and Woolstaplers' Hall, can now go left to walk down what has been called the showpiece of the Cotswolds. Almost every house has a notable history and the wide street has occasional buildings in its centre including the early sixteenth century Hicks Market Hall and the partly fourteenth century Town Hall.

If instead the visitor goes right, away from Grevel House to Leysbourne End, on the right is the Ernest Wilson Memorial Garden, planted in memory of a Campden-born man responsible for the introduction of thousands of oriental shrubs and trees to the west. 'Chinese' Wilson, as he was known, became director of the famous Arnold Arboretum at Harvard University in the late 1920s.

The arrival in 1902 of the Guild of Handicrafts in the town has stimulated the establishment of many craft workshops; local shops have examples of the work. One workshop that can be visited is the pottery in the Leysbourne district,

45

at the church end of High Street. The shop on the premises also sells the work of other local craft workers, together with work from further afield. In Calf Lane, which runs parallel to High Street, there are footpaths that lead to two old mills, still complete with their large, overshot waterwheels.

Chipping Campden is also a good centre for short expeditions to other, smaller, villages on the northern edge of the Cotswolds. To the north and east there are a number of interesting places that lie outside the AONB – there can be few villages with a more Cotswold 'feel' than **Ebrington**, despite the thatch on the Cotswold stone cottages, or **Ilmington** (which is held to be home of Cotswold Morris Dancing). Ebrington can be reached by path from Campden; the return journey by the lane running south from the village is a good introduction to country lane walking in the Cotswolds (total 8kms - 5 miles - 2 hours). Ebrington, apart from being a delightful village, is also the butt of local 'village idiot' jokes. Here they manured the church tower to make it grow taller; it is the place where they boiled a donkey to get his harness off; it was a local who carried his wheelbarrow for 11kms (7 miles) so that the wheel would not dent the road; as if to agree, the locals refer to the village not by its correct name, but as Yubberton.

Also within a short distance of Chipping Campden are **Hidcote Manor Gardens,** near Mickleton, laid out over his lifetime by Major Lawrence Johnston and presented by him to the National Trust. Hidcote is especially interesting to the amateur gardener because it is

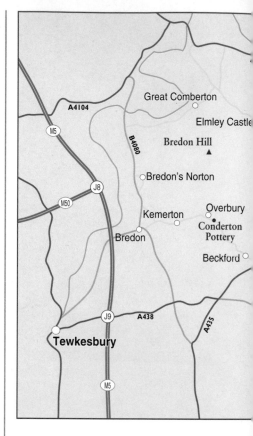

not one large expanse, but a series of small gardens, each hedged around and planted with a single class of flower. For those who love gardens the day can perhaps be rounded off with a visit to the more formal **Kiftsgate Court Gardens**, also close to Mickleton. There are rare shrubs here, and the collection of roses is one of the finest in Britain. The roses include one that is unique to Kiftsgate and claimed to be the largest rose in Britain.

Opposite page: Chipping Campden's sixteenth century market hall

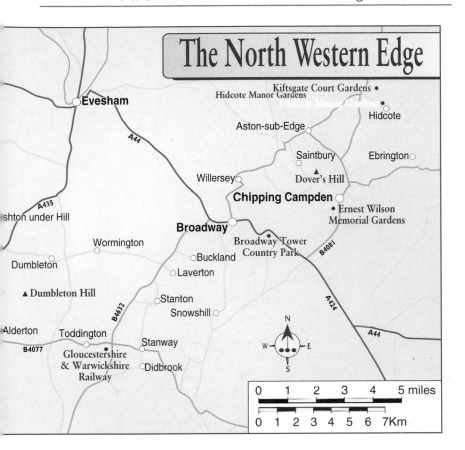

The North Western Edge

Evesham

Kiftsgate Court Gardens •
Hidcote Manor Gardens

Hidcote

Aston-sub-Edge

Saintbury

Ebrington○

A44

Willersey○

Dover's Hill ▲

Chipping Campden○

A435

• Ernest Wilson
Memorial Gardens

shton under Hill

Broadway○

Wormington

Broadway Tower
Country Park

B4081

Dumbleton

○Buckland

○Laverton

▲ Dumbleton Hill

○Stanton

A424

Snowshill ○

B4632

Alderton

Toddington

Stanway

N

A44

B4077

Gloucestershire
& Warwickshire
Railway

○Didbrook

W — E

S

0	1	2	3	4	5 miles

| 0 | 1 | 2 | 3 | 4 | 5 | 6 | 7Km |

In 1660 William Harrison, a steward employed by Lady Juliana Noel of Campden, the daughter of Sir Baptist Hicks whose tomb is in Campden church, disappeared. A search of the area the following day revealed his blood-stained comb and hat-band, but no other trace of him. Because of the blood-stains, and because Harrison had been a rent-collector and was, therefore, carrying a large amount of money, foul play was suspected.

Suspicion fell on John Perry, Harrison's manservant, whose behaviour on the night of the disappearance was curious. Perry had an alibi which was checked and found to be accurate, but then, astonishingly, during questioning his story changed and became increasingly bizarre. He first claimed Harrison had been murdered by a wandering tinker, and then that his mother, and brother Richard, had killed him. After further questioning, he admitted that he had been present when the murder was committed, but that his only action was to tell the others of Harrison's movements. To prove his story, he led his questioners to the millpond where the body had been thrown. The pond was dredged, but nothing was discovered. Despite this, and the protests of Mrs Perry and Richard, the three were accused of murder. The judge was obviously uneasy about the lack of a body and refused to try them, but early in 1661 a more enthusiastic judge was found, and the three were found guilty of murder and sentenced to death. They were executed above Chipping Campden, close to the road linking Stow to Broadway, in the early summer. A large crowd was present, and because of a local belief that Mrs Perry was a witch, she was hanged first, in case she had bewitched her sons and the spell might be broken. Before Richard died, his pleas to his brother were so impassioned that the crowd joined in shouting for John to admit his brother's innocence. John remained silent until his turn came, and then he too protested his innocence and that of his family. After his execution his body was left to rot in chains.

The body, or what remained of it, was still there 2 years later when William Harrison walked back into his home in Chipping Campden. He had a remarkable story to tell: of kidnappings and beatings; of being sold as a slave in Turkey, of escaping and fleeing across Europe to Portugal; of gaining passage on a boat to London; and of walking to Campden from there. The story is amazing enough, the more so when we consider that Harrison was about 70 at the time.

Now, over 300 years later, it is hard to arrive at the truth, but the general opinion is that Harrison was embezzling money from the Noels, and conspired with John Perry to fake a violent robbery when he feared that his crime would be discovered. Though this may be true, it leaves many questions unanswered. Why did Perry confess and why did he involve his family? And why did both Harrison and, even more remarkably, Perry remain silent through the trial, sentence and execution? There were those who doubted Harrison's story even then, but the Noels continued to employ him until he died aged over 80. After his return, his wife, who should have been overjoyed, even if shocked, committed suicide.

BROADWAY

Between Chipping Campden and Broadway is the Fish Inn, a curious building, once a coaching stop where horses would be changed after the long pull up the steep hill from Broadway. Close by is a picnic area, while a little further off - and on the line of the Cotswold Way - is **Broadway Tower**, which is now the centrepiece of the Tower Country Park, devoted exclusively to the study of the countryside.

There are two barns, each of original design, though reconstructed on site. One is an information centre; the other houses several exhibits on the local area, its geology, wildlife and country crafts, particularly the dry-stone walling for which the Cotswolds are famous. There are also two nature walks, one taking approximately half an hour, the other an hour. The tower itself has an interesting history: it was built in 1799 by the Earl of Coventry as a present for his wife, who was impressed that she was able to see a bonfire lit on Broadway Hill (part of their local estate and, at 320m (1,024ft) the second highest point of the Cotswolds) from their Worcestershire estate and wanted the tower as a permanent landmark and reminder of her Cotswold home. The view from the roof gallery is reputed, as are so many others, to be the most extensive in Britain. It is certainly true that, before county boundaries were redrawn, thirteen counties could be seen from the tower; the Wrekin and Welsh Hills are visible, as well as other nearer landmarks such as Worcester cathedral and Pershore Abbey. Even with re-drawn boundaries twelve counties may be seen.

The tower was not constructed of local stone, as the earl wanted it to be darker. Later repairs in the local, lighter, stone can easily be identified. Major repairs have been required several times, as the tower has fallen into disrepair. Once it was saved by the Pre-Raphaelite artists, Morris, Rossetti and Burne-Jones, and more recently by the Batsford Estate who now run the country park.

Broadway itself, which is in Worcestershire rather than in Gloucestershire, is the tourist centre of the Cotswolds and has, as a result, a considerable number of shops. Most are aimed at the visitor, many being outlets for local craftsmen. The world-famous furniture factory of Gordon Russell is just off the main street, while in the main street is the Teddy Bear Museum with a collection of old teddies, dolls and toys. The village name derives, quite naturally, from the width of the main street. Its width is due to the covering of two streams that run down each side of the original, narrower road. When it was originally covered, dip-holes were left for buckets as the village did not have piped water; they have been filled only within living memory.

Despite the high degree of commercialisation of the town, there is much that is very beautiful and fascinating. Especially notable is **Prior's Manse**, one of the oldest houses in Worcestershire. It was constructed in the fourteenth century for the Prior of Worcester, but the dormer windows give it a very modern look.

Above: Kiftsgate Court Below left and right: Hidcote Manor gardens, owned by the National Trust

1 The Cotswold Edge

From Chipping Campden go west along High Street continuing where the B4081 goes left for Westington to take Dyer's Lane up to the Cotswold Edge. At the crossroads (where Dover's Hill and its car park are ahead) go left. Along this road, about 350yd on the right, is the Kiftsgate Stone. At the T-junction turn left, and go right at the junction with the main A44. To the right now is the Fish Hill picnic site. At the bottom of the hill is Broadway. Leave Broadway along the A46 for Winchcombe. To the left now are three no-through roads, one to the village of Buckland (and its rectory) and two to Laverton. The fourth lane to the left goes to Stanton and continues to Stanway (Stanway House). Through the village the B4077 is reached. Go left and up to Stumps Cross. There go left on the minor road past Stanway Ash Wood to Snowshill (Snowshill Manor). Take the top road out of the village and follow it to the Broadway Tower Country Park. Beyond is the A44 and the Fish Hill picnic site again. Go right for 1.5 miles to the B4031 that goes left to Chipping Campden.

Snowshill Manor

2 Bredon & Alderton Hills

From Bredon (tithe barn) take the B4079, but leave it for a lane to Kemerton (The Priory) and on to Overbury and Conderton. The lane continues to Beckford Silk, and from there it heads south-east. Leave it leftward for a lane to Ashton-under-Hill and on to Elmley Castle. These lanes from Bredon have now taken the traveller half-way round Bredon Hill, and a full circuit can be made by way of the Comberton villages and Bredon Norton. Alternatively, go right in Elmley Castle following another lane for 4 miles to Hinton Cross on the A435. Go right and after 1.25 miles go left on the B4078 through Sedgeberrow and on to the A438. Go right and after less than a mile go right again to Alderton. Go ahead now to reach the A435 again. This last section has gone around Alderton Hill. Go over at the A435 to Beckford and reverse the route to Bredon.

Waterloo in trees

Broadway's Lygon Arms, a marvellous building, commemorates General Lygon, a local eccentric who had his estate planted with clumps of trees in the same formation as the troops at the battle of Waterloo, so that he could re-enact the battle. The inn also commemorates Broadway's past as a staging post on the coaching route from Worcester to London. Because of the steepness of Fish Hill the stage coach stopped here to take on extra horses, and the town became a fashionable overnight stop. At the height of its popularity the town, which was smaller than now, had more than twenty such inns.

To the north of Broadway are the villages of Willersey and Saintbury in Gloucestershire, not Worcestershire. **Saintbury** is built on the escarpment as it starts to swing eastwards, and there are fine views of the Vale of Evesham from above the town. **Willersey**, closer to the foot of the escarpment, has some typical north Cotswold stone cottages clustered around a duck pond and green.

Weston-sub-Edge was the home of William Latimer; his house, Latimer House, far older than any of the others in the village, still stands. Latimer was a friend of Sir Thomas More and Erasmus. He helped William Tyndale to translate the New Testament into English. He was a fine Greek scholar who promoted the study of Greek civilisation at Oxford, and translated the works of Aristotle. One of the cottages is called Ryknield, a reference to the Roman road – Ryknield Street – that passes close to the village.

At nearby **Aston-sub-Edge** the Manor House, a fine building, was once the home of Endymion Porter, a famous patron of the arts in the time before the Civil War, who was instrumental in the setting up of Robert Dover's games on the nearby escarpment. When Prince Rupert visited the games he stayed with Porter. His life of luxury came to an end with the Civil War, when he was banished as a Royalist and lived in great poverty in Holland. He eventually returned to England and is buried in the church of St Martin's-in-the-Field, London.

BROADWAY TO CHELTENHAM

On the road to Cheltenham, between Broadway and Winchcombe, there is a collection of typical Cotswold villages strung out along the spring-line at the base of the escarpment, with one, Snowshill, equally fine, set on the wold above them.

Buckland is the first spring-line village from Broadway, and is famous for its rectory, once the oldest and most complete 'working' parsonage in the country, possessing a stained-glass window from the mid-fifteenth century containing the arms of Edward IV. It is now a private house. The village's church has an equally exceptional window, in the east wall, arguably the finest in the Cotswolds. It so delighted William Morris, then resident at Broadway Tower, that he paid to have it re-leaded.

Laverton, the next spring-line

village, is quiet, almost secret, but though it is bigger than Buckland it has nothing to compare with the latter's rectory.

Snowshill, on top of the escarpment above Buckland and Laverton, is renowned for its manor, now administered by the National Trust. It is interesting architecturally as a typical fifteenth to sixteenth century manor house, with a very good dovecote. The terraced gardens were designed by Charles Wade as a series of cottage gardens, complete with rockeries and stone walls. The house is especially noted for the fascinating collection that he left to the National Trust. There are bicycles, musical instruments, toys, oriental furniture, mechanical objects, lace, clocks, keys, locks, domestic items, scientific instruments: the list is almost endless. Of major importance is a collection of Japanese Samurai armour, the finest collection outside Japan. Wade bought and restored the building to display his collections, which he started when he was seven years old, while he lived alone in a nearby converted barn. He was an archetypal English eccentric, but an artist and craftsman of some skill. He rescued from destruction many interesting objects. Interestingly, Wade did not live in the manor, preferring the Priests's House in the grounds so that the main building could be given over to his collection. The Priests's House, furnished as he left it, and the gardens beside the manor complete a fascinating site.

Stanway, back at the spring-line, is a treasure house of ancient buildings. **Stanway House** was built by the Tracy family in the mid-seventeenth century. The house's recently restored Baroque watergarden, complete with 21m (70ft) fountain,

Grand Canal and pyramid is open to the public. The gateway to the house is oddly positioned between a high wall and the church and, although an is an architectural gem, its elaborate design does not fit well with the simple dignity of the church. The village also has a massive tithe barn in the grounds of the house, and a cricket pavilion set up in typical fashion on staddle stones so as to combat damp.

Thomas Dover and Robinson Crusoe

One resident of Stanway House was Thomas Dover, a grandson of Robert of Dover's Hill fame. Thomas was the inventor of a mercury-based medicine reputedly worse than the diseases it claimed to cure, and a privateer who rescued Alexander Selkirk – the real Robinson Crusoe – from his desert island.

At **Didbrook**, the church is of considerable interest, rebuilt in 1475 following, it is said, the massacre of refugees from the Battle of Tewkesbury in the earlier church. The door is original and still shows the marks of bullets. This act was seen as a desecration and the older church was demolished. The village also contains a noteworthy pair of cottages that show at one end the 'cruck' method of construction, an external inverted V of substantial timbers to hold up the roof.

Finally **Stanton**, perhaps the best of the villages, has a superb situation and a single street full of individual Cotswold-stone cottages and houses. Their preservation and restoration is due to the efforts earlier this century of the architect Sir Philip Stott. This is truly a place to savour both the warm colouring of the buildings and a quiet Cotswold village with its backdrop of wooded hills.

To the west of these spring-line villages the Cotswolds seem to point a finger towards the Malvern Hills and Wales. Alderton Hill and Dumbleton Hill, reaching about 200m (650ft), are quite low in comparison with the escarpment at this point, but the great mass **Bredon Hill**, a true outlier, reaches almost 300m (1,000ft). The first two hills, really twin summits on a single stone mass, are ringed by a series of villages. **Toddington** is only 3kms (2 miles) from Stanway. The main A438 runs by it and appears to touch it, but the true centre is tucked away in a valley to the side. It has a collection of fine houses, and a

---

 ## Short Cycle Rides

The steep escarpment slope can make cycling hard work in this area of the Cotswolds. Here are two rides, one at the top and one at the bottom of the slope, that reduce the climbing to a minimum.

1 Spring-Line Villages *(15 miles)*
Map: OS Sheet 150 – Worcester, Malverns & surrounding area. From Broadway take the A46 to the Toddington roundabout (Gloucestershire and Warwickshire Railway). Go ahead towards Winchcombe, but take the first lane left to Didbrook (cruck cottage) and on to Wood Stanway. Ahead the lane reaches the B4077. Go over and on to Stanway (Stanway House). Go through the village and on to a T-junction. Go right and into Stanton. At the next T-junction go left and down to the A46. Here go right, taking each of the short no-through roads to Laverton and Buckland (Buckland Rectory) before returning to Broadway. Plenty of places for refreshment.

2 High Wolds *(15 miles)*
Maps: OS Sheet 151 – Stratford-upon-Avon & surrounding area; Sheet 150 – Worcester, Malverns & surrounding area. From the Dover's Hill car park go left and down to the crossroads. Go right (the Kiftsgate Stone is about 350yd along on the right-hand side). At a T-junction go left and on to the crossroads with the A44. Go over and follow the lane past the Broadway Tower Country Park to Hill Barn Farm. Just beyond at a crossroads go right to Snowshill (Snowshill Manor). Return to the crossroads near Hill Barn Farm, but now go straight over. Go over again at the next crossroads and follow the lane to the A44. Go left and follow the main road along the beautiful Five Mile Drive to the crossroads near the Fish Hill picnic site. Reverse the route to Dover's Hill.

Bredon

beautiful manor set in nearly 500 acres of excellent parkland. Its distinguished church has a spire which account books show was erected for just £4,400 in the late nineteenth century. It was built by the Tracy family, one of whose early members, William de Tracy, was among the four knights who murdered Thomas à Becket. Memorials to the family, who are descended from King Ethelred the Unready, can be seen inside. Next to the church are the ruins of the Tracys' original seventeenth century manor house, now sadly ruined and dangerous.

Close to the village – between Toddington and Stanway, beside the main road – the village railway station on the old Cheltenham to Stratford-on-Avon main line has been restored to its former GWR (Great Western Railway) glory, but the initials now stand for the Gloucestershire and Warwickshire Railway. Steam trains occasionally run again on a stretch of restored line from the station to Winchcombe.

BREDON HILL

North of Toddington is **Wormington** on the very edge of the Cotswold AONB where, in the church, is one of Britain's most outstanding Christian treasures, a very rare Saxon crucifix probably a thousand years old. It may be a relic of Winchcombe Abbey. The stream that flows past the village, the River Isbourne, flows to Winchcombe. On either side of the hill are: and **Dumbleton,** two small villages whose fine views of the Cotswold edge can be enhanced by climbing the hill along the path from Alderton, or the track from Dumbleton, the two routes meeting at Hill Farm (5kms - 3 miles - 1 hour). The actual summit of the two hills, named from the villages themselves, are wooded, the woods being privately owned. Since the triangulation station that stands on a third peak is also on private land, this walk has no firm objective in terms of a viewpoint, but the views to the edge and to the Evesham and Severn Vales more than make up for this shortcoming.

Beyond Dumbleton/Alderton hill the Carrant Brook flows down to Tewkesbury, the last part of its course forming the border between Worcestershire and Gloucestershire. It runs through **Beckford,** where there was an Augustinian monastery in the early twelfth century on the present site of Beckford House. The stream itself was anciently used to power mills. Visitors to Beckford Silk can watch the hand printing of silk.

Bredon Hill - Local Barometer

Because of its position, standing alone, Bredon Hill collects the weather and is used locally as a barometer:

When Bredon Hill puts on its hat
ye men of the Vale beware of that
when Bredon Hill doth clear appear
ye men of the Vale have naught to
fear.

Beyond Beckford is Bredon Hill, looking 'like a stranded whale'. The hill can be ascended by very many paths from each of the villages that ring its base (7kms - 4 miles - 2 hours). The summit area of the hill has many interesting spots. The tower is Parson's Folly, built in the eighteenth century by a gentleman of that name from Kemerton, and is an ideal shelter. It stands within the ramparts of an Iron Age hillfort which, when excavated, revealed the mutilated bodies of fifty men who, it is assumed, were the defenders of the fort when the last battle was fought there. The bodies were not buried but left where they fell, and were gradually overlaid with wind-blown soil as the fort fell into

disrepair. Also within the ramparts is the **Banbury Stone**. It has been considered to be either a sacrificial stone for the Druids or a Roman altar. At over 4m (14ft) high and 18m (nearly 60ft) round, it is unlikely to have been brought here and is, indeed, a natural outcrop. The Cotswolds abound with single stones, some natural, some not, and all seem to have been considered supernatural at some stage. It has long been held that this stone descends the hill to drink at the Avon each time it hears a church clock strike twelve.

To the south of the hill is **Overbury**, perhaps the prettiest village in Worcestershire. The number of half-timbered houses shows clearly that the village is at the limit of the Cotswolds, but there are fine stone buildings as well, particularly Overbury Court, a largely eighteenth century house. Nearby **Conderton** has a fine craft pottery where the process of manufacturing hand-thrown stoneware can be seen, and the Elaine Rippon Studios where the hand painting of silk can be watched. The Studio also has a shop on site, and another shop in Broadway.

At **Kemerton**, to the west, there is the tomb of a man killed in the Charge of the Light Brigade. Also here at The Priory is a beautiful, large garden with borders laid out for colour, and a good sunken garden. On the nearby hill above Westmancote are two more natural rock outcrops imbued with supernatural powers. These are called the King and Queen, and to pass between the two was considered a cure for all ills. Until quite recently – if indeed the custom has stopped – children were passed between the stones to ensure their good health.

Next is **Bredon** village itself. This has a fine tithe barn, one of the best of its kind, dating from the fourteenth century and now in the care of National Trust. The barn has excellent porches, one with a most unusual chimney cowling.

Bishop Prideaux's Appetite

When he was sacked from Worcester by Cromwell, Bishop Prideaux came to Bredon where he lived in poverty on a miserly pension. He survived only by selling his personal effects. Once, when asked how he was faring he replied: 'never better in my life, only I have too great a stomach ... I have eaten a great library, a great deal of linen, much of my brass, some of my pewter and now I am come to eat my iron and what will come next I know not'.

From Bredon a 5kms (3 mile) walk around the base of the hill to Great Comberton (1 hour) passes **Woollas Hall**, a fine early seventeenth century gabled mansion. The return can be made over the hill. Great Comberton itself is another mainly half-timbered village which has two good dovecotes, one containing 1,425 nest holes, the largest number of any such building in England. The village also contains many thatched houses and is surrounded by orchards – it is clear we are leaving Cotswold country for the Vale of Evesham.

Elmley Castle, to the east of Comberton, once had a moment of glory when Elizabeth I stayed here. She did not stay at the castle itself: although slight ruins remain, the Norman castle had been destroyed by Henry VII. She was on her way back to London, and further along the route at the county boundary near Ashton-under-Hill she stopped to thank the Sheriff of Worcestershire for his hospitality, although it is not known where she stayed. She also commanded him to commend her 'heartily' to the Bailiffs of Worcester itself. This was probably because she had just borrowed £200 from them, money she never returned, and probably never intended to.

TEWKESBURY

To the south of Bredon is **Tewkesbury**, just outside the AONB, but not to be missed. The town is distinctly non-Cotswold, the older buildings being almost entirely half-timbered, in keeping with the upper reaches of the River Severn, and with the Vale of Evesham from Pershore to Stratford. The Avon, which flows through the Evesham Vale between those two towns, joins the Severn at Tewkesbury. But even though it lacks the architecture and stone of the Cotswolds, it is a Gloucestershire town and a place of considerable interest.

Tewkesbury Abbey is one of the largest churches in Britain, and also one of the best; it has some remains of a Benedictine monastery, and contains some excellent Norman work. Some of the memorial tombs are very old and considered to be the finest of their type. When the abbey was demolished at the Dissolution of the monasteries, the townsfolk bought the abbey church – now called Tewkesbury Abbey – from Henry VIII for £453.

The Battle of Tewkesbury

On a calm day the abbey at Tewkesbury seems a tranquil place, but it was not always so. On 14 May 1471, survivors of a battle at Bloody Meadow, south of the abbey beside the A38, sought shelter inside it. The battle had ended with the defeat of the Lancastrians by the Yorkists, who then proceeded to massacre the defeated army. The Duke of Somerset and many knights fled there, although their leader Prince Edward was already dead. There is a legend that the monks at the abbey broke up the fighting that took place in the church itself. Many knights received sanctuary, but it was short lived; they were dragged from the church the following day and executed at the town cross.

Tewkesbury Abbey

Selected Walks

↑1 **Bredon Hill** 6 miles *Strenuous* *750ft climb*
Maps: OS Sheet 150 – Worcester, Malverns & surrounding
area. Start at Elmley Castle. Go north-west – away from the 'Queen
Elizabeth' – and bear left on the lane to Hill House Farm. From the
farm a bridleway leads on, bearing right between the woodlands of
Fox Hill and Doctor's Wood. At a gate and stile go over and sharp left
along the wood edge, then uphill to Long Plantation Wood. Go right
when this is reached and follow the path to the top of Bredon Hill.
The tower here is known as Parson's Folly, after an eighteenth
century owner of Woollas Hall below. Here too is the Banbury Stone.
Reverse the route, but bear right along a fence to the Long Plantation Wood. Follow the wood edge until a yellow crown waymarker
(for the Wychavon Way) directs you left and easily downhill to a lane.
Go left and back to Elmley Castle.

↑2 **Chipping Campden** *2.5 miles* *Moderate/Strenuous* *300ft climb*
Map: OS Sheet 151 – Stratford-upon-Avon & surrounding area.
Start at Chipping Campden. This route follows the Cotswold Way to
Dover's Hill. Go west along High Street to the signed lane (the
Cotswold Way sign is a white or yellow arrow and dot) to the right.
Soon Hoo Lane leaves leftwards. Take this and follow it to a metalled
road. Go left and soon take a signed path right that leads to Dover's
Hill. Go left past the summit triangulation point and on to the
panorama dial and car park. From the car park go left and down to
the crossroads. Go over to Dyer's Lane and follow this back to
Chipping Campden.

↑3 **Stanton to Buckland** *9 miles* *Strenuous* *1,100ft climb*
Map: OS Sheet 150 – Worcester, Malverns & surrounding area.
Take the signed path northward from Stanton church, crossing fields
and a couple of streams, to Laverton. Go right on the road where the
path emerges, then left through the village. At a T-junction go ahead
on a signed path across fields to Buckland. Go right past the rectory
and follow the village lane uphill past fish ponds. At the top of the
climb a fenced track goes right. Go along this, following the
Cotswold Way. From its end the Way is well signed past old quarries,
and over Shenberrow hillfort. After the fort bear right – watch for
yellow arrows – down a steep valley back to Stanton.

BECKFORD

Beckford Silk
☎ 01386 881507
Open: all year, Monday-Saturday
9am-5.30pm. Closed 24 December -
2 January
Evening lectures on silk making can
be arranged for groups by appointment.

BREDON

**Bredon Tithe Barn
(National Trust)**
☎ 01684 850051
Open: April to November, Wednesday, Thursday, Saturday and Sunday
10am-6pm or sunset. At other times
by appointment.

BROADWAY

Broadway Tower Country Park
Fish Hill
☎ 01386 852390
Open: April to October, daily
10.30am-5pm; November to March
Saturday & Sunday 11am-3pm.

Fish Hill Picnic Site & Nature Trail
near Broadway
Open: at all reasonable times.

Broadway Teddy Bear Museum
76 High Street,
☎ 01386 858323
Open: all year, daily 9am-6pm (5pm
from November to March)

CHIPPING CAMPDEN

Ernest Wilson Memorial Gardens
☎ 01386 840764
Open: all year daily 9am-7pm.

**Hidcote Manor Gardens
(National Trust)**
Hidcote Bartrim
☎ 01386 438333
Open: April to early November, daily
except Tuesday and Friday 11am-
7pm (6pm in October). Also open on
Tuesday from mid-May to July. No
entry after 6pm, or 1 hour before
sunset.

Kiftsgate Court Gardens
near Hidcote Bartrim
☎ 01386 438777
Open: April, May, August and
September, Wednesday, Thursday,
Sunday and Bank Holiday Mondays
2-6pm.
June and July Wednesday, Thursday,
Saturday, Sunday and Bank Holiday
Mondays 12noon-6pm.

CONDERTON

Toff Milway's Conderton Pottery
The Old Forge
Conderton
☎ 01386 725387
Open: all year, Monday-Saturday
9am-5pm.

**Elaine Rippon Handpainted
Silk Studios**
☎ 01386 725289
Open: February to December,
Monday-Saturday 10.30am-5pm.
January, Saturday 10.30am-5pm.

Kemerton
The Priory Garden
☎ 01386 725258
Open: June to September, Thursday
and certain Sundays 2-7pm.

Snowshill
Snowshill Manor (National Trust)
☎ 01386 852410
Open: April to October daily except
Monday and Tuesday 1-6pm. Also
open on Mondays (including Bank
Holidays) in July and August.

Stanway
Stanway Water Garden
☎ 01386 584469
Open: August and September,
Tuesday and Thursday 2-5pm.

TEWKESBURY
John Moore Countryside Museum
41 Church Street
☎ 01684 297174
Open: April to October, Tuesday-
Saturday and Bank Holiday Mondays
10am-1pm, 2-5pm. Also open most
Saturdays in winter.

Little Museum
45 Church Street
☎ 01684 297174
Open: April to October, Tuesday-
Saturday and Bank Holiday Mondays
10am-1pm, 2-5pm.

Old Baptist Chapel
Church Street
☎ 01684 299893
Open: daily, except Christmas Day
9am-dusk.

Tewkesbury Abbey
☎ 01684 850959
Open: May to September Monday-
Saturday 7.30am-5.30pm; October-
April Monday-Friday 7.30am-5pm,
Saturday 7.30am-4.30pm. Sunday all
year 7.30am-6pm. Services at 8am,
9.15am, 11am, 6pm.

Tewkesbury Town Museum
64 Barton Street
☎ 01684 295027
Open: Easter to October, daily 10am-
1pm, 1.30-4.30pm. November to
Easter by appointment only.

TODDINGTON
Gloucestershire & Warwickshire Railway
☎ 01242 621405
Open: Steam rides mid-March to
October, Saturdays, Sundays and
Bank Holidays, and weekdays during
school holidays 11am-5pm.

Cheltenham and the Surrounding Area

This area comprises Cheltenham, the escarpment north of the town, and a slice of high wold across to the A429. Although a little artificial, the area contains an excellent cross-section of the landscapes that make up the Cotswolds.

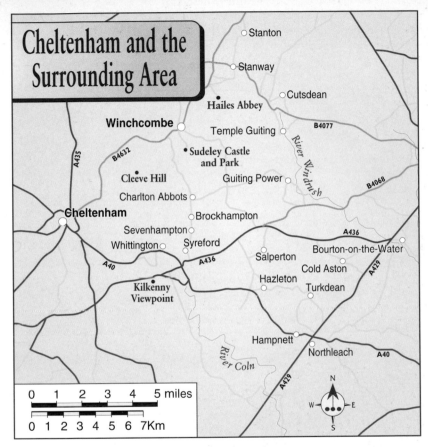

Cheltenham is now a spacious and splendid town, but until the latter part of the eighteenth century it was just a small village tucked underneath the Cotswold edge, on the road between the important towns of Gloucester and Winchcombe. Henry VIII did endow a grammar school here, but it seems likely that the importance of the village was due more to its proximity to Gloucester and a Royal Manor than to its own merits.

Then, in 1716 a Quaker farmer, William Mason, wondered why flocks of pigeons gathered to feed in one of his fields. On investigation he found that the birds were pecking at salt crystallizing near a spring in the field. Cheltenham was close enough to Bath and Clifton for Mason to realise that if this water was drinkable he could have a valuable asset. He had it analysed and, after confirmation that it was pure mineral water, he had a locked shed erected over the spring, surrounded with a stout fence. Water was bottled and sold, some being sent as far as London.

Mason however was a man of only limited ambition for when his daughter and son-in-law, Capt Henry Skillicorne, a retired merchant seaman, inherited the land in 1738, the spring was 'open and exposed to the weather'. But Skillicorne was a good business man and so Cheltenham Spa was born. The early history of the spring in the early eighteenth century may be read on Skillicorne's 587-word epitaph – the longest in Britain – in the parish church.

Skillicorne, after building four brick arches over the spring, dug it out to produce a well and he installed a pump. A road was then made to the well from the village. The beginnings were small, but steady; a report in 1740 on mineral waters in Britain stated that those in Cheltenham were the best. It was claimed to have 'action' without 'dryness, sickness, gripings or dejection of the spirit', and was effective for 'bilious conditions, obstruction of liver, spleen and perspiration, and all disorders of the primae viae'.

Dr Johnson came, as did **Handel**, but Cheltenham was off the beaten track, three days by fast coach from London, and trade slackened. After Skillicorne died the spa seemed doomed, despite his son's efforts, but in 1788 George III visited the village to take the waters. The king with his queen and children, and the queen's lady-in-waiting **Fanny Burney**, stayed for a month. The construction of the elegant modern town now began, and its popularity increased. Jane Austen even deserted her beloved Bath for a few weeks; the racecourse, still famous today, was laid out; and new pump rooms were constructed. Cheltenham rode the crest of the social wave, but by the time Cobbett presented his differing view the social bubble was indeed bursting. The socialites and water-takers departed, and left Cheltenham almost as it is today.

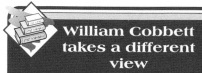

William Cobbett takes a different view

Not everyone was impressed with Cheltenham. William Cobbett in his *Rural Rides* in 1821 thought that the town was 'a nasty ill-looking place, half clown, half cockney', peopled with 'East India plunderers, West Indian floggers, English tax-gorgers, together with gluttons, drunkards and debauchees of all descriptions, female as well as male', here at the suggestion of 'silently laughing quacks, in the hope of getting rid of the bodily consequences of their manifold sins and iniquities'. He returned in the following year and noted with delight that building work was decreasing. It was 'the desolation of abomination. I have seldom seen anything with more heart-felt satisfaction. The whole town ... looked delightfully dull'. He noted 'it is curious to see the names that the vermin owners have put upon the houses there'. The townspeople were not amused, and burned his effigy.

Regency Cheltenham, and it is worth remembering that it is the most complete Regency town in Britain, is best seen by taking the leisurely promenade for which it was constructed. To prove the point The Promenade leads into the new town centre from the Lansdown/ Montpellier area. The town walk (3kms - 2 miles) should start from Montpellier Gardens: **Lansdown Place**, behind, was constructed in the early nineteenth century, about 60 years after Bath's Royal Crescent. The difference is quite striking; the buildings here seem altogether more modern, less spacious and elegant. Cheltenham was indeed laid out on a grand scale and the gardens at Montpellier are a delight. It is difficult to understand, standing here, why the town's unofficial motto is 'Pretty, poor and proud'. Pretty and proud are easy to see. But poor?

Montpellier itself, the streets that border the gardens, was built by the architect, John Papworth, who designed Lansdown Place. Montpellier Walk, with its caryatides (female figures) supporting the upper storeys, and the Rotunda (now a bank) have more character. The Rotunda itself, which is distinctively different from anything else in the area, was the pump room of Montpellier Spa. At the east end of Montpellier is the Ladies College for which Cheltenham is famous. The college was founded in 1853 and was a very bold venture for the period. Thirlestaine House, one of the college's complex of buildings, is of considerable architectural interest.

From Montpellier the broad, beautiful, tree-lined Promenade runs towards the new town centre, where there is a statue to a famous son of Cheltenham, Dr Edward Wilson, who died with Captain Scott in the Antarctic on the successful polar expedition. The statue is actually by Scott's wife. To the right of the Promenade is the Town Hall, where some of the Festival events are held. The Hall stands in Imperial Square which has another fine garden area. Beyond the square is Trafalgar Street, where Captain Hardy lived. In Clarence Street, a little way north of the Promenade, is the museum and art gallery. Here there is a fine collection of local prints, many local exhibits including the finds from the Belas Knap long barrow, and a collection of memorabilia of Edward Wilson.

Cheltenham's Gardens

C heltenham prides itself as once having been described as 'a town within a park' and also on being the 'garden town of England', the latter supported by the town having won more Britain in Bloom competitions than any other town. It has also won the Prix European d'Excellence in the *Entente Floral* competition. Throughout the summer there are masses of hanging baskets to add to the more formal gardens. Close to the Promenade are Imperial Gardens, while a little wat south are the Montpellier Gardens. South-east of the town centre is Sandford Park, while in the opposite direction is the Winston Churchill Memorial Garden with its rose garden and fine trees. Northwards is Pittville Park, split into two by the road to Evesham.

To the north of High Street, at the end of the Promenade, is **Pittville Park**, where the last of the

Cheltenham spas was situated. It is named after Joseph Pitt who 'used to hold gentlemen's horses for a penny, when, appearing as a sharp lad, an attorney at Cirencester took a fancy to him and bred him to his own business.' Pitt became a lawyer, self-taught, and used his money for land speculation, amassing a fortune with which he was to develop the park and the surrounding area. His pump room is a remarkable building being, on three sides, a copy of the Temple of Ilissus in Athens. **The pump room** is open to visitors and the spa water can still be taken. The pump room's museum/gallery of fashion portrays the history of Cheltenham's Regency period by tableaux of costume and jewellery.

Between Pittville Park and the town centre is the **Gustav Holst Birthplace Museum** in Clarence Road, in the house in which Holst was born in 1847. Much of his early work was inspired by the Cotswold countryside, particularly around Bourton-on-the-Water and Wyck Rissington, where he had his first professional engagement.

Prestbury, sandwiched between Cheltenham (of which it is now a suburb) and Cleeve Hill, is famous for its links with the turf and many famous horses have been trained here. The Racecourse's Hall of Fame explores the history of the races, horses and jockeys. Prestbury is also famous as the most haunted place in the Cotswolds – and as the second most haunted village in England. Among others, a Black Abbot walks the streets, a Cavalier rides the lane with news of the Battle of Worcester and there is the Phantom Strangler of Cleeve Corner. A little

Pittville Park, Cheltenham

Above: Imperial Gardens, Cheltenham

Right and below: The Promenade Cheltenham, (right) Neptune's statue and (below) Edward Wilson's statue

further on, towards Cleeve Hill, is **Southam** where the Sui Generis Art and Design Gallery shows the work of contemporary artists – painters, sculptors, potters, photographers etc - in a refurbished eighteenth century barn.

For those who would like a guided tour of Cheltenham, guided walks are organised by the tourist information office.

High Wolds East of Cheltenham

About 13kms (8 miles) to the east of Cheltenham is a group of six small villages and hamlets set on the high wolds which capture the feel of the old Cotswolds as no other area does. They are small collections of fine stone farmhouses clustered around churches, getting what shelter they can from a protective ring of trees, and defying the winter winds that sweep across the wolds. Here it is quiet, an almost secretive quiet.

The first of these villages is Cold Aston. Originally the village was just Aston, but this was changed to Cold Aston in the thirteenth century, then to **Aston Blank** three centuries later. Some say the change was to avoid confusion with Cold Ashton further south, but the timing of the change suggests that this was not so. Today most villagers use the older name, as – to the confusion of the visitor – do some signposts and maps. The older name does have the advantage of being very descriptive of the village well when winter winds sweep across the wold. The grey and sturdy houses seem to have been built especially to take this weather. At their centre the village green has a huge and magnificent sycamore. Equally fine is the rugged yew in the churchyard, at least 15ft around its trunk. The church itself is curious

in not having an east window, a distinctly Celtic feature in an obviously Norman building.

The first village reached from Aston Blank is **Turkdean**, which is divided into two villages by an avenue of beautiful beech trees; beyond is **Hampnett**. Here there are fine views towards Northleach and its church. Hampnett's own church is interesting: a Victorian vicar attempted to recreate the feel of a medieval church by painting the wall and ceiling. The painting is a geometric pattern rather than the usual medieval scenes of saints and sinners, but the bursts of colour must be similar to the effect that the older wall painters hoped to achieve.

Westward at **Hazleton** churchyard is a stone coffin thought to be 800 years old. The tithe barn here burnt down in 1885, a barn so big – it was reputedly the biggest ever built in Gloucestershire – that it took two weeks to burn.

Salperton, not to be confused with Sapperton further south, seems the loneliest and bleakest of all the villages. The nearby trackless railway embankment makes one feel that the village has been forgotten. Yet Salperton has as fine an early nineteenth century house as exists in the Cotswolds, set in an equally fine park. In the churchyard is a memorial with an inscription mentioning that James Harter of the Salperton Park house died of wounds in 1917 near Jerusalem, while helping to free the Holy Land from the hand of the infidel. One of his ancestors had fought in the Crusades of the thirteenth century, for the same cause.

Nearest to Cold Aston (Aston Blank) is **Notgrove**, to the west of which is a very famous long barrow

45m (150ft) long, now in the care of English Heritage. The excavated contents of the barrow, chiefly the bones of nine persons, are now in Cheltenham museum. The village itself spreads wider than Aston Blank and is, perhaps, more picturesque because of this lack of order. An old poem in the church suggests that the village name derives from its original position surrounded by hazelnut trees, though modern scholarship is at odds with this charming idea.

Closer to Cheltenham are villages strung out along a tributary headstream of the Coln, or the Coln itself. The first is little more than a hamlet at **Syreford** and from there a good walk (3kms - 2 miles - 1 hour) by path along the stream leads to Sevenhampton – often said to be the source of the Coln, though it actually rises further north – from where a lane or pathway (now on the other side of the river) leads on to Brockhampton. Each of these larger villages has a fine manor house, the latter standing in a substantial deer park. An extension of the walk, also by pathway along the river, can be made by passing the stream spring itself and reaching **Charlton Abbots**, another charming village with a good manor house. One spot in the village is known as Lepers' Yard, a memory of the time when the monks of Winchcombe Abbey had a leper colony in the village.

Continuing towards Cheltenham, the visitor passes **Whittington**, where the church stands on the lawn of the old court: around it are still the signs of an old moat – it was originally built as a fortified mansion. North from here is **Cleeve Hill**, the last unenclosed piece of high wold land left in the Cotswolds.

Cleeve Hill

At 328m (1,075ft) is the highest point of the Cotswolds. The summit is marked by a triangulation point which can be reached by a walk of a few yards from a car park. It is near a wall that overlooks it, as do the nearby radio masts. The land on each side slopes so gently that any one of dozens of spots could have been used to mark the summit. As a place of pilgrimage, it is disappointing and sad, though the same cannot be said of the common itself, a Grade I Site of Special Scientific Interest because of its beauty and plant life. There are several old quarries and rock outcrops where the fossil hunter will be well rewarded, the fossil bivalves being easy to extract from the soft oolitic limestone.

By walking from the hill's masts along the common, the visitor gains an idea of the original form of the wold, and has excellent views of Winchcombe and Sudeley in the valley to the north-east and of the Malverns and Wales to the west. Since Cleeve is unenclosed there is no danger of trespass, and walkers can wander at will – but they must beware of golf balls! The most worthwhile walk (allow 2 hours), however, is to visit the Cotswold summit and then go north to follow the edge of the common with its views to Winchcombe. At the next triangulation point, to the west, a panorama dial points out the distant hills. On the summit of Cleeve Cloud, a cliff of the local limestone,

The Holy Blood of Hailes

At the height of its prosperity it was one of the most important abbeys in England as it possessed what was said to be a phial of Sacred Blood collected at the Crucifixion. Mentioned by Chaucer, the relic drew pilgrims from all over England, who paid money to be absolved of their sins in its presence. At the Dissolution the relic was opened and publicly exposed as honey coloured with saffron. It was also said that the monks had obtained money from pilgrims by fraud. The glass phial was said to have been opaque on one side and clear on the other and the pilgrim was told that only those not in mortal sin could see the blood. On being shown the opaque side the fearful visitor then paid in full and 'miraculously' the blood appeared.

Hailes Abbey

is an Iron Age hillfort whose ditches have now been utilised to defend a golf green.

WINCHCOMBE

By descending from Cleeve Hill to the valley of the River Isbourne, the visitor can pass Winchcombe and arrive at Hailes Abbey. Postlip Mill on the River Isbourne is the county's only paper mill. The best way to reach Hailes Abbey from Winchcombe is by the Pilgrims' Way along the quaintly named Puck Pit Lane. This 1 hour route, very muddy in wet weather, is on the Cotswold Way and is well signed.

Hailes Abbey is now administered by the National Trust. It was built around 1250 and dissolved in 1539. In the museum on the site there are some of the more finely worked pieces of stone. Of the silver and other treasures, nothing remains, the abbey having been stripped of everything including the lead roof, at its dissolution. The nearby church contains some remarkable medieval wall-paintings that have been carefully restored. They depict not only the expected ecclesiastical scenes but also hunting scenes and other smaller secular pictures including a beautiful owl.

Winchcombe

![icon] **Scenic Car Tour**

Around Winchcombe

From Winchcombe take the lane south-east to Guiting Power (passing Sudeley Castle), going up steep Round Hill, and pass Guiting Wood. Go through the village to a junction. Go right then left at a Y-junction and down to the B4068. Go over and through Aylworth to the main A436. Go over and take the lane to Cold Aston. Go back along the lane, now taking one to Notgrove (the Notgrove long barrow is beside the A436 a mile from the village). Go south to Turkdean and through it to the A429. Go right. At the roundabout go right on the A40 to Cheltenham, taking a lane right for Hazleton. Follow lanes to Brockhampton, crossing the A436 again just beyond Salperton, and from there go on to Charlton Abbots. Beyond that village the road falls steeply down to the A46 and Winchcombe (Belas Knap long barrow to the left).

Short Cycle Rides

↑1 **Wold Villages** *(15 miles)* Map: OS Sheet 163 – Cheltenham &
Cirencester area.
From Cold Aston (Aston Blank) take the lane to Notgrove. Go through
the village and at the T-junction go left for Turkdean. Go through that
village, and about half a mile beyond the church a very sharp right turn
is taken. Go down towards the A40 but a few yards before it go right on
a lane for Hazleton. This goes steeply down at one point but is quite
safe. Take the road for Salperton/Brockhampton, and go off it for
Salperton itself. Go through the village and down to the A436. Go right
and along the main road (Notgrove long barrow) for 2 miles to a turn,
right, for Notgrove. From there go back to Cold Aston.

↑2 **Winchcombe to Charlton Abbots** *(10 miles, but with a very steep
climb)* Map: OS Sheet 163 – Cheltenham & Cirencester area.
A route for the enthusiast. From Winchcombe take the lane south-
eastwards for Guiting Power (Sudeley Castle) that rises steeply up
Round Hill. As the top of the climb is reached the road bends right-
ward, and about 400yd on take the right fork at a Y-junction. This lane
is mercifully flat and reaches a point from which the view over the
Sudeley estate and Winchcombe is as breathtaking as the ride up Round
Hill. Go on to Roel Gate, a crossroads, where the route goes right. The
road goes steeply down at one point, beyond which go right into
Charlton Abbots. From the village the lane to Winchcombe is taken, a
lane that is very steep in several places as it nears the town. The Belas
Knap long barrow is off this road, to the left, beyond Humblebee Wood.

Winchcombe is the largest town
on the north-eastern edge. There
was once an abbey here but, unlike
Hailes, nothing is now visible except
a cross (on private land) that marks
the position of the altar.

The town was a capital of Saxon
Mercia and has, in St Peter's church,
the stone coffins that may be those
of a Mercian King, Kenulf, and his
son, the boy-saint Kenelm. Kenelm
was murdered in Shropshire by order of his ambitious sister and his
body was brought back here by
monks from the abbey who had been
guided to the spot by a heavenly
shaft of light. His sister, stunned by
the finding of the body, appeared at
the window as it was being carried

by, reading Psalm 108 backwards
and 'at that moment her eyes, torn
by divine vengeance from their
hollow sockets, scattered blood
upon the verse'. Until the discovery
of the coffins the story was believed
to be entirely legend, but the presence in the smaller coffin of not only
the bones of a boy but also a large
dagger – the reputed murder
weapon – has now suggested that
parts of the story may be true.

As well as the church, there are
other points of interest in the town.
Many of its inns, particularly the
George and the Corner Cupboard,
are very ancient and full of character. **The Folk and Police Museum**
sheds light on the area's history and

includes an interesting collection of police uniforms and equipment. There is also a small railway museum which the enthusiast should not fail to visit. The old stocks exist, opposite the George Hotel. There is a wide variety of shops, and on the Broadway Road out of the town is a **Pottery** specialising in hand-thrown stoneware, together with other craft-workshops which include sculpture, jewellery making and wood turning.

Close to Winchcombe is **Sudeley Castle**, a marvellous site, in private ownership. The castle has a long and distinguished history. It was so beautifully sited that Edward IV arrested Ralph Boteler, the owner, for treason, in order to acquire it for himself. As Boteler was taken away he turned to take his last look and said 'Sudeley Castle, thou art the traitor, not I'. The castle was of major importance at the end of the reign of Henry VIII. Henry came here with Katherine of Aragon and with Anne Boleyn. Thomas Seymour, brother of Jane, Henry's third wife, not only owned the castle but also married Katherine Parr, Henry's widow. Both Queen Mary and Queen Elizabeth spent time here as princesses and from here Lady Jane Grey, Thomas Seymour's niece, set out on the journey to London which

Tobacco

On the western edge of Winchcombe there is a street called Tobacco Close, an odd name for the Cotswolds but one which has its roots in a curious aspect of Cotswold farming.

Following the Civil War, the area from Cheltenham to Winchcombe became well known for growing tobacco. It was first planted by William Stratford near Winchcombe and, when it proved successful, the fields from there to Cheltenham were rapidly taken over for its production. Indeed there were isolated fields of tobacco as far south as Bristol. The crop was soon worth the remarkable sum of £1,500 a year.

The Government became fearful that this new, home-produced crop would harm the prosperity of the new colonies in America (especially Virginia) which were almost entirely dependent on their tobacco crop, and so made its cultivation illegal here. The decision was not popular and a series of pro-tobacco propaganda pamphlets was issued. The best of these was Henry Hangman's Horror, or Gloucestershire's request to the smokers and tobacconists of London. This was a nice piece of black humour, for it claimed that the hangman's trade had declined locally since the lawful growing of tobacco had become widespread, and that the real aim of the ban was to produce a crime wave and hence an increase in executions.

The propaganda, however, was unsuccessful and illicit growing was stamped on hard. Riots were frequent as soldiers arrived to destroy crops. The locals were referred to as a 'rabble of men and women calling for blood for the tobacco', and blood they got when they attacked an army detachment, killing men and horses. Henry Hangman got his way and the growing ceased. But a large field near Bristol continued to grow the crop for a further fifty years.

Selected Walks

1 **Hailes Abbey and Sudeley Castle** *6 miles* •*Moderate/ Strenuous*• *1,000ft climb* Map: OS Sheet 163 – Cheltenham & Cirencester area.
Start at Winchcombe. Go north on the A46 towards Broadway and after crossing the River Isbourne take the second lane to the right, Puck Pit Lane, and follow a section of the Cotswold Way to Hailes Abbey. The route goes across farmland, but is well signed and beaten. From the abbey go uphill southward, following Salter's Way, an old salt route. After a steep uphill section, 400yd beyond a small wood, a signed path right beside a stone wall is taken. Follow this through two gates (at the second a path to the right offers a short cut back to Winchcombe.) Go on, passing St Kenelm's Well to a lane. Go left, and almost immediately right on a lane to Sudeley Hill Cottages. Near them a signed path right leads through fields to the parkland of Sudeley Castle. Follow the path through the park to Winchcombe.

2 **Cleeve Hill** *10.5 miles* •*Strenuous*• *900ft climb* Map: OS Sheet 163 – Cheltenham & Cirencester area.
Start at Winchcombe and follow the Cotswold Way southward, leaving on the lane to Sudeley Castle, then going across fields to the Wadfield Roman Villa and Humblebee Cottages, and uphill to the Belas Knap long barrow. Beyond is Wontley Farm and High Cleeve Common. The Way here goes right, but head instead for the masts, the high point of the common and the Cotswolds. From the masts follow the wall rightwards as you approach it, to its end, and go ahead skirting the hillfort and the rock outcrops of Cleeve Cloud. Continue to the Cleeve Hill Golf Club House. Take the signed, worn track east, reaching and following the wall of Postlip Hall. Continue through Postlip Mill (go towards 'Reception', then past the fire station) and take the lane beyond. Where it bends sharply left go ahead through the field to a road. Go right, over the river and left on a signed path beside the river to Winchcombe.

3 **Wold Villages** *5 miles* •*Moderate*• *200ft climb* Map: OS Sheet 163 – Cheltenham & Cirencester area.
The high Wolds are not well supplied with footpaths, but use can be made of the quiet lanes to explore the area. Start at Cold Aston (Aston Blank). Go west towards Notgrove, but take a lane left to Bangup Farm and on to the stream. Beyond, the lane continues to Turkdean. From there take the lane to Notgrove. In Notgrove a path beside the church, to the left, goes through a delightful piece of woodland to a lane. Go right to return to Cold Aston.

Opposite page: Sudeley Castle

75

was to end so tragically for her. Katherine Parr is buried in the castle church.

In addition to the castle itself, which has many art treasures, there is a ruined wing of the castle, gardens and a pond with wildfowl. In the parkland around the castle is an excellent children's playground complete with a huge wooden fort. Each year there is a calendar of special exhibitions and events in the castle or grounds.

There are several good walks from Winchcombe, and two of the best include visits to ancient sites. The first (8kms - 5 miles - 2 hours) follows the Cotswold Way past the beautiful Wadfield Farm and Humblebee Cottages to the long barrow, returning down the country lane towards the A46, but following the river back to the town before the main road is reached. The Belas Knap long barrow is one of the best preserved of the many such Stone Age burial chambers that can be seen in the Cotswolds. Much of its dry stone walling is original – a local craft that has remained unchanged for some 4,000 years. The wallers who, in 1798, were offering 'New Dry walling [at] Sixteen pence per Perch 4ft high' would recognise the style of these walls. The apparent doorway of the barrow is, in fact, false: it was built either to fool grave robbers or, perhaps, to confuse evil spirits.

The other walk visits **Spoonley Roman Villa**. This walk (also 8kms -5 miles - 2 hours) actually goes through Sudeley Park and then by path and track to the woods that now surround the villa (at OS reference 045177). A circular route can be taken from here, but it is better to return by the same walk. The villa

site has not been extensively excavated, but rooms and the courtyard can be discerned. The site has the feel of a ghostly ruin.

ABOVE WINCHCOMBE

High on the wolds above Winchcombe is the source of the Windrush, and (at Cutsdean) of the Cotswolds name itself. In wet weather the stream has come a short distance by the time it reaches **Cutsdean**, but in dry weather it is barely a trickle until Ford, about 800m further down the valley. It is only slight even there but it will become the most truly Cotswold of all the rivers whose valleys split the high wolds. It was high in this valley that an Anglo-Saxon called Cod had a farm on the wolds.

The walk along the footpath that follows the Windrush back towards its source from Cutsdean to Taddington, returning by the lane through the original wolds, is a link with history. If the stream is barely visible, the walk can be made along it, further down the valley from Ford to **Temple Guiting**, again returning along a high wold lane.

Temple Guiting is a beautiful village, set among trees at the side of the stream. The stream has given it the second word in its name, derived from the same root as 'gushing'. Temple recalls the twelfth century ownership of the manor by the Knights Templar. From here to Guiting Power the Windrush is not followed by footpaths, although the lane that connects the Guitings is delightful. **Guiting Power** is set on a tributary of the Windrush and is a straggling village, less picturesque than its more romantically named neighbour.

Cheltenham and the Surrounding Area

CHELTENHAM

Cheltenham College
Bath Road
☎ 01242 513540
Open: any reasonable time, by arrangement with the bursar's office.

Cheltenham Town Museum & Art Gallery
Clarence Street
☎ 01242 237431
Open: all year, Monday-Saturday 10am-5.20pm. Closed Bank Holidays.

Gustav Holst Birthplace Museum
4 Clarence Road
☎ 01242 524846
Open: all year, Tuesday-Saturday 10am-4.20pm; closed Bank Holidays and Christmas Eve.

Hall of Fame
Cheltenham Racecouse, Prestbury Park
☎ 01242 513014
Open: all year Monday-Friday 9.30am-4.30pm

Pittville Pump Room and Museum
Pittville Park
Albert Road
☎ 01242 523852
Open: all year, daily except Tuesday 10am-4pm (4.30pm from May to September).

Sui Generis Art and Design Gallery
The Barley Barn, Southam
☎ 01242 252610
Open: all year, Wednesday-Sunday 10am-6pm

WINCHCOMBE

Folk and Police Museum
Town Hall, High Street
☎ 01242 602925
Open: April to October, Monday-Saturday 10am-5pm.

Hailes Abbey (English Heritage and National Trust)
near Winchcombe
☎ 01242 602398
Open: April to October, daily 10am-6pm (5pm in October); November to March, Saturday and Sunday 10am-4pm; closed 24-25 December.

Sudeley Castle
☎ 01242 602308
Open: April to October, daily 10.30am-5.30pm.

Winchcombe Pottery
Off the B4632 (Broadway) road about 1½kms (1 mile) north of the town
☎ 01242 602462
Open: all year Monday-Friday 8am-5pm, Saturday 10am-4pm.
Also open Sunday 12noon-4pm (May to September)

Winchcombe Railway Museum
23 Gloucester Street
☎ 01242 620641
Open: Easter to October, Saturday, Sunday and Bank Holidays 1.30-5pm, Wednesday-Friday 10am-2pm. Open daily in August 1.30-5.30pm.

he north-eastern Cotswold villages differ little in character from those of the north-western edge. There are still warm, stone villages nestling beneath tree-clad hills, but here, rather than the edge of the escarpment the hill is the side of a valley cut deep into the limestone. The north-eastern area, however, is also true high wold, bleak and free of woodland. Indeed the town of Stow is rightly 'on-the-Wold', having been built in an exposed position on the highest land.

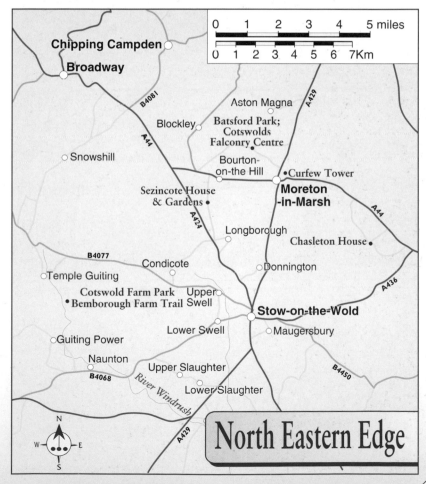

North Eastern Edge

A further effect of this uniformly high wold is the limitation of the view. It does not extend across to the Welsh hills, but it is an equally inspiring vista of rolling wold-land.

MORETON-IN-MARSH

Moreton-in-Marsh is the principal town, not only of this section of the Cotswolds but of the entire northern area. The name - often, and quite incorrectly, given as Moreton-in-the-Marsh - is something of a misnomer, as it is doubtful whether the area around the town was ever marshland. It is more likely that 'marsh' is a corruption of 'merche' or 'march', the ancient name for a boundary. To support this theory, there is, about 3kms (2 miles) east of the town on the A44 to Chipping Norton, a Four-Shires Stone which formerly marked the boundary of the counties of Gloucestershire, Oxfordshire, Warwickshire and Worcestershire. Following the re-drawing of county boundaries in 1928, however, there are now only three county boundaries meeting at the stone, the county of Worcester having withdrawn about 15kms (10miles) north-west.

The **Foss Way**, an important road in Roman times, was the effective western boundary of Roman Britain for some time, as the Romans attempted to subdue the Silurian tribesmen to the west of the River Severn. Moreton straddles the Foss Way (now the main A429) in elegant fashion; the broad, tree-lined High Street with its occasional wide, grassed verges being a perfect foreground for the rows of late eighteenth- and early nineteenth-century houses. The majority of these houses were built when the town was an important coaching stage, and also the centre of a linen weaving industry. Linen weaving grew up after the decline of the woollen industry, first using locally grown flax and then imported material.

The town is worth exploring in detail as it is a fine example of a late Cotswold market town. The church, St David's, is mid-nineteenth century, though it may incorporate very much earlier work. It used to contain perhaps the most amusing epitaph in the Cotswolds:

Here lie the bones of Richard Lawton whose death, alas, was strangeley brought on,
   trying one day his corns to mow off the razor slipped, and cut his toe off

West of the church the old parsonage is of comparable age, although tiled in Welsh slate rather than the local stone. At the corner of Church Street and High Street is the Manor House Hotel, one of the older houses in the town, dating from the mid-seventeenth century. This provides a direct comparison with Chipping Campden which has many houses of considerably greater age. The influence of Moreton's linen industry is clearly visible in the number of later houses.

The Manor House is said to be haunted. Further along High Street is the White Hart Hotel where Charles I is said to have spent a night in the summer of 1644 during the Civil War, although an inscription suggests a construction date of 1782!

Moreton's Curfew Tower

The Curfew Tower, on the corner of Oxford Street, is sixteenth century and is the oldest building in the town. The tower still contains the last curfew bell, dated 1633, which was rung daily until the mid-nineteenth century and even later to call the local fire brigade. The word curfew derives from 'cover-fire', and a bell was rung nightly from the time of the Norman Conquest to try to prevent house fires. In view of the survival of the tower it is perhaps fitting that today Moreton is a centre for the training of firemen.

High Street is dominated by the imposing lines of **Redesdale Hall**, in the middle of the old broad road. The building is also known as Market Hall, a reminder that this has long been the local market town, a tradition maintained by a weekly market held on Tuesdays, with stalls laid out along the west side of the High Street. In Broadway Road, close to the High Street the Wellington Aviation Museum and Art Gallery has a collection of items not only from the Wellingtons of the name, but other aircraft. There is also a gallery of art with aviation themes.

AROUND MORETON

Close to Moreton is **Bourton-on-the-Hill**. This was also once 'on-the-Merche', as was Moreton, but although it is now 'on-the-Hill', it is in fact just below the level of the high wolds; the village straddles the A44 as it descends towards Moreton. It is an unlikely site for a village, but still excellent and very popular with local artists, its tiers of cottages, each with a colourful, terraced garden, being a picture composer's dream. The church – dedicated to St Lawrence – holds a Winchester bushel and peck, volume standards laid down in the time of Elizabeth I. The two standards are very rare, having been produced just before the change from the Winchester to the Imperial scale.

At the base of the hill, the visitor arriving from Moreton passes **Bourton House**, which still contains some sixteenth-century work and has a superb tithe barn, the largest in the area, inscribed 'R. P. 1570'. R. P. is for Richard Palmer, and is a link with a murder that, in its day, was as famous as the Campden Wonder. Palmer was, by marriage, connected to the remarkable Overbury family.

South of Bourton-on-the-Hill is **Sezincote**, famous for its house and garden. The house was remodelled in the early eighteenth century by Sir Charles Cockerell whose wealth derived from his work with the East India Company. He obviously enjoyed the East, and had the house constructed in Indian style with oriental gardens. The architects for the house and garden were Daniell and Repton, assisted by Cockerell's brother. The park is clearly the work of a great British eccentric; Sir Charles obviously had a good pedigree for the task, his parents having christened his brother Samuel Pepys Cockerell. In its day the park was a very bold venture and impressed the Prince Regent so much during a visit in 1807 that he decided to use a

The Overbury Murder

Sir Thomas Overbury wrote the first detailed account of the Campden murder but, before that in 1613, an earlier Thomas Overbury was the victim of a real and very unpleasant murder. Thomas opposed the marriage of his friend and favourite of James I, Robert Carr, to Frances Howard, Lady Essex, not least because she was already married. To silence him, Lady Essex had him wrongfully imprisoned in the Tower of London where he was poisoned with cakes containing 'arsenic, aqua fortis, mercury, powder of diamonds, lapis costitus, great spiders and cantharides'. The combination did not kill Sir Thomas quickly. Indeed he was in great agony for months and was reduced to a skeleton, his doctor maintaining that his illness was due to natural causes. Eventually it was decided that he was to be released, and a large dose of a 'corrosive' substance was administered as a coup de grâce. Some three years later the young apothecary who had obtained the poison confessed and Lady Essex, now Carr's wife, Carr himself and several others were committed to the Tower. Saved by their rank, the Carrs were released after five years, but several of their accomplices were hanged.

similar but more subdued design for his own planned extravaganza, the Brighton Pavilion. There is a profusion of exotic trees, and one should not miss the bridge over the landscaped valley north of the house, or the Wellington Memorial which serves also as a chimney for the greenhouse heating system.

Also close to Bourton-on-the-Hill is **Batsford Park**. The house here was built in the late nineteenth century, the park having been landscaped by Lord Redesdale a little earlier. Redesdale was the British Ambassador to Japan around 1850 and imported many oriental ideas as well as statues and plants. A bronze Buddha, deer and dolphins were all brought back from Japan and there is a replica of a Chinese temple. The park is now an arboretum with what is considered to be the finest private collection of rare trees and shrubs in Britain. The higher areas of the park offer fine views of the Evenlode

Valley. As well as the arboretum there is a garden centre which sells many of the trees and shrubs that grow there, and the Cotswolds Falconry Centre with flying demonstrations by eagles, owls, hawks and falcons.

Nearby is **Aston Magna**, a pleasant village grouped around a green which still has the base of its medieval village cross. The village pool, which is actually within the Batsford estate, offers excellent fishing. Licences can be obtained from the estate office.

BLOCKLEY AND LONGBOROUGH

Blockley, in a valley below Bourton-on-the-Hill, is well worth a visit. It is a delightful place, perhaps the finest and most unspoilt of the larger Cotswold villages. Like many other Cotswold communities it suffered from the decline of the woollen industry, which affected all the

Redesdale Hall,
Moreton-in-Marsh

northern towns and villages, alleviated in its case by the continued production from its eight silk mills, powered by the fast flowing stream in its secluded valley. Because of them it has survived remarkably well, the old workhouse, in the High Street, has even been converted into an antique shop. Some of the old mills have been similarly converted: many of the houses on Blockley Brook at the southern end of the village were mills in the sixteenth and seventeenth century. The village also possesses a fine collection of genuinely ancient inns, now selling real ale.

The history of the village during the last 300 years has been closely linked to that of the Northwick family who built nearby Northwick Park and its mansions. Particularly noteworthy was John Rushout, the second Lord Northwick, who once sailed with Lord Nelson and Sir William and Lady Hamilton. He constructed the Five Mile Drive which is such a feature of the A44 above Blockley, and also landscaped the valley at the south end of the village now known as Dovedale, to the fascination and confusion of lovers of the Peak District. A little way south of the village **Mill Dene Garden** is a lovely garden surrounding a mill (not open) in a tight valley. The flower beds, flower-types selected for their scent, are explored by secret paths which wind close to the mill stream and pool. Please note that the garden is not suitable for children or wheelchairs.

From the end of Blockley High Street, which actually leads nowhere, a fine 1 hour walk follows a track through Dovedale to Bourton Woods and through them to the Five Mile Drive. Apart from this one track on the southern side, the woods are

private, though access is allowed at most times, with excellent woodland walking. Returning to the village, look for Fish Cottage –in the (private) garden of the cottage is a memorial stone to commemorate a fish that would feed from the owner's hand, and lived for 20 years until 1855!

South of Sezincote is a trio of picturesque villages on the high wold, snatching what cover they can from the folding of the landscape. **Longborough** has a church with Norman doorways; it contains both a monumental bust of Sir Charles Cockerell of Sezincote Park and a fine effigy in armour that dates from the early fourteenth century. Nearby is **Condicote**. The Victoria County History of Gloucestershire notes that 'except that the land was sometimes owned by important people, Condicote has no associations with figures or events of national fame or notoriety. Its remoteness and its physical condition are the kind to have made the life of the community as uneventful as it is austere'! Be that as it may, the village has much of interest. Its church contains a large amount of Norman work, and a group of beautiful eighteenth century Cotswold farmhouses surround an old village green that still has its ancient cross. The cross could be 600 years old, but is modern in comparison with the site now exposed on the eastern side of the village. This site is believed to be a Neolithic ceremonial or 'henge' site and, as such, pre-dates the cross by several thousand years.

SOUTH TO THE WOLDS

Condicote Lane, the Roman Ryknield Street, runs through the

village down towards the Foss Way at Stow. This can be followed over the local high point, at around 880ft, returning by lanes to the village. This is a most interesting walk of 6^1/$_2$kms (4 miles) - allow 2 hours - following in the steps of the Romans and giving a very good view of the high wold. This area, to the west of Condicote, is a superb expanse of enclosed and cultivated wold. Cleeve Common gives a good impression of how the original wolds must have looked, but this area, between Condicote and the Guitings, is an excellent example of the more modern landscape.

Donnington is the third of the villages, and is famous as the place of surrender of Lord Astley and his army in 1646 in the final battle of the first Civil War. Astley is famous for the couplet:

Lord I shall be verie busie this day
I may forget Thee, but doe not
Thou forget me

coined before the Battle of Edge Hill. Astley had reached Stow on his way to join the king at Oxford. History records his final act of surrender after the battle, painting a sorry picture of an old and tired soldier: 'taken captive and wearyed in his fight, and being ancient – for old age's silver haires had quite covered over his head and beard'. His 'soldiers brought him a Drum to sit and rest himselfe upon' and he told them and his captors to 'sit downe and play, for you have done all your worke' adding, prophetically, to the Parliamentarians, 'if you fall not out among yourselves'.

On a more cheerful note there is, between the villages of Condicote and Donnington, a brewery that produces real ale. The site, on a long lake, appears most incongruous in the wold land, but is the result of the extension of an old mill pond. The old mill-wheel still helps to power the brewery, which is housed in an old mill building with a dovecote in one wall. The brewery grows its own barley and so is completely self-contained; it produces beer that, when bottled, requires skilful pouring, as it also contains old-fashioned sediment. Near the brewery is **Donnington Fish Farm**, a very modern trout farm based in a beautiful seventeenth century barn. All stages in the life of the trout can be seen, and a shop on the premises sells fresh and smoked trout, and salmon in season. Trout fishing is available on site and there is a picnic area.

At Bemborough Farm, the **Cotswold Farm Park** concentrates on the breeding of ancient species of domesticated animals. The co-director of the park was a founder of the Rare Breeds Survival Trust, and the animals on show are part of the most comprehensive collection of breeds in the trust. Soay sheep, one of the oldest breeds, live on seaweed on the islands of St Kilda, and Manx Loghtan sheep are of Viking origin and have four horns. The pigs include the beautifully coloured Tamworth Gingers and the hardy, and local, Gloucester Old Spot; these do not need cover and can survive on fallen apples. There are also goats and geese, cattle and chickens. In addition to the penned animals there is a pets' corner with sheep, goats and pigs to feed, rides in a shire-drawn cart and barns containing educational exhibits, souvenirs and refreshments. The large car-parking field is ideal for picnics and there is an adventure playground.

Blockley

Cotswold Farm Park

Cotswold Farm Park

In 1968, two Cotswold farmers, Joe Henson and John Neave, decided to help save the last remnants of Gloucestershire's three farm animal breeds.

Two hundred years ago, white-tailed Gloucester cattle filled the dairies of the Severn vale, producing Double Gloucester cheese and quality beef for the London market. By 1972 there was just one herd of pure Gloucesters left.

The Romans brought the Roman Longwool from Italy to replace the scraggy native sheep. In medieval times the Wool Merchants grew rich from the golden fleece off the back of these huge, long-wooled Cotswold sheep. When Libby Henson founded her flock, only 300 ewes remained.

In Victorian times every cottage had a pig sty where a lop-eared Gloucester Old Spot pig lived on the household waste. Fat, of course, means flavour; and local restaurants are now featuring Old Spot pork, bacon and sausages as gourmet fare.

The Cotswold Farm Park opened to the public in 1971 with 30 different breeds of sheep, cattle, goats, pigs and horses, together with assorted poultry and water-fowl.

Visitors to the Park can also see fascinating examples of Britain's living agricultural heritage, walk the farm nature trail, buy local craft work in the gift shop and enjoy home cooked Cotswold food in the restaurant.

South of the Farm Park is **Naunton**. This village, which has an excellent church containing some Saxon features and a fine gabled dovecote with over a thousand nest holes, is on the River Windrush and could be perfect. But it is just a little too long, and appears to straggle. Perhaps the view from the A436, south of and above the village where too much of the village can be seen, betrays it, for the limited aspect from the northern approach by country lanes is much more pleasant. The view from the south, with the church and a cluster of cottages close to it against a backdrop of wold, is well known.

Naunton, as with all villages close to Stow, shows evidence of the Civil War. As if to represent the feelings of the majority of the ordinary people at that time who waved Parliamentarian and Royalist flags with equal vigour at various times, the town's evidence is double-headed. In St Andrew's church there is a marble memorial Ambrose Oldys recording that he was 'barbarously murdered by ye rebells' in 1645 after having 'escaped many and eminent dangers in battles for ye honour and service of his King'.

By contrast, further down the Windrush is **Cromwell House** built before the war, but renamed by the Aylworth family in honour of the Protector. Indeed it was Richard Aylworth who stopped the King's army at Stow in 1644. The Aylworths are also commemorated at a hamlet of that name which can be reached by a path across the wold and along a tributary stream of the Windrush, from the A436 above Naunton, returning there by country lanes (5kms - 3 miles - 1 hour). The hamlet was part of a larger estate that extended over much of the land in this area south of the Windrush.

An attraction of Naunton is the Windrush, and the walk from Harford Bridge to the Foss Bridge near Bourton-on-the-Water is as delightful as any of the 'softer' river valleys to the south. The route (5kms - 3 miles - 1 hour) is straightforward enough, leaving the minor road from Harford Bridge just after crossing the Windrush. From there the route follows the river as it meanders gently towards Foss Bridge. At the Foss Bridge end an old, now trackless, railway embankment is crossed, and the walker can use a redundant railway bridge to cross the river, as both banks of the river have pathways.

Taking the A436 from Harford Bridge towards Stow the traveller drops down to cross the Eye valley. Here, to the south of the road, are the villages of Upper and Lower Slaughter, pictures of which have, rightly, adorned almost every book ever compiled on the beauties of the Cotswolds. Massingham, the writer on the English countryside, maintained that the two villages, together with the two Swells a little closer to Stow, 'perfectly exemplify, as no other group quite does, the unique and local genius of the Cotswold style'.

THE SLAUGHTERS AND SWELLS

Massingham preferred the Slaughters and particularly **Upper Slaughter**. Even a car driving through the village seems to disturb the timelessness of the cottages grouped around the church and manor. From the Eye Bridge on the A436 a walk of only 2¹/₂kms (1¹/₂ miles) is needed to

reach both villages and, a further kilometre beyond the second, the A429 is reached. For those who have to make the visit by car, the road about 2¹/₂kms (1¹/₂ miles) north of Harford Bridge, dropping down the side of the valley and giving superb views of both Slaughters in the wooded valley floor, should be used.

The River Eye is known in its 3km (2 mile) section between the main roads as the Slaughterbrook. The name Slaughter has no evil connotations, as it derives from the Saxon for either 'the place of the Sloe trees' or 'the place of the pools'. Only the latter is now appropriate. Upper Slaughter is so rich in interest and beauty that travellers should wander at will, but they should not miss the ford, which is still used, nor the farms, cottages and superb trees gathered around it. There is a fine dovecote up-river of the ford. The church has been 'modernised' several times, not always successfully, but is still worthy of note. One rector was the Reverend F. E. Witts who wrote *The Diary of a Cotswold Parson*.

At the true village centre there is a small reminder of the green and, beyond, two manors. One is the original manor house, a largely Elizabethan house built on earlier foundations. It has been described as the most beautiful domestic house in the Cotswolds, with its row of dormer windows and Jacobean doorway. Sadly the manor is not, at present, open to the public. The other manor was 'The Manor': it was the old parsonage but took a new name in the nineteenth century when the rector became Lord of the Manor. It is now a hotel.

Lower Slaughter also has a ford, but here the brook follows the road closely for much further, the village being grouped around it. One added advantage of the brook is that one side of it allows a car-free walk past excellent stone cottages. Indeed, this array of cottages beside the stream can lay claim to being the prettiest village in the Cotswolds. At one end of the village is the old mill complete with an occasionally moving waterwheel. The mill is now a museum of milling and a crafts showroom. The mill has a brick chimney which, strangely, seems in no way incongruous. At the other end of the village opposite the Manor House is a tree-sheltered green beside the brook. Next to the manor is a sixteenth century dovecote, one of the largest in Gloucestershire.

In the valley of the Dikler, a stream that, like the Eye, flows to Bourton-on-the-Water, are the Swells, named from a shortening of 'Our Lady's Well'. **Upper Swell** is only 1km ($^1/_2$ mile) south of the Donnington brewery. As car parking is banned on the narrow road through the village, the interested traveller must walk from laybys on the B4077. Those walking from the direction of Stow reach a right-angled bridge with excellent views of the mill and mill-pond, before turning into the village itself. The round trip from here (3kms - 2 miles - 1 hour) is best accomplished by going along the lane from Upper to Lower Swell, returning by track and path along the Dikler.

Lower Swell is, in fact, away from the river and seems to suffer as a result. It has some interesting corners, however; the visitor who has been to Sezincote will undoubtedly have a sense of déjà vu when he sees Spa Cottages. To the west of the villages are several long barrows and other reminders of prehistory. The solitary, enigmatic Hoar Stone, about 800m south-west of Lower Swell, is also thought to be the remnant of a long barrow.

Short Cycle Ride

The Slaughters and the Swells (17 miles)
Map: OS Sheet 163 – Cheltenham & Cirencester area.
From Stow-on-the-Wold follow the B4077 to Upper Swell. Go left beyond the village to Lower Swell. Go right immediately on a lane that rises gently to cross the Roman Ryknield Street, now called Condicote Lane, and then falls to a junction near a huge quarry. Right from here is the Cotswold Farm Park and its picnic area. Go left and follow the lane to the B4068. Go over and on past Manor Farm, going left beyond it to Upper Slaughter. From there take the beautiful lane to Lower Slaughter, and from there follow the equally excellent lane to Lower Swell. In the village the lane meets the B4068 that is followed back to Stow-on-the-Wold.

Lower Slaughter, the old mill

Above: **Upper Slaughter**

Below and right: **Lower Slaughter**

STOW-ON-THE-WOLD

Visits to the Slaughters and the Swells inevitably lead the traveller to **Stow-on-the-Wold**. This delightful market town is, with Moreton, perhaps the best known of the small Cotswold towns. The addition to the name is as recent as the sixteenth century, the town having been previously called Stow St Edward. The religious name was given by the Abbot of Evesham who sited the town here at the crossing of many major roads at about 800ft with no sheltering hill on any side. The locals say it has no earth, fire or water, but plenty of air, and a local couplet maintains:

Stow-on-the-Wold
where the wind blows cold

When the Cotswolds became rich during the wool boom, Stow, with its two annual fairs, was a centre of considerable importance. **Daniel Defoe**, during his journey through the area, recorded that at one fair over 20,000 sheep were sold, and that such huge numbers were not uncommon. The size of the market place, around which the town is built, is indicative of these fairs at which both sheep and horses were sold. Such was their importance that they became a unit of time and certainty – 'three years next fair' and 'as sure as the fair'.

The town church is dedicated to St Edward; its continued existence is remarkable when one recalls that, after the Civil War battle at Donnington in 1646 in which a large Royalist army was totally defeated, prisoners were incarcerated in it. The conditions of their imprisonment were, to say the least, primitive and their behaviour was, not surprisingly in view of the executions that were frequently carried out on prisoners at that time, appalling. After this use as a prison, the church was declared ruined. Fortunately in the latter part of the seventeenth century it was restored, although further major work was required 200 years later. Despite numerous deaths, the churchyard contains only one marked grave of a soldier from the battle or its aftermath – that of a Captain Keyte.

The church is on the west side of the market square. Walking around the square and the rest of the town, the visitor is faced with an elegant array of Cotswold town houses. **St Edward's Hall**, now the county library, is Victorian, and dominates the centre of the square, whilst St Edward's House is perhaps the best of the eighteenth century houses. At one end is the town cross, of which only the base is ancient; at the other are the original town stocks. In Park Street, follow Digbeth Street from the corner of the Square, the **Toy and Collectors Museum** has a collection of toys and teddy bears, books and other childhood collectables. The museum is attached to a shop.

Despite the association of Stow with the Foss Way, and the references to the road in several house and hotel names, the Way does not actually pass through the town, which is 2kms (about a mile) north. But it does pass through **Maugersbury**, an excellent village, just a little way from the town. Just before Maugersbury the Way passes yet another reminder, in name, of the town's ecclesiastical beginnings – St Edward's Well – an artificial pond and stream that marked one

Scenic Car Tours

↑1 Around Stow-on-the-Wold

From Stow-on-the-Wold take the A429 southward towards Bourton-on-the-Water – from the right fork where the A424 goes off left to Burford, the main road follows the line of the Roman Foss Way. Take the minor road right to Lower Slaughter, about 2 miles from the A424 junction, and go through the village and on to Upper Slaughter. Circle the village in order to go through its well known ford. Go back towards Lower Slaughter, but turn right after a few yards on a narrow lane to a T-junction. Go right and take the first left, a narrow lane, which has a steep final section as it falls to Harford Bridge and the B4068. Go over this and into Naunton. Turn left at Grange Hill Farm, after the village, and follow signs to Guiting Power. Go through the village to a crossroads after 1 mile and go right to Kineton. Ahead now is the Cotswold Farm Park. Take the road past it (to Upper Slaughter and Bourton-on-the-Water), turning left before a huge quarry towards Lower Swell. Beyond that village is Stow.

↑2 Around Moreton-in-Marsh

From Moreton-in-Marsh take the A44 westward to Bourton-on-the-Hill (Batsford arboretum) and beyond it turn right along the B4479 to Blockley. Go left beyond the church, ignoring a lane to Chipping Campden for one that reaches the A44 again at Five Mile Drive. Go left and fork left, where the A422 goes ahead, to take the A44 back towards Bourton. Before the village go right along a lane (Sezincote) that leads to the A424 near Longborough. Follow the main road to Stow-on-the-Wold. Leave the town by the A436 eastwards following it for about 5 miles to a lane left for Chastleton (Chastleton House). Go right beyond the village to meet the A44 again. Go right and down to the crossroads and pub. Go ahead towards Chipping Norton, but just beyond the pub go left on a lane that leads to the Rollright Stones. Go back along the lane to one for Little Compton, going through the village to the A44. Go right and follow this (Four Shires Stone) back to Morton-in-Marsh.

Chastleton House

Rollright Stones

Selected Walks

↑1 ***Blockley and Bourton-on-the-Hill*** 5 miles •Moderate/Strenuous• 400ft climbs. *Map: OS Sheet 151 – Stratford-upon-Avon & surrounding area.*
Start at Bourton-on-the-Hill (tithe barn). Go east, towards Moreton-in-Marsh, along the A44, taking the lane towards the Batsford Estate (Batsford arboretum). At the lodge go left through a gate and on to a second gate. Beyond go left on a track. At an obvious sharp bend in the track take the path right to the park wall and follow it to a road. Go over, and take the path through a copse and across farmland to a road. Go right into Blockley. Leave the village along the B4479 – the same road as you have joined – towards Bourton, taking the second lane to the left. Go right at the obvious track which is followed into Bourton-on-the-Hill.

↑2 ***The Slaughters*** 3.5 miles •Moderate• 250ft climb *Map: OS Sheet 163 – Cheltenham & Cirencester area.*
Start at Lower Slaughter. Follow the east bank of the stream, i.e. on the left, to the post office. Beyond it go left between buildings, through two kissing gates and past the millpond. Ahead now the path crosses farmland using gates and stiles at field boundaries before reaching the road at Upper Slaughter. Go right to the stream. Cross it and go left to the ford and footbridge. Go over and up the short hill to the village green. Go right at the green on a lane to a T-junction. Take the bridleway through the gate ahead. At the top go diagonally right across a field to a covered reservoir in its corner and out onto a lane. Go left. Pass a quarry on the right, then another one on the left, before reaching an obvious track to the left. Take this to a lane junction. Ahead the lane leads back to Lower Slaughter.

↑3 ***Guiting Power to Naunton*** 4.5 miles •Moderate• 100ft climb *Map: OS Sheet 163 – Cheltenham & Cirencester area.*
Start at Guiting Power (Cotswold Farm Park nearby). Follow a signed path to the right of the church over two stiles to open land. Ahead, a footbridge leads to more fields and a lane junction. Go across and take the lane running southward for 200yd to a gate on the left. Go through and across three fields to a gate onto another lane. Go left and into Naunton. To return to Guiting Power, reverse the outward route to the lane junction at the halfway point, but instead of continuing to reverse the route, go right and follow the lane back to the village. The lane is quiet, crosses the River Windrush and also passes through a section of fine woodland.

extreme of a nineteenth century pleasure garden designed in Romantic style. Stow has had some remarkable, or at least strange, inhabitants. Richard Enoch built a tower on the Oddington road and there he planted what was, he claimed, the one grain of corn that was buried with an ancient Egyptian. Although it was about 2,500 years old, it grew fifteen stems and yielded over 1,600 grains – each counted by Enoch.

Eight kilometres (5 miles) northeast of Stow is **Chastleton House**, a Jacobean manor built around the turn of the seventeenth century on land bought from Robert Catesby, a Gunpowder Plotter. The house is more famous for its interior than its exterior, being lavishly furnished in true period style.

Some 7kms (4 miles) further east from Chastleton are the prehistoric **Rollright Stones**. There are three monuments on an extended site: a stone circle, 100ft across with seventy stones known as the King's Men; a solitary stone – the King; and a group of five stones – the Whispering Knights. They are the remains of a long barrow and ceremonial circle about 4,000 years old, but like most such prehistoric remains are the subject of lore and superstition. Local legend has it that they were a boastful king and his followers that had been turned to stone by a local witch. The stones were long held in awe by the locals, and there is a story that a farmer, ignoring superstitions, tried to move one away. His team of horses toiled all day but dragged it only a few yards. Convinced of the stone's power, he decided to restore it to its original position, a feat accomplished by one horse, with ease.

Chastleton's Secret Room

Chastleton's very fine panelling contains a secret chamber which was used to good effect in 1651 by a member of the family, fleeing from the Battle of Worcester. His pursuers evidently thought he was the king himself and, having failed to find him, they decided to spend the night in the room that contained the chamber! Luckily the man had a brave wife who drugged the soldiers with laudanum, thus giving her husband time to escape. A poignant relic of the earlier phase of the Civil War is the Bible carried by Charles I to the scaffold. The gardens are as great an attraction as the house: they include work from the seventeenth and eighteenth centuries, and fine topiary shrubs.

Cheltenham and the Surrounding Area

BLOCKLEY
Mill Dene Garden
☎ 01386 700457
Open: April to October Monday-
Friday 10am-6pm.

BOURTON-ON-THE-HILL
Batsford Park Arboretum
Batsford
☎ 01386 701441
Open: March to mid-November, daily
10am-5pm.

Cotswold Falconry Centre
Batsford Park
☎ 01386 701043
Open: March-November daily
10.30am-5.30pm (4pm in November). No dogs.

GUITING POWER
Cotswold Farm Park
☎ 01451 850307
Open: April to October, daily
10.30am-5pm.

DONNINGTON
Donnington Trout Farm
Condicote Lane
☎ 01451 830873
Open: April to October, daily 10am-
5.30pm; November to March,
Tuesday-Sunday 10am-5pm.

LOWER SLAUGHTER
The Old Mill
☎ 0451 820052
Open: all year, daily 10am-6pm

MORETON-IN-MARSH
Chastleton House
Open: all year, daily, but only by
advance booking. ☎ 01494 755572

**Wellington Aviation Museum
and Art Gallery**
Broadway Road
☎ 01608 650323
Open: all year, daily except Monday
10am-12noon, 2-5.30pm

Sezincote House & Gardens
Sezincote
☎ 01386 700444
Open: May, June, July and September, Thursday and Friday 2.30-
5.30pm. No children.

STOW-ON-THE-WOLD
The Toy and Collectors Museum
8 Park Street
☎ 01451 830159
Open: April and June to September,
daily except Tuesday 10am-4.30pm
(Opens at 11am on Sunday); October
to March, daily except Tuesday
11am-4pm.

I n the eastern Cotswolds the streams that drain down from the high Wolds are becoming rivers as they cross towards the Oxford Vale and the Thames. But the country is still Cotswold, even if the first village, or small town, visited – Bourton-on-the-Water – is slightly out of Cotswold character as it is an obvious tourist centre. The commercial nature of Bourton should not prejudice the traveller against its great merits, and even some of the tourist traps are, in themselves, of considerable interest.

BOURTON-ON-THE-WATER

In best Cotswold tradition, the village is grouped around a river, the Windrush, already described as the typical Cotswold river. In its journey to the Thames Valley the Windrush is here wide and shallow, and is well set off by broad grassy banks. There are a number of bridges across it in the village, many of them only footpaths. Undoubtedly there have been bridges here for many years; indeed Bourton bridge that carries the A429 was once a Roman bridge supporting the Foss Way. Since bridges do not easily survive periods of neglect or age, the oldest now is around 230 years old.

The village itself is much older; an Iron Age hillfort has been excavated at Salmonsbury, a little to the east. The original Norman church on Saxon foundations was largely demolished in 1784 and rebuilt with a dome, a unique feature in the Cotswolds. **The Manor House** in High Street was built in the twelfth century, rebuilt in the sixteenth century, rebuilt again in the late nineteenth and 'restored' in the early

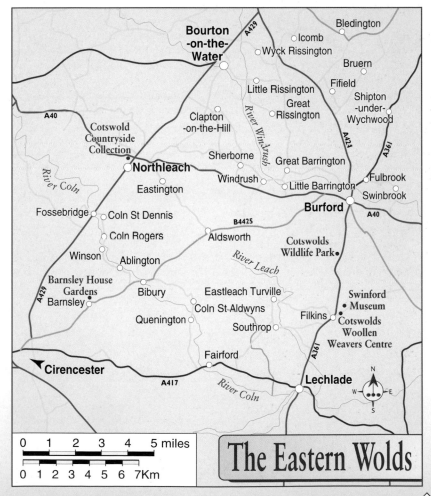

twentieth. The dovecote is noteworthy, and is believed to be of the sixteenth century. An even better example of a dovecote can be seen in Sherborne Street where one house has the nest holes in its walls. Visitors to Bourton should not hurry, but those who can take only a short walk around it, seeing the church, houses and one or two of the bridges, will be well rewarded.

In Bourton High Street, behind the quaintly named Old New Inn, is the **model village**. The village modelled is Bourton itself and so, of course, the model includes a model of the model! It is constructed on a 1:9 scale and is actually made in Cotswold stone. On The Green, **Miniature World** is an amazing collection of models and scenes by Britain's finest model makers. Some of the models are truly astonishing, including such things as real bone china cups and saucers.

The **Cotswolds Motoring Museum and Toy Collection** is housed in an old barley mill in the centre of the village. Here there are not only cars but motorcycles, caravans and bicycles, as well as a good range of original die-cast models and one of Britain's largest collections of old advertising signs. Also in the High Street is the model railway where several hundred square feet of superb, detailed layout support a collection of British and overseas trains. Youngsters are even allowed to try their hands as drivers. Visitors to **The Cotswold Perfumery** are allowed free access to perfumes and other trial products and can watch the manufacturing processes, including the perfume blending laboratory. Most of the products are made on the site, but some processes are carried out only in the quiet months

of winter. There is an exhibition of perfumery, and a perfume quiz for those wanting to pit their noses against the experts. Not far from the Perfumery the **Cotswold Pottery** is run by John and Judy Jelfs. All the pots here are made from local ingredients and hand-thrown.

Also worth visiting is **Birdland**, several acres of park with hundreds of different species of birds, the majority of which are free-flying. In addition to the birds there is a tropical house. The park has good flower borders and a small art gallery devoted to paintings of wildlife. Birdland is on the Rissington Road, as is the **Dragonfly Maze**, one of Bourton's newer attractions. The maze is the work of Kit Williams, famous as the author of *Masquerade*, the book whose illustrations gave clues to the whereabouts of a buried statuette.

About 4kms (2½ miles) to the west of Bourton, off of the A436, is **Folly Farm Waterfowl**, a farm specialising in rare poultry and waterfowl. The site includes a picnic area. To the north-east of the town and on the Oxfordshire Way, a long-distance footpath that starts from Bourton, is **Salmonsbury Camp**, an Iron Age fort that was also occupied in Roman times. Finds from the camp can be seen in the Cheltenham museum. About 1,350 years ago the camp was the scene of a fierce battle between local Saxon kingdoms.

THE RISSINGTONS

To the east of Bourton are the Rissingtons of which (unusually in the Cotswolds) there are three rather than two. The best way to reach the first, Wyck Rissington, is to follow the Oxfordshire Way from Bourton.

Wyck Rissington is the smallest of the villages. The church is a massively-constructed building where Gustav Holst was once organist. The 17-year-old Holst had his first professional engagement on its hand-pumped organ: he lived in the last cottage on the left of the lane from the village towards the Foss Way. The churchyard is as interesting as the church. It has a living cross trimmed from a yew tree 3m (10ft) high, and a headstone on the grave of a gipsy, marked 'of no fixed abode'. To the east of the village is Wyck Beacon, its summit marked by a triangulation pillar beside the road.

Wyck Maze

Within Wyck Rissingotn's church is a plaque commemorating a maze that once existed close to the church. The maze's origin was equally remarkable. After World War II the local vicar had a dream in which he saw large numbers of people following paths in a maze: an unseen figure explained how the maze was to be constructed. Mazes have always been regarded as a form of spiritual pilgrimage, the pathway with its wrong turns being seen as the path of life and the centre as heaven (Wolsey's Hampton Court maze was constructed with a similar purpose.) For several years, the vicar laboured to construct the six hundred metres of path and to plant the hedges of willows, and it was opened on Coronation Day 1953. Sadly the maze fell into disuse and was eventually sold and lost.

The next village, **Little Rissington**, lies in the shadow of a large, but now almost disused, RAF airfield. From Little Rissington a path beside the church can be followed to Bourton (8kms - 5 miles - 2 hours), meandering between ponds created by the filling of gravel pits, after passing Rissington Mill, inscribed 'Richard Lane, Carpenter 1754'.

Great Rissington is the most southerly and largest of the three villages, sporting two village greens. As with the northern pair it is a typical Cotswold village, though perhaps the only one whose main street rises 55m (200ft) so sharply. It overlooks the broad water meadows of the Windrush. The church still contains traces of a fourteenth, century wall painting.

On the opposite side of the broad Windrush valley from the Rissingtons is **Clapton-on-the-Hill**, another village whose name is almost as big as itself. Everything about Clapton appears tiny. The church is one of the smallest of all Cotswold churches, and the tiny collection of cottages surrounds a delightful gabled manor house. On a pleasant day the walk from Bourton to Clapton is a fine way of seeing the Windrush valley at close quarters, and from a high vantage point.

To the east of the Rissingtons is the A424 Stow-Burford road, and east again is the most easterly strip of the AONB, bordered on its Oxfordshire side by a railway line. In this eastern strip is a collection of small villages leading down through largely uninhabited high Wold to Wychwood, Icomb, Westcote, Idbury and Fifield, each in its way delightful. **Icomb Place** is

to the position of the villages beneath the Wychwood Forest, which once extended over a large area around Burford and even towards Bourton. It was famous as a deer forest and the inhabitants of Burford enjoyed the right to hunt there on one day each year. This privilege, together with poaching which was limited to the other 364 days, produced a saying that 'a Burford labourer ate as much venison in a week as a London Alderman in a year'. The forest is now much depleted. Indeed no part of it now lies within the Cotswold area, although the last surviving large area, a National Nature Reserve, is only 3kms (2 miles) east of Shipton-under-Wychwood.

Shipton-under-Wychwood had a considerable reputation in the eighteenth and nineteenth centuries for lawlessness, presumably arising from the poaching in Wychwood Forest. It had inns that were clearly poaching inns, and the poachers and petty criminals seem to have carried on with little fear of detection. One stranger who called at an inn in the late nineteenth century opened his purse too readily and was buried in an unnamed grave in the churchyard. The poachers were not always successful. One man brought news of a remarkably fine deer that browsed each night at the edge of the forest. A gang went out that evening and shot the animal, a gipsy's donkey; but such was the honour among thieves that the men were forced to buy another. The quaintly named **Shaven Crown Inn**, which looks remarkably similar to Prior's Manse in Broadway, is one of the village's most picturesque buildings. The inn's sign is said to be unique in England.

The Ghost of Shipton Court

Shipton Court, at the southern end of the town, is a lovely building, surrounded by fine yew trees, said to be haunted by the ghost of Sir John Reade. Sir John was a drunkard who owned the house in the mid-nineteenth century. His drinking partner was his butler and one night after a particularly heavy session the butler attempted to ring for yet more bottles. Sir John, sufficiently drunk, threw the bell rope over a picture to stop him, but the butler climbed up to retrieve it. He slipped (or was pushed) and fell into the fireplace, where he was impaled on a fire dog. Shipton was alive with the story of murder, but accidental death was recorded. Whatever the truth, Sir John never went drinking again and he died a deeply troubled man in 1868. His ghost was often seen afterwards and even an exorcism has not, apparently, stopped the haunting.

Further south, **Swinbrook**, like the majority of local villages, also has a wealth of poaching stories. In the most famous, two Swinbrook men were out one night when they discovered a well liked keeper who had been shot. The two men carried him back to the Hit and Miss Inn in Swinbrook – the name itself indicating poaching. The keeper, John Millins, died, and the two men were tried for murder, found guilty and hanged. Some years later a man dying in nearby Leafield confessed that he, not the Swinbrook men, had killed Millins accidentally, thinking he was a deer. The tree under which the keeper was found is still known as Millins' Oak. In Swinbrook Church is the Fittiplace monument, a pair of wall tombs where six men of the family are stacked in threes, one on top of the other, each lying on his right side and looking at the visitor.

From here it is only a short drive to the beautiful ruin of **Minster Lovell Hall,** constructed around 1430 by Lord Lovell. It is close to the Windrush, and although there is little to see – only a part of the Great Hall and a tower – the ruin is overwhelmingly romantic. The medieval dovecote has withstood the ravages of time a little better, some nesting boxes still being complete. The small village church is dedicated to St Kenelm, whose tomb may be seen in Winchcombe.

Tom, Dick and Harry

Fulbrook, close to Minster Lovell, was the home of Tom, Dick and Harry, perhaps the first of all such trios. In this case they were the Dunsdons, sons of a respectable family, who turned to theft, at first on a small scale. Emboldened by success they turned highwaymen, robbing the Oxford to Gloucester coach, a crime which made them famous and much sought after. Their nightly haunt was an inn with another poaching name, The Bird in the Hand, at Capp's Lodge. Though the inn has long gone, the name survives at Capp's Lodge Farm, a kilometre or so out of Fulbrook to the right on the Shipton road.

One night at the inn, where they seem to have been safe from capture, they drank too much and boasted of their scheme to rob the local manor of Tangley Hall. Their plan was passed to the householder who called in the constables. A shutter for looking at visitors normally guarded a hole in the front door of the manor, but that night the shutter was removed; an arm, put through the hole to feel for the door key, was lassoed by the constables and tied to the doorhandle. Outside, there was much swearing, followed by a shout of 'Cut it' and the arm fell through the hole on to the floor. The door was opened but the brothers had escaped. Dick was never seen again, and it was assumed that he had bled to death following the amputation.

The other brothers continued in crime until they over-reached themselves one day by quarrelling with the landlord of The Bird in the Hand. They were promptly arrested, taken to Gloucester for trial, found guilty and sentenced to death. Tom, hurt during their arrest, limped to the scaffold. Harry kept encouraging him, telling him that it made small difference that he had only one leg since he had only a little time to stand. After execution the bodies were brought back and gibbetted, probably on the Gibbet Tree to the side of the Fulbrook-Shipton road a little north of Capp's Lodge. Such executions and gibbeting were very common at that time and not far from this tree is the sinisterly named Habber Gallows Hill, about 5kms (3 miles) north of Burford on the A424 to Stow.

Burford

Keith Harding's Wortld of
Mechanical Music, Northleach

The Dunsdon brothers of Fulbrook owned a cottage at **Icomb** which was reputedly connected by an underground passage to the nearby wood where their horses were stabled and the loot was hidden.

BURFORD

From Fulbrook it is only a short journey to **Burford**, an elegant town with a wide, steep, main street leading down to the river Windrush from the wolds. For a town that is now so solid a part of the landscape it is remarkably young, for when the Romans wanted to cross the Windrush they brought Akeman Street down river to Asthall shunning, perhaps, the north-facing slope at Burford. In early Saxon times there was a settlement here, grouped around the fort of the same name, and by AD752 the ford had become important, on the route from Wessex to Mercia. In that year the two kingdoms fought here at Burford. (As a link with history, a midsummer festival was recently held here at which the dragon and giant, the standards of the two Saxon armies, were carried in procession).

Burford has one of the best of Cotswold churches, one famous for the number and quality of the woolsack tombs in its churchyard. Inside, as well as the inscription on the font, the visitor may also notice the monument to **Lord Chief Justice Tanfield**, an imposing tomb erected by his wife, with a Latin inscription bemoaning the burial in such a backwater of so important a man as her husband.

There is only one way to see Burford – on foot. It has a quite remarkable collection of fourteenth- to sixteenth century houses. **The almshouses** in Church Lane date from the mid-fifteenth century while the cottages in High Street near the bridge are 100 years older. High Street itself has many notable buildings. The **Corner House** is sixteenth century, slightly older than the delightfully named Rampant Cat. Hill House, on the western side, is mainly fourteenth century. **The Tolsey**, or Court House (now housing a museum), is a sixteenth century

The Burford Mutiny

In 1649, following the Civil War, Burford was again the scene of bloodshed. At nearby Salisbury, some of the Parliamentarian soldiers mutinied after losing faith in Cromwell, who they believed had become a tyrant; they further feared being posted to Ireland. They marched to Burford where they were arrested with little gunfire and no bloodshed. The men were imprisoned in the church for three days while Cromwell decided what to do next. Finally a token group of three men was taken into the churchyard and shot. To ensure that the other mutineers were 'encouraged' by the executions, some were forced to watch. One of these was Anthony Sedley and in the church the visitor can still see, scratched on the rim of the font: 'Anthony Sedley Prisner 1649'.

house with elegant bay windows. Here can be seen the charters of the original town dating from the thirteenth century, together with seals which may be as old, and the sixteenth century town mace. There is also a fine Regency dolls' house.

South of Burford on the A361 is the **Cotswold Wildlife Park**. Here a variety of animals, both large and small, are kept in expansive enclosures. There are special houses for reptiles, tropical birds and butterflies, and an aquarium. In addition, there are landscaped gardens, a narrow gauge railway, adventure playground and pets' corner. The park occupies the 120-acre estate of a fine manor in Gothic style where there is a brass-rubbing centre.

THE WINDRUSH VALLEY

There is superb walking along the country lanes that link Burford to the Barringtons on each side of the Windrush (13kms - 8 miles - 3 hours). The walker in the meadow on the northern side of the river, just beyond the **Windrush Bridge** at the bottom of High Street, stands amongst grasses, reeds and farm animals, while across the water the town starts instantly, a whole collection of interesting town houses being just a stone's throw away. The return journey on the other side of the river passes the fifteenth century Lamb Inn and the Priory, which still houses a monastic order.

The first village towards the Barringtons, **Taynton**, is famous for the quality of the building stone that came from its quarries. Blenheim Palace and some Oxford colleges are built of Taynton stone. The village itself is a tapestry in stone, set at

such an angle of the Windrush Valley that it may be seen in almost complete detail as the traveller aproaches. Above Taynton, the Windrush has crossed from Gloucestershire into Oxfordshire and a kilometre or so beyond the border are the Barringtons, Great and Little.

Barrington stone was not much sought after as a primary building stone, but it was once used to repair Westminster Abbey, being floated down the Windrush and the Thames to London. If the stone was less sought after, however, its masons were not. The most famous, Thomas Strong, considered by Wren to be the finest in England, was a leading mason contractor on St Paul's Cathedral. He actually laid the foundation stone himself, though he died before the cathedral was completed. He left money in his will 'to make a way between the Barrington Bridges that two men may go a front to carry a corpse in safety'. The road, still known as Strong's Causeway, is included in the walk described at the end of this chapter. After Thomas's death his brother Edward took over as Master Mason of England and laid the final stone of St Paul's.

Great Barrington church is famous for its marble monument to two children of the Bray family who died of smallpox in 1720. The monument, a sculpted marble mural, amongst the finest in England, was long thought to be the work of Francis Bird, Sir Christopher Wren's favourite sculptor, but experts now believe that it is actually by Christopher Cass. There is also a notable memorial to Captain Edmund Bray, clad in Tudor armour but wearing his sword on his right side, not his left. He murdered a man in anger but was pardoned by Elizabeth I, after swearing never again to draw his sword with his right hand. Barrington Park was, and is, a walled deer park in which Earl Talbot built his fine mansion after the style of Palladio. The mansion sits on a natural terrace, but as this was too far from the river for a good view, the river was moved slightly!

To reach **Little Barrington**, **Strong's Causeway** is crossed between the two arms of the Windrush. The land between the two teems with plant and animal life. Little Barrington itself is spread out along the southern Windrush bank to such an extent that it seems larger than its 'greater' neighbour.

Upstream of the Barringtons is **Windrush**, a tiny village, far smaller than its name leads the visitor to expect. A picture book village, almost every building is a fine example of its type. Special note should be made of the seventeenth century corn mill.

From Windrush village mill, a path crosses the water meadows near the river with its lilies and trout, and then follows the Sherborne brook back to Sherborne village. To return, the lane back to Windrush is a delight (total 5kms - 3 miles - 1 hour).

Sherborne village is strangely positioned, strung out along the stream, but distinctly divided by Sherborne Park, another large manor house. This originally belonged to Winchcombe Abbey and was used by the abbot when he came to check the sheep shearing; the Sherborne Valley has always been good farming land.

The Dutton Memorial

While in Sherborne, be sure to visit the church to see the Dutton Memorial in which a life-size angel crushes skeletal Death beneath her feet, her left wing emblazoned with the profiles of James Lennox Dutton and his wife. Many claim this to be the most extraordinary tomb in the entire area.

Continue along the Sherborne Brook valley to **Farmington**, the last village on the minor road from Burford to Northleach. The village is an ancient site, with a long barrow and some old fortifications to the west.

NORTHLEACH

From Farmington it is a short journey to **Northleach**. This very special village, or small town, is best viewed from a distance particularly along the minor road from Farmington. Northleach is then seen in the valley below, as the visitor drops off the Wold, in front of an unfortunate backdrop of electricity pylons and lines. But from this northern side the church stands up from behind the houses.

In villages all over the Cotswolds the cottages are grouped around churches, most of which are not only at the heart of the village, but also at the heart of its interest and history. But where the wool merchants' money was used to finance complete buildings, so that the church is all of one architectural period and enriched by fine stonemasonry, the church is not only at the heart of the village but dominates it completely. It is generally agreed that the three finest wool churches in the Cotswolds are at Cirencester, Chipping Campden and at Northleach. Cirencester is a major town and absorbs the church's presence; Campden, though smaller, is a town nonetheless; but here at Northleach the church does truly dominate.

It was constructed in the fifteenth century on the site of a previous church, though of that very little indeed survives; as notable for its exterior work as for its interior, it is the interior that holds the attention, for there is a unique collection of memorial brasses, the finest in Britain, almost exclusively of the wool merchants who raised the church. Most of the figures on the brasses have the traditional wool pack at their feet and some have sheep as well. The brass of John Fortey who died in 1459 is the largest (5ft), and it dates from the best period of brass engraving. Within the church a leaflet details the brasses, giving their ages, and translating the Latin inscriptions. The inscriptions include a mix of Latin and Arabic numerals, and the arms of the English City of Calais. Few of the buildings in the rest of the village can compare with the church, but there are other buildings of interest. One, Oak House in High Street, is a seventeenth century wool merchant's house and contains **Keith Harding's World of Mechanical Music**, an excellent collection of clocks, musical boxes and mechanical musical instruments.

The Cotswold Heritage Centre

A little to the west of the village, at the crossroads on the A429, is the **old village police station** and prison, built in 1790 by Sir Onesiphorus Paul, a gentleman who had not only an extraordinary Christian name, but also an interest in penal reform and the welfare of prisoners. At a time when a miscreant could expect his sentence to include not only imprisonment but a straw bed, no water or sanitation, no exercise and typhus, Sir Onesiphorus built this prison with exercise yards, separate rooms for sleeping, baths and a sick bay. It was not just a prison, but also a 'house of correction'. It is now a museum. There is a history of the prison in the cell block and a collection which explores the history of agriculture in the Cotswolds area built mainly around the Lloyd-Baker collection of implements and wagons.

THE LEACH VALLEY

To the south of the A40 from Northleach to Burford, the Cotswolds are split by fertile river valleys, along which the villages have grown. The wolds of this southern section are perhaps more sparsely populated than in the north. Certainly the difference between populated valley and empty wold is very striking.

The first valley was cut deep by

the River Leach that flows by Northleach itself; indeed it springs close to the village. In its upper reaches the Leach drains bleak wold, but it does not have the character of the Windrush. Neither does it have, except in its lower reaches, the prettiness of the Coln. Nevertheless it is a fine valley, and gives its name to Lechlade, the town that actually separates the Cotswolds from the Thames Valley.

Short, enjoyable walks on the wolds around the **Roman Akeman Street** can be linked with some country lanes to make a complete route of 13kms - 8 miles - 3 hours) from Northleach to Eastleach which is never far away from the river. It is best to go by way of the villages, the essence of the Cotswolds. First is **Eastington**, one of two Gloucestershire villages of the same name. This is the prettier, a hamlet on the banks of the stream. A kilometre or so on from the village is **Lodge Park**, another deer park, which has a very fine long barrow. The lodge was built around 1630 by John Dutton, a friend of Cromwell, who was allowed to stock it with deer from Wychwood Forest. The building was only used to watch coursing in the park. The coursing was by greyhounds, as usual, but the quarry was deer, not hares. This cruel practice was regarded as good sport by the rich gentry; one needed to be rich, because Dutton allowed anyone to try his dogs at a price of half-a-crown for each dog, together with ten old pence for the 'slipper' who released the deer.

Aldsworth is accepted as a Leach Valley village, even though by now the river is 1^1/$_2$kms (1 mile) away. It is really a high wold village, and an attractive one with a fine set of

gargoyles on the church.

The prettier end of the Leach Valley is reached at Eastleach. This is divided by the river into two villages each having its own church. **Eastleach Turville** is the larger, the second half of the name derived from that of an early Norman lord. **Eastleach Martin** is named from its church, although this part of the village is known locally as Bouthrop. The whole village was granted to Gloucester Abbey in the thirteenth century by the lord of the manor, who set the yearly rent at one pound of wax!

An interesting sidelight on the power of the church in such villages only 250 years ago is shown by the Eastleach parish records. These show that in 1747 a small group of village folk was 'presented' by the vicar to the Bishop of Gloucester at Cirencester. One was accused of not having been to church for at least three months. The parish clerk was presented 'for defamation and scandal in saying that I had wronged him!' But worst of all, Anne Cock was presented 'as lying under a common fame of fornication, which I verily believe to be upon just grounds, she being in all appearances big with child'!

In Eastleach one must visit **Keble's Bridge**, the most photographed part of Eastleach, perhaps also of the Cotswolds. The most famous of the Kebles whose name is commemorated here is John Keble, the poet and leader of the Oxford Movement in the early nineteenth century. Keble was rector of both Eastleach churches, and of Southrop, for eight years. The footpath-only bridge, made of large, flat stone slabs on low supports, is little different from the clapper bridges of prehistory.

Macaroni Down

The walk from Northleach enters Eastleach by crossing Macaroni Downs, probably named from the late eighteenth century London **Macaroni Club**. The Macaronis were young rich playboys who frequented the nearby Bibury racecourse. They were famous for extravagant Italian clothes and enormous wigs, though it is not known why the Downs and one or two local farms should be named after them.

The best walk in the Leach Valley is not that described above, but from Eastleach down to **Southrop** (3kms - 2 miles - 1 hour). It follows paths beside the river and returns along a path and lane, crossing the river at each of the villages. At Southrop the Leach is a beautiful sight, as wide as a road and only a hand's breadth deep. The village itself is as attractive as Eastleach, though less well known, perhaps because it lacks a photogenic footbridge. But it does have a fine sixteenth century manor house, a very old and tiny church, an array of excellent stone cottages, and a carefully restored seventeenth century corn mill.

To the east of the Leach, just the other side of the A361, is the village of **Filkins**, where the **Swinford Museum** specialises in agricultural and rural domestic exhibits. Also in the village are two excellent craft centres. The **Cotswold Woollen Weavers Centre** has an exhibition that traces the history of the Cotswold woollen industry as well as carrying on the tradition of weaving. There is also a small gallery exhibiting the work of local artists.

THE COLN VALLEY

The other river valley in the area south of Northleach is the Coln. It runs under another Foss Bridge on the A429 Cirencester to Stow road, and then flows through a succession of delightful villages before flowing through Fairford to join the Thames near Lechlade, and for almost its entire way it can be followed on foot by path and country lane. The walk described at the end of this chapter follows one particularly fine section.

From Foss Bridge the first village is the tiny **Coln St Dennis**, with a Norman church on the banks of the river. Its tower has a strange opening couplet to a memorial on its inner, northern, wall to Joan Burton who died in 1631. It reads 'Heare lyes my body fast inclosed within this watery ground; by my precious soule it cannot nowe be founde'. St Dennis is a corruption of the French, St Dionisuis, a Parisian church which was granted to the village by King William after the Norman conquest. Beyond Coln St Dennis is the tiny hamlet of Calcot, a typical Cotswold valley hamlet, with pretty stone cottages and river.

Coln Rogers has an even older, Saxon, church. The name here is also Norman, deriving from Roger de Gloucester, the lord of the manor in the mid-twelfth century. The village was then known as Coln on the Hill, but this was changed by the grateful Abbot of Gloucester when Sir Roger granted him the manor.

Winson has the West Country's smallest post office, a neat, thatched cottage, a fine manor house and a

Selected Walks

↑1 Bourton-on-the-Water *5 miles • Moderate • 100ft climb*
Map: OS Sheet 163 – Cheltenham & Cirencester area.
Start at Bourton-on-the-Water (many items of interest). From the
main street go south-east towards the Model Village, but go left on
the main road before it is reached. Opposite the car park go right
beside the cemetery. Near a group of houses, about 400 yards further
on, go left on a signed path that leads through the Bourton Pools.
Beyond the last pool take the signed path for Rissington Mill which is
passed on the way to Little Rissington. The village of Little
Rissington does not have to be visited, as the route goes left as soon
as the church is reached, crossing three fields to a track for Wyck
Rissington. Go through that village, passing the church, maze and
green, to a signed path, left, that is followed easily back to Bourton.
This last section is on the well signed Oxfordshire Way.

↑2 The Coln Valley *6 miles • Moderate • 100ft climb*
Map: OS Sheet 163 – Cheltenham & Cirencester area.
One of the best routes in the Cotswolds. Start at Bibury (Arlington
Row and Mill). Pass the cottages of Arlington Row and continue
uphill to a Y-junction. Take the left fork and go straight on at a
junction of paths. Go across two fields and at the far corner of the
second go left on a broad track to a road. Go left. After a lane, left,
take the signed bridlepath to the Coln bridge at Coln St Aldwyns.
Just before the bridge a signed path follows the Coln westward
through woodland and along the river's bank. Where the river bends
right, the well trodden path goes across fields to meet a track that is
followed past Bibury Court and on to a road. Go left, and left again
when the main road is joined, to re-enter Bibury.

↑3 The Barringtons *4 miles • Moderate • 200ft climb*
Map: OS Sheet 163 – Cheltenham & Cirencester area.
Start at Windrush. Go past the church, eastward on a road to the
Barringtons and after 100yd go right through a kissing gate to farm
land. Cross fields on the obvious path to Green Drive Farm. Go down
the farm lane to Little Barrington. Go northward through the village
and take the lane that goes right after the green. The lane becomes a
pathway and a footbridge to the left is used to cross the River
Windrush. Beyond, a path leads to Barrington Mill beyond which a
lane leads to Great Barrington. Leave that village on the lane for
Windrush, a lane that crosses Strong's Causeway to reach the Fox
Inn. Go right here and follow the lane past the wood end on the
right. About 200 yd further on a stile, right, gives access to a path to
Windrush Mill. Go up the mill lane to a stile on the left, with
'Windrush' marked on the step. Beyond an easy path leads to
Windrush village.

Scenic Car Tours

↑1 Bourton-on-the-Water & Wychwood

From Bourton-on-the-Water (many places of interest) take the minor road from the main street that goes southwards to Clapton-on-the-Hill. Do not go to that village, however, but continue along narrow lanes to Farmington. Here go left, again on narrow lanes, along the Sherborne Brook to Sherborne village, and on to Windrush. Take the lane to Great Barrington and on to Taynton and into Burford (Tolsey Museum). Leave Burford on the A361 through Fulbrook to Shipton-under-Wychwood. There, opposite the church, go left to Milton-under-Wychwood, and go left there at the T-junction for Fifield. Continue to Idbury, and by lane to Nether Westcote and Church Westcote to the A424. Go right. At the next crossroads go left, passing Wyck Beacon to Wyck Rissington. Go through the village to the A429. Go left and back to Bourton-on-the-Water.

↑2 Burford & the Coln Valley

From Burford go south on the A361 towards Lechlade, passing the Cotswold Wildlife Park to Filkins (Swinford Museum, Cotswold Woollen Weavers, Filkin's Gallery). Beyond the village go right to Southrop and from there go north to Eastleach Turville. Leave the village westward to a T-junction. Go right and bear left to the Akeman Street Roman road that is followed to Hatherop and Coln St Aldwyns. Go right for Bibury (Arlington Row, Arlington Mill). Where the A433 goes left over the Coln in Bibury, go straight on to Ablington and follow lanes beside the Coln to Coln Rogers and Coln St Dennis, and on to Fossebridge on the A429 (Foss Way). Go right to Northleach (Cotswold Countryside Collection). At the roundabout go right on the A40 to return to Burford.

River Coln, near Bibury

Bibury

long stretch of river before the next village, Ablington, which has not one, but two large houses – the Manor from the late sixteenth century and the House from about 100 years later. The House is distinguished by its stone lions which came from the Houses of Parliament.

Bibury, the largest and most famous of the Coln Valley villages, is split by the main A433. As at Coln Rogers there is a Saxon church here, a truly great one. Some of the Saxon work was so fine that the originals were taken to the British Museum, and one sees casts on show here. Part of the churchyard is known as the Bisley Piece. William Morris, the Pre-Raphaelite artist, also connected with Broadway, described the village as the most beautiful in England. It is easy to understand his judgement when one walks along the road beside the Coln. On one side are the cottages of **Arlington Row**, across a clear stream in which large trout swim, and on the other the more substantial houses and the Swan Hotel, dating from the late 1700s and among the best restaurants in the area.

Modern Bibury is actually an amalgam of several pieces and the visitor will find much of interest. Bibury hamlet is grouped around the church, but there is a second hamlet at Arlington, on the hill behind Arlington Row. Further downstream, where the walker has to leave the Coln for a short time, is **Bibury Court**, a well-proportioned mansion of the early seventeenth century superbly sited near the river with a fine backdrop of trees. The Court is now a hotel. At the road bridge over the Coln is Arlington Mill, a seventeenth century building on a site mentioned in the Domesday Book. It was both a cloth mill and a corn mill, but as well as a working water mill it now houses a museum of country crafts, including exhibitions of arts and crafts. There is also a collection of William Morris memorabilia, perhaps in deference to his opinion of the village. At the side of the mill is the Bibury trout farm which breeds for release as well as for eating. The various stages of rainbow trout development can be followed, and the fish can be seen underwater in a floodlit mill race. Trout can be bought, and fishing with hired tackle is available.

Arlington Row

The cottages of Arlington Row, Bibury are now owned by the National Trust, but were originally weavers' cottages, built for the outworkers who supplied cloth for fulling at Arlington Mill. Many believe the cottages to be the finest group in the whole Cotswolds. When admiring them, please remember that though owned by the National Trust they are private houses and the privacy of the owners must be respected. Opposite Arlington Row is a stretch of water meadow known as Rock Isle, where the cloth woven in the cottages and fulled in the local mill was dried. At the end of the Row more cottages pile up on the aptly named Awkward Hill.

Just outside Bibury, near the hamlet of Arlington at OS Ref 108094, is an interesting burial long barrow known as a Beehive Chamber.

The final villages of the Coln before it heads for Fairford and the Thames are **Coln St Aldwyns** and **Quenington**. The former has a green dominated by a magnificent horse chestnut tree, and is as good as any of the more northerly villages. It is separated from Quenington by part of Williamstrip Park; the house here was built by a Speaker of the House of Commons.

Between Coln and Cirencester is another stretch of high wold. Barnsley Wold is named from the village Barnsley on the A433 Cirencester to Bibury road. The village is set on the Welsh Way, an old track over the wolds used by the Welsh cattle drovers. The number of such drove roads through the area explains the number of inns called 'Butcher's Arms' as the slaughtering of the cattle occurred at various points on the journey to London. The most famous attraction here is **Barnsley House**, set in Barnsley Park, a Georgian mansion of the early eighteenth century with an excellent garden containing numerous rare shrubs. There is also a vegetable garden and plants are available for purchase. The Gothic summerhouse and the temple in the garden have been brought here recently.

FAIRFORD AND LECHLADE

To the east lie the last two towns that can be considered to lie within the Cotswolds. John Keble, the founder of the Oxford Movement, was born in **Fairford** in 1792, his father then being the vicar of Coln St Aldwyns. His birthplace, now called **Keble House**, can be reached by a longish walk along the London Road from the Market Place. The Market Place, and the High Street leading from it, give an indication of why the elder Keble might have preferred Fairford to the Coln village, delightful though the latter is to the modern visitor: Fairford is a lovely town and, in the eighteenth century, was a lively and prosperous place, as the fine array of houses from that time indicates.

The town stands beside the Coln, its waters used to power the mills of the wool trade. Today the Coln offers a quiet walk (follow the lane between Leo's restaurant and the White Hart Court to reach the river; the wooden bridge crossed on the way must be the only one in the Cotswolds named for a dog.) To the south as you follow the river is the huge Fairford airfield, built during the 1939-45 war, but achieving national fame when it was the test site for **Concorde**. Latterly it has been a controversial USAF base, and some very strange aircraft can still be seen rising from it.

Fairford's great pride is its church, reached by heading northwards from the Market Place along High Street, your approach across the churchyard watched by a grotesque guardian on the tower. **St Mary's** is like a miniature cathedral in appearance and is famed for its windows, having the only complete set of medieval glass of any parish church in the country, although repairs were required to the west windows after a severe storm in 1703. The original work was carried out under the direction of Barnard Flower, Henry VIII's Master Glass Painter, the windows portraying the life of Christ, scenes from the Old Testament, the Evangelists, Apostles and Prophets. Though ageing has affected some of

Lechlade

the detail of the figures, the bold use of colour on some of the glass can still be appreciated.

While in the church, look too for the misericords on the chancel stalls which depict some unusual scenes including a woman attacking her husband, a drunk and a thieving dog.

Lechlade, the final town of the Cotswolds is dominated by the spire of St Lawrence's Church, rising above the flat lands of the Thames Valley. The site, close to where the Leach meets the Thames, has been sought-after for thousands of years. There are numerous Neolithic sites in the surrounding area, some of them identified only recently by aerial photography. The sites include an example of that most enigmatic of structures, a cursus, its parallel ditches some 40m (130ft) apart. There is also a henge site, and a number of barrows.

The Romans also settled here, two villas having been excavated, but the most remarkable find is a **Saxon cemetery** (to the north-west of the sports ground) from which some beautiful jewellery has been excavated. Remarkably, the cemetery seems to have been in use until the seventh century, a time when it is usually assumed Wessex had become Christian.

St Lawrence's Church is built on the site of an early thirteenth century hospital of St John, run by an Augustinian prior. When this foundation was suppressed in 1473 the present structure was raised. The construction was completed quickly, so that the church is entirely perpendicular in style, a fact that has led many to claim it as one of the finest in Gloucestershire. The claim is enhanced by the soaring elegance of the spire (which the Elizabethan traveller Leland called a 'pratie pyramis of stone'). Inside there are some good brasses from the fifteenth and early sixteenth century, and a sixteenth century carved figure of St Agatha. Though a little crude, the figure is a powerful emblem. St Agatha, a third century martyr, was tortured to death, the torture including mutilation of her breasts (she has become a symbol of women undergoing mastectomy as a result) which is unsparingly depicted. Look, too, for the remarkable memorial to Anne Simons in the chancel.

Outside the church (on the town side) is a plaque in the wall commemorating Shelley's *Stanzas in Lechlade Churchyard* written during his stay at the New Inn in 1815. The path that leads eastwards from the plaque is **Shelley's Walk** and can be followed to St John's Bridge and Lock on the Thames. The first bridge here, built in the fourteenth century, perhaps even earlier, was one of the first ever across the Thames. At the lock is Monti's statue of Old Father Thames, carved in 1855 for the Thameshead site. After years of vandalism there it was brought to the lock for safe-keeping. From the lock, follow the southern bank of the Thames to reach **Halfpenny Bridge** and the delightful **Riverside Park**. The bridge is eighteenth century and still has its original, tiny tollhouse: those who crossed were charged the halfpenny of the name. Turn right over the bridge to return to the centre of the town.

Finally, visitors heading north towards Filkins and Burford will pass the **Lechlade Trout Farm** where fishing is available. Those wanting to acquire trout with less effort can buy them at the farm shop.

Keble's Bridge. Eastleach Turville

Coln St Aldwyns

BARNSLEY

Barnsley House Gardens
☎ 01285 740561
Open: all year except Christmas to end of January, Monday, Wednesday, Thursday and Saturday 10am-5.30pm.

BIBURY

Arlington Mill Museum
Open: all year, daily 10am-6pm (5pm from October to April)
☎ 01285 740368

Arlington Row (National Trust)
Not open to the public. Exterior viewing only.

Trout Farm
☎ 01285 740212 or 740215
Open: all year Monday-Saturday 9am-6pm (5pm in winter), Sunday 10am-6pm (5pm in winter).

BOURTON-ON-THE-WATER

Birdland
Rissington Road
☎ 01451 820480
Open: April to October, daily 10am-6pm; November to March, daily 10am-4pm. Closed Christmas Day.

Cotswold Motoring Museum & Toy Collection
The Old Mill
☎ 01451 821255
Open: March to October, daily 10am-6pm.

Cotswold Perfumery
Victoria Street
☎ 01451 820698
Open: all year, Monday-Saturday 9.30am-5pm, Sunday 10.30am-5pm.

Cotswold Pottery
Clapton Row
☎ 01451 820173
Open: all year, Monday-Saturday 9.30am-5.30pm, Sunday 10.30am-5pm.

Dragonfly Maze
Rissington Road
☎ 01451 822251
Open: all year, daily 10am-5.30pm or dusk

Folly Farm
☎ 01451 820285
Open: all year, daily 10am-5pm (3.30pm from October to March)

Miniature World
☎ 01451 810121
Open:March to October, daily 10am-5pm; November to February Saturday and Sunday 10am-5pm.

Model Railway
High Street
☎ 01451 820686
Open: April to September, daily
11am-5.30pm; October to March,
Saturday, Sunday and Bank Holidays
11am-5pm.

Model Village
Old New Inn
☎ 01451 820467
Open: all year, daily 10am-5.45pm
(4pm in winter).

BURFORD
Cotswold Wildlife Park
☎ 01993 823006
Open: all year, daily 10am-6pm or
dusk. Closed Christmas Day.

**Minster Lovell Hall and Dovecote
(English Heritage)**
Open: Any reasonable time.

Tolsey Museum
126 High Street
☎ 01367 810294
Open: Easter to October, Monday-
Friday 2-5pm, Saturday, Sunday and
Bank Holidays 11am-5pm.

FILKINS
Cotswold Woollen Weavers
☎ 01367 860491
Open: all year, Monday-Saturday
10am-6pm, Sunday 2-6pm. Closed
25-31 December.

Swinford Museum
☎ 01367 860209
Open: May to September 1st Sunday
in month 2-5pm. Other times by
appointment.

Lechlade
Lechlade Trout Farm
Burford Road
☎ 01367 252663 or 253266
Open: April to October, daily 10am-
5.30pm; November to March,
Tuesday-Sunday 10am-5pm.

Northleach
Cotswold Heritage Centre
☎ 01451 860715 (summer) or 01285
655611 (winter)
Open: April to October, Monday-
Saturday 10am-5pm, Sunday
2-5pm. Open all Bank Holidays.

**Keith Harding's World
of Mechanical Music**
Oak House
High Street
☎ 01451 860181
Open: all year, daily 10am-6pm.
Evenings by appointment.

T his section of the guide deals with the southern end of the northern Cotswolds, the strip of country between Gloucester and Cirencester sandwiched between the A40 and the A417. It is not, in fact, as arbitrary as it seems. It has been said that if you scratch Gloucestershire then you find Rome beneath. This is the heart of Roman Gloucestershire and, therefore, of Roman Cotswolds. This is the land between Corinium and Glevum including, at Chedworth, some of the finest remains of any Roman villa in Britain.

CIRENCESTER

Cirencester was the second largest town of Roman Britain, with an area of 240 acres (only London was bigger). It grew up around a fort built about AD50, about 100 years after Julius Cæsar had come, and gone. He did not get as far as Cirencester: his visit was a reconnaissance rather than an actual invasion. Not until AD43 was there a true invasion of Britain.

The town was built at the intersection of three crucial roads – the Foss Way, Akeman Street and Ermin Street. To find out more about Roman Cirencester there is no better place than the **Corinium Museum** in Park Street. There, besides the many finds that have been unearthed during excavations from beneath the present town, there are reconstructions of numerous aspects of Roman life including a mosaic-maker's

Corinium – Cirencester

Following the invasion of AD43 the Roman names of some of their towns reflect the military nature of the campaign. Caer Coryn was the native name for the original settlement, from Caer a 'fort' and Coryn the 'top part'. The latter is interesting because it probably refers to the Churn, the river that runs through Cirencester, being the highest source of the River Thames. As the frontier moved and the area became more peaceful, the town's name was changed to Corinium. The Saxons who followed the Romans changed it back to the original name. Since, however, the Saxons used Ceastre for Caer the town was then Ceastre Coryn which was reversed to become Coryn Ceastre or Cirencester.

Corinium Museum, Cirencester

workshop. Also on display, and indeed one of the most famous Roman relics in Britain, is an early link between the Romans and the Christian church, a world-famous word square painted on plaster and found in the nineteenth century in New Road. The museum also has many other fine exhibits on later Cotswold history. The Roman amphitheatre is still visible on the south side of the by-pass road that passes south of the town, while a section of the old Corinium town wall has been restored in the abbey grounds.

The town remained Roman, or rather Romano-British, until 577, when it was destroyed by the Saxons. The destruction was so total that when the Saxons built their own town on the site, the Roman square plan was not used. However, the town was soon important again; it was a royal city in Saxon times and was visited by King Canute; in Norman times a great abbey was built here. Nothing now remains of the abbey as it was destroyed at the Dissolution, but the abbot was also rector of the parish church, and that building still survives.

As Cirencester is the largest of the truly Cotswold towns, it naturally has a fine church. The town was important in medieval times as a wool centre; the benefactions of the local merchants were extremely generous; the church is not only the largest in the Cotswolds but one of the largest in England: indeed it is larger than several British cathedrals. It is not in a formal encircling churchyard but amongst the other town buildings.

Inside, the church is a rare treasure house, the plate being among the most interesting in England. The **Boleyn Cup**, a gilt cup made for

Queen Anne Boleyn in 1535 and bearing her family crest, is the most famous, although a pair of jug-shaped flagons from 1570 is, perhaps, the finest. The memorial brasses are also worthy of notice – their chief interest lies in the matrimonial achievements of the wool merchants depicted on them. William Prelatte had two wives, while Reginald Spycer had four. Robert Page had only one wife, but six sons and eight daughters. A much later brass shows Rebecca Powell with her two husbands.

Reginald Spycer, commemorated here, was instrumental in the arrest and execution, in the town, of the earls who led a rebellion against Henry IV. The action prevented a civil war and the grateful king gave the town a handsome reward with which the church tower was built.

No trip to Cirencester is complete without a tour of the town. The church is in the Market Place and a street market is still held there twice a week. South through the **Market Place** towards Dyer's Street, the Corn Hall, a fine Victorian building, is on the right: it is the site of a Saturday craftsmen's market and exhibition of local crafts. In Dyer's Street the **Bear Inn** is a classic timber-framed house with overhangs. At the end on the right is Lewis Lane and, on the right again, Cricklade Street. To the left here is **Brewery Arts**, a collection of craft units housed in an old brewery. There is a gallery, shop and coffee house.

Cricklade Street leads back past the Market Place again and allows a left turn into Blackjack Street, reputedly named from a statue of St John on the church, whose stone became dark with age. Straight on from here is Cirencester Park. The Corinium

Museum is on the right as one enters Park Street. On the right, in Thomas Street, is Weavers Hall or St Thomas' Hospital, an almshouse set up in the early fifteenth century for destitute weavers. Coxwell Street, running almost parallel to Thomas Street, is narrow and can hardly have changed over the centuries: on one side are the houses of the rich wool merchants, while on the other are those of the poor weavers.

At the end of Thomas Street, a left turn leads into Dollar Street (named from Dole Hall, the abbey almonry);

this leads on to Gloucester Street where there is a further set of almshouses known as St Lawrence's. Spital Gate Lane contains the town's third group of almshouses, St John's Hospital, originally founded by Henry II but rebuilt early in the last century. Spital Gate, named from this building and known locally as Saxon Arch, was actually a Norman gatehouse of the abbey – standing at the junction with Grove Lane. From the arch the walker returns to Lewis Lane by following the River Churn across the abbey grounds.

Cirencester Park

To the west of the town is Cirencester Park, famous for its polo tournaments. The house itself was built in the early eighteenth century and is not open to the public. Externally, it is generally considered to be a failure; even Lord Bathurst, who commissioned it, apparently agreed. Thinking aloud to Alexander Pope, after seeing what he had received for his money, he wondered 'How comes it to look so oddly bad?' The park itself is open to the public and there are several picnic sites and forestry and farm trails which can be followed. Polo is played on Sundays during the polo league season and the very quiet or lucky walker may see one of the fallow deer that still roam the park.

The park is, strictly, entered only from the town end. Although it is private the public is allowed in under certain conditions, but no dogs. To the north, Overley Woods, and to the west at the end of Broad Ride, certain areas of the park can be reached directly, but it must be borne in mind that the parkland is private, and entrance depends upon the goodwill of the landowner. It offers fine walking, particularly along the Broad Ride to the Ten Rides meeting point (10kms - 6 miles - 2 hours). To the north-east is Alfred's Hall, a folly of Lord Bathurst, from about 1720. It is dated 1085(!) and was built complete with black oak and rusty armour. An early visitor is said to have commented on its antiquity to the caretaker, and received the astonishing reply 'Oh this is nothing, my lord intends building one 200 years older shortly!'

As the boundary of the AONB on this southern edge near Cirencester has been drawn along Akeman Street, certain villages have been removed from the Cotswolds. Although this guide attempts to maintain the strict boundary, straying only to visit an especially fine attraction, an exception must be the four villages close to the Ampney Brook, 3kms (2 miles) east of Cirencester.

AROUND CIRENCESTER

The largest of the villages is the first, **Ampney Crucis**, not named from the remarkable and ancient cross in the churchyard but from the church itself, dedicated to the Holy Cross. The church contains the remains of wall paintings at least 600 years old. The village also has a tiny green and an excellent mill. **Ampney St Mary** is away from the brook that gives the villages their name. It, too, is named from its church which contains a superb collection of wall paintings, some of which make the 600-year-old Crucis paintings appear young. Sadly, as with most such medieval wall paintings, the Puritans, who felt that such works were idolatrous, mutilated much of the work. The church is known locally as Ivy Church, a memory of when it was badly neglected. The original village was wiped out by Black Death and its site moved slightly when it was re-occupied leaving the church behind a little.

South of St Mary is **Ampney St Peter**, which is on the brook. The stone cottages of the village and the nearness of the stream are typically Cotswold. Close to the village is Ranbury Ring, a Neolithic camp, while to the south is a fourth Ampney, Down Ampney, famous as the birthplace of Ralph Vaughan Williams. Just south of the Ampney villages is the **Cotswold Water Park** at South Cerney which offers most water-based sports. The associated **Keynes Country Park** has a golf course and waterside barbecue area.

Opposite top: Cirencester Park Opposite bottom: The Bear Inn, Cirencester

THE UPPER COLN VALLEY

The area between Cirencester and Cheltenham-Gloucester is dominated by the valleys of the rivers Churn and Coln. It is the latter that will first be described. **Chedworth** is not on the Coln itself but on a steep-sided tributary. The village is attractively placed on both sides of the steep valley. Those who find the village from Denfurlong do not get the full flavour of this side of the valley, which is better approached from Foss Bridge up the quaintly named Pancake Hill – certainly not as flat as a pancake. The village clings to the steep sides of the valley, the cottages appearing to grow out of it; indeed they have more rows of windows that open away from the hill than open on to it.

The village once had a railway line, and the skill with which the engineers laid its track, in view of the steep and deep sides of the upper Coln Valley and the limited gradients necessary for locomotives, is astonishing. The travellers on this line, from Cheltenham to Cirencester, passed through some excellent countryside, even if the line did have considerable lengths of embanked track. The idea of creating a footpath along the disused trackway has not been pursued with great vigour: as it penetrates the heart of Chedworth wood, visitors could visit these, while keeping away from some of the nature reserves that the woods now house.

The woods themselves stretch from the outskirts of Chedworth village right across to the Coln Valley and the Roman Villa, and follow the valley itself from Stowell Park, near the Foss Way – the A429 – up to Withington. This is the first section of wooded valley that so characterises the Cotswolds in the area around the Stroud Valley. The wood is true British deciduous forest intermingled with some conifers. The roads that follow the Coln Valley from Yanworth past the Roman Villa towards Cassey Compton, and then left through the wood, or from Chedworth to Withington, are delightful. On occasions they are unfenced, the wood ending at the roadside. The visitor can sense the past in the silence.

Chedworth Roman Villa

To reach Chedworth Roman Villa one does not go to Chedworth village, as the villa is in the Coln Valley on a road going west from Yanworth. A more suitable way to approach the site is through the woods from Chedworth village. There are, in fact, several paths and bridleways from the village into the woods and on to the villa. The walker can choose to go from the village or, perhaps better, take the minor road to

The hypocaust at the Chedworth Villa

Stowell, under the railway bridge, and use the bridlepath that leaves this after it has risen steeply (3kms - 2 miles - 1 hour). This allows the benefit of excellent views of Chedworth itself.

The Roman Villa is often regarded as the finest in Britain. It is very large, with thirty two rooms and separate bathrooms. Only when faced with the enormity of the building does the sophistication of the Romans strike home. The medieval period in Britain, with its hovels and superstitions, tends to obscure the fact that the Romans were a people of culture and builders of great skill. The villa remains have been covered to preserve them, and the best of the domestic articles that have been found are in a museum at the site. An interesting by-product of the Roman occupation is that the large European edible snail can be found at the site and in the nearby area.

Yanworth, mentioned as being on the route to the villa from the east, is a small hamlet set above the Coln, with fine barns near a church that includes an ancient wall painting of a skeleton as Old Father Time. Further down river from Yanworth is Stowell and **Stowell Park**, where the mansion was constructed on the site of a house owned by the Tames, a rich woolstapler family from Northleach. The views from the outskirts of the park towards Chedworth woods and the river are breathtaking. The best are obtained by following the river to and from a well sited pub, taking the path from Foss Bridge to Stowell Park and returning by path and lane on the opposite side of the river (5kms - 3 miles - 1 hour).

Withington is at the other end of the road from Yanworth that goes past Chedworth Villa. Its fine older part is set in the Coln Valley which is not too steep or deep at this point. The pleasant village has an inn, The Mill, constructed with stone from Northleach prison.

Above Withington the Coln is difficult to follow, because the headwaters are not a single stream: one rises near Brockhampton and another towards Dowdeswell. The western branch, towards Dowdeswell, flows past the pleasant hamlet of **Foxcote**, having sprung from below Foxcote Hill and the Kilkenny viewpoint, a nicely situated series of tiered car parks. The view is over the Gloucester Vale and the Severn, a wide vista not only towards the vale with the major towns of Gloucester, Cheltenham and Tewkesbury, but also of the distant Malverns.

Another head water flows to **Andoversford**, mainly modern and suburban, and not really comparable with the villages of the lower valley. Beyond Andoversford is Dowdeswell where the reservoir is one of the few large expanses of water in the Cotswolds. The village looks out across this water, with the woods beyond, and from this distance has a fine view. To the south and east are two more parks. Sandywell Park, to the east, was described by Horace Walpole as containing 'a square box of a house, very dirtily situated', but Upper Dowdeswell Manor, to the south, is a much nicer late sixteenth century house. The name Dowdeswell is said to derive from a Saxon chief Dodo who, with another called Odo, founded Tewkesbury.

Returning towards the Foss Way the village of **Compton Abdale** sits on the edge of high wold, above the Coln Valley. The village's beauty is enhanced by the small stream flowing down the main street. It is on the White Way, a very ancient trackway leading across the high wold. Before the advent of freezing, salt was used for preserving freshly-killed meat, and from earliest times tracks, known as Salt Ways or White Ways, were made across Britain to saltings.

This particular way heads back across the wolds towards the Midlands, probably to the salt town of Droitwich. A 2 hour walk along the Way takes the traveller down to the Coln and up into Chedworth Woods. Beyond is open wold again. At the exit from the wood one is suddenly in the middle of a disused airfield. The White Way then crosses the high wolds of North Cerney Downs on a perfectly straight 6$\frac{1}{2}$ kms (4-mile) section of trackway. Beyond the Down, the road drops

129

Scenic Car Tour

Around Chedworth

From Cirencester take the ring road going northward, following signs for the A417 to Birdlip and Gloucester. After the roundabout where the A429/A417 leaves right for Stow-on-the-Wold and Fairford, go ahead and take the road right for North Cerney. This minor road crosses North Cerney Down, an excellent stretch of high wold, bypassing North Cerney village, and reaching the old airfield near Chedworth Woods. A signed road here leads to the Chedworth Roman Villa and Cassey Compton. From the latter continue to Compton Abdale from where a narrow, steep lane leads to Withington. Go out of the village westward, forking right at the Y-junction for Upper Coberley. Go down through the village to the A435, and cross it to Cowley. Go left beyond the church on a lane to the A417, the Roman Ermin Way. Go left along this, but soon take a lane on the left, to Elkstone, returning to the A417 after going through the village. Go left again at the main road to return to Cirencester.

down to Spital Gate in Cirencester, but instead take the Churn valley, and follow it back towards Cheltenham.

THE UPPER CHURN VALLEY

Baunton is the first village in the Churn valley, a neat hamlet whose church contains a lifesize fourteenth century wall painting of St Christopher wading through a stream with fish. The whole painting is 4m (13ft) by 3m (10ft) and is the largest and best in the county.

From Baunton, the river can be followed by a path on its eastern bank all the way to North Cerney, but the western bank is accompanied by the A435, good for motorists, but not for walkers. Instead, they should leave the road and go up the escarpment east of North Cerney to the Downs and follow the fine lane that was White Way, back towards Baunton (11kms - 7 miles - 4 hours).

Bagendon, a pleasant hamlet, is set a little way back from the river. It gives little indication now of the importance it once had in the Iron Age, for excavations suggest that the village is on the site of the massive and well fortified capital of the Dobunni tribe.

Next up-river is **North Cerney**, with its exquisite church. It is not of one period, and has been lately renovated completely, in keeping with its original work. Outside it has lovely carved corbels, and on the south wall, a manticore can be found, with the body of a lion, red hair, the face and ears of a man, three rows of teeth and a tail complete with scorpion's sting. The beast also had a fine singing voice.

Opposite page left: Devil's Chimney, Leckhampton Hill

Opposite page right: Looking down on Cheltenham from Leckhampton Hill

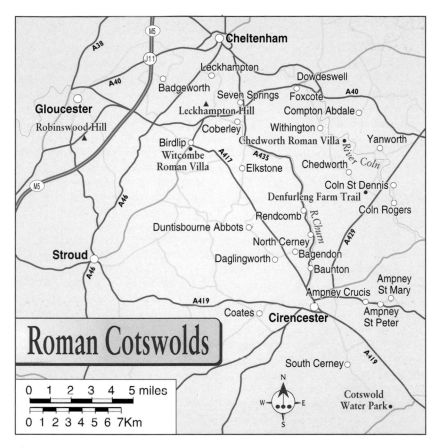

Roman Cotswolds

0 1 2 3 4 5 miles

0 1 2 3 4 5 6 7Km

5555555

For food it was said 'it myght fede on thy Braynes'. Inside, the notable fifteenth century nave roof has supports resting on carved corbels.

Near the church is **Cerney House Gardens**. This beautiful old country estate of some 30 acres comprising gardens and woodland is open to the public between Easter and September. It is especially known for the walled rose garden, the herbaceous borders, the specialist herbs and wild flowers.

Rendcomb is the next village from North Cerney, a pretty collection of riverside cottages with another park, constructed for another member of the Northleach Tame family. Between Rendcomb and Colesbourne there is no public river footpath, but there is one between Colesbourne (which also has a park, containing a good collection of rare shrubs) and Cowley, whose manor has a water garden fed from artificial lakes, themselves fed from the Churn. Above Colesbourne is the tiny village of **Elkstone** noted for the curious parish records of the Rev. Prior, vicar from 1682 to 1725. He notes in 1704 that he 'buried the stinking residue of William Gwylliams', and in 1724 that he married Joseph Still and Mary Pool – 'For future reference: he gave me what he gave to the sexton: a single miserable shilling'. The church has a fine, and rare, tympanum above the main doorway.

Further up the Churn Valley, as the water in the stream bed becomes shallower, is **Coberley**, where Sir Richard Whittington once lived at the hall (no longer extant). Sir Richard, the Dick of pantomime fame, was Lord Mayor of London on three occasions. His mother, Joan, married Sir William Whittington, after

being widowed by Sir Thomas Berkley, the local squire. Sir Thomas survived the battle of Crecy and died about 1350. The church has a fine collection of monuments; the oldest, dating from 1295, is of Sir Giles de Berkley, an ancestor of Sir Thomas. The tomb is, in fact, above a heart burial, the effigy knight clutching a heart. Such burials were common at the time, the heart being interred separately from the rest of the body. In this case the body of Sir Giles is at Little Malvern.

Coberley's Horse Burial

On the other side of the church wall from the heart burial of Sir Giles de Berkeley, a recent stone marks the spot where Sir Giles' favourite horse, Lombard, is buried. Animal burials in consecrated ground are unusual – Sir Giles must have been very influential.

The Churn rises at **Seven Springs**. They are at the side of the A436 and can be reached by descending to a small copse below road level. A tablet claims, in Latin, that this is the source of the Thames. Nowadays it is generally acknowledged that the Thames rises at Thameshead, a little way south-west of Cirencester. The claim of the Churn to be the true source is strong however, in that it rises about 15kms (about 10 miles) further from Lechlade than the more southerly headwater.

An excellent 2 hours walk from Seven Springs follows the Cotswold Way to the **Devil's Chimney** on

Leckhampton Hill. It follows the escarpment slope around Charlton Kings Common and Leckhampton Hill. The view of Cheltenham in the valley below, and of the edge, is very good. The Devil's Chimney is a rock pinnacle, a remnant of quarrying on the hill. The spot is an excellent viewpoint, but do not climb the pinnacle which is extremely unstable.

Leckhampton itself had interesting manorial lords. One, Gilbert de Clare, killed at Bannockburn when he was just 23, is buried at Tewkesbury. Another family, the Giffards from nearby Brimpsfield, built the original court. One of the lord's four sons founded Worcester College, Oxford, two were prominent local gentry, and the fourth was hanged for robbing the King's baggage train near Birdlip.

To the south is the **Crickley Hill Country Park**, built around the most completely excavated hillfort on the Cotswolds. In the summer months visitors can frequently watch excavations in progress and receive a guided tour. At other times there is little to be seen, but diagrams at the site vividly portray the fort in its phases from the Stone to Iron Ages. A later entrance gateway was a particularly ingenious piece of work. To the north-east of the park is Short Wood, a superb small wood of large beeches. Beyond the park is Gloucester.

GLOUCESTER

Gloucester does not actually lie within the AONB, being down in the Severn Vale below the Cotswold edge, though protected by two outliers of the hills –Robinswood Hill and Churchdown.

The city site is an ancient one,

probably earlier than the Roman city of Glevum – built here at a crossing point of the Severn, as the western bastion of early Roman efforts to subdue the tribesmen of Wales. There have been major excavations of this important Roman city, and finds can be seen in the **City Museum** in Brunswick Road, along with other items of local interest such as the Birdlip mirror. In addition, and in keeping with the city's decision to retain its past as part of a lively present, the excavations of the Roman city's Eastgate (in Eastgate Street) have been opened up close to the main shopping precinct. Here a glass-topped plinth set at street level allows a view of the remains below street level. At certain times the underground excavation itself can be viewed.

Gloucester remained an important city when the Romans had been replaced by the Saxons, not only because of its position on the Severn but because it stood on the boundary of Mercia and Wessex, two of the three great Saxon kingdoms of England. The Cotswolds themselves represented a high-level route between the kingdoms, jealously guarded because of its strategic importance, and as a garrison city Gloucester was critical. Its importance can be gauged by the many centres for monastic life created there. Several Saxon rulers endowed convents or monasteries, and the Mercian king Ethelred, brother of Alfred the Great, brought the body of St Oswald from Lincolnshire here and founded a priory around the tomb. The remains of the priory, or at least those of the Norman modifications to the original building, can still be seen to the north of the cathedral.

Short Cycle Rides

↑1 Chedworth Woods (13 miles)
Map: OS Sheet 163 – Cheltenham & Cirencester area.
From Yanworth take the signed road towards the Chedworth Roman
Villa. Before the villa a lane leaves this road – just after the Coln
bridge – to Compton Abdale. Take this lane, which falls steeply into
the village. Go left past the church and left at the Y-junction on a
lane that rises and falls steeply through Chedworth Woods and then
crosses the old airfield before reaching Chedworth village. The
village is entered sharply downhill, and left by an equally sharp rise
by the lane returning to Yanworth.

↑2 Cirencester Park (19 miles)
Map: OS Sheet 163 – Cheltenham & Cirencester area.
Leave Cirencester by the minor road that goes over the ring road
northward to Somerford Keynes. Follow this until a lane right leads
to Ewen, and go through this to Kemble. Go over at the main A429
through the village on a road that goes under the railway and meets
the A433. Go over this taking the lane to Tarlton. There go right for
Coates. Where the road goes over the canal, just before it goes under
the railway, go left to see the Sapperton Tunnel portal. At a T-
junction outside Coates go left past the church and continue
westward to the main A419. Go left, then right for Sapperton, but do
not reach the village, going right at a crossroads for Park End, and
right there for Daglingworth. From the village take the lane to
Stratton and the A417 that is used to regain Cirencester.

Compton Abdale

Gloucester Cathedral

There was a Saxon royal palace near the priory, and Ethelred was buried here. Certainly at that stage Gloucester was the central city of Mercia and the only city comparable with Winchester, the capital of Wessex. When England was finally united against the Danes, power shifted to the east and to London, the capital accepted by the Norman conquerors. But Gloucester remained important, early Norman kings holding a council here in the autumn of each year. Indeed it was here, in the chapter house of the cathedral, that William the Conqueror drew up his plans for the Domesday Book.

The chapter house is the oldest surviving part of the cathedral, one of the most architecturally important buildings in Britain, a fine and early example of the Perpendicular style of architecture. Within, there is a treasury of fine work. The cloisters are one of the few surviving examples of this most obvious feature of monastic life. They are roofed by marvellous fan-vaulting, and include the monks' lavatory, or wash-house, on one side. The very ancient east window is the largest of any British cathedral, constructed to commemorate victory at the battle of Crecy. The cathedral is the only site apart from Westminster Abbey to have been used for a coronation for over 700 years; Henry III was crowned here as a nine-year-old, and with his mother's bracelet, a few days after the death of King John. The Coronation was a hasty move – John had been dead only nine days – to avoid civil war, and was carried out here to avoid the delay of a journey to London. The tomb of Edward II, murdered at Berkeley Castle, is in the north ambulatory.

Facing the cathedral is a memorial to **Bishop Hooper**, burnt at the stake here in 1555 for being a Lutheran. He spent the night before his execution in a half-timbered building in Westgate Street. The building, a beautiful three-storeyed house with double overhangs, is now known as Bishop Hooper's Lodgings and contains a folk museum, which has a replica of a wheelwright's shop.

The Siege of Gloucester

A little less than 100 yearsafter Bishop Hooper had perished at the stake there was more fire and death in the city when the Parliamentarian govenor Sir Edward Massey was besieged by a Royalist army under the king himself. At that time the city stood between the king's capital at Oxford and his main support in Wales, and its occupation was vital to both sides. When eventually a relief army arrived, the city was down to its last three barrels of powder, and the king withdrew. Puritan supporters were so pleased that a rhyme was constructed for Massey

He that doth stand so well upon his guard
I hope shall never miss a good reward.

It includes, in the last five words, an anagram of his name rendered as Edward Massie Governor.

As a port and a centre for light industry, Gloucester has continued to prosper, but its past history is recalled in a fine series of reliefs on buildings in the city centre. Another place of interest is the **Tailor of Gloucester's house**, a Beatrix Potter Museum, the one actually used as the model for the book and containing scenes from it.

Two further monastic remains are **Blackfriars**, founded in the early thirteenth century which contains, in the church, a superb roof from that time; and **Greyfriars**, a sixteenth century building near the new covered market. There are also a number of fine, mainly Norman, churches, and many beautiful houses. A walk around Gloucester is worthwhile: in Bearland , between Southgate and Westgate streets the **Transport Museum**, visible from the road, has a small collection of antique vehicles including a horse-drawn tram. Those who prefer a formal guided tour can join one at **St Michael's Tower** at the junction of the four 'gate' streets. These tours also take in the city docks which have been extensively restored. Here is the **National Waterways Museum** of canal items. Nearby, the **Soldiers of Gloucestershire Museum** explores the history of the local regiment, the Glorious Glosters. The docks are also close to the Gloucester Antiques Centre which includes a reconstructed Victorian shop row.

To the south of the city is Robinswood Hill with a country park and one of **Britain's largest dry ski slopes**. But strangest of all is the Prison Museum, housed in an old lodge of the prison. This, Britain's only museum in a working jail, has information on the prison service and sells the handiwork of the inmates.

Finally, just outside the city there are two more fascinating visitor sites. A little way north, on the A38 near Twigworth, is **Nature in Art**, a collection of wildlife art in various media. The collection is claimed to be the only one of its kind in the world. There are both indoor and outdoor exhibits, a shop, a play area and coffee house, the whole arranged in and around Wallsworth Hall, a fine Georgian building. And mid-way between Gloucester and Cheltenham, is the Staverton (Gloucestershire) airport, formerly the home of the **Jet Age Museum** a collection of very early jet aircraft and cockpits. The museum celebrated Gloucester's position in the history of jet aircraft travel: Britain's first jet aircraft flew from close to the city and the Gloster Meteor was a very successful early jet. Sadly the musuem has recently had to move from its Staverton premises and is seeking new ones.

Gloucester docks with the Cathedral in the background

Selected Walks

↑1 **Chedworth Roman Villa** *4.5 miles •Moderate• 100ft climb*
Map: OS Sheet 163 – Cheltenham & Cirencester area.
Start at Yanworth (tithe barn). Leave the village westward to a road junction where the road ahead is signed for the Roman Villa. Follow this road towards the villa, crossing the River Coln just before the villa is reached. To return, retrace your steps from the villa to the river and go onto a signed track, right, that follows the river's southern bank through the beautiful Chedworth Woods. When a road is reached go left. Just over a bridge go right through a gate and follow the river's northern bank until the path swings away across fields to a lane. Go left to return to Yanworth.

↑2 **Seven Springs and Leckhampton Hill**
7 miles •Moderate/Strenuous• two 300ft climbs
Map: OS Sheet 163 – Cheltenham & Cirencester area.
Start at Seven Springs (Source of Churn – or Thames?). The next section of the walk follows the Cotswold Way and so is extremely well waymarked. Take the minor road leaving the A436 north of the river source and the track that leaves this road. The track traverses Charlton Kings Common to the hillfort and triangulation point on top of Leckhampton Hill. A short distance westward is the Devil's Chimney and a superb view over Cheltenham and the upper Severn Vale. The walk continues to follow the Cotswold Way passing a quarry and Salterley Grange to reach the Ullenwood golf clubhouse. There the Cotswold Way goes right, but go straight on down the lane to the main A436. Go over onto the lane for Cowley and immediately go right through a gate to a path up South Hill. At the top of the hill go left passing Cuckoopen Barn on a bridlepath that descends to a road junction. Go ahead and, where the road goes right, ahead again. Immediately go left on a path past Close Farm to Coberley. Now take a signed path beside the school across the fields to the A436. Go right to Seven Springs.

↑3 **The Ampneys** *5 miles •Moderate• Level ground*
Map: OS Sheet 163 – Cheltenham & Cirencester area.
This is an excellent short and easy walk through very pleasant country. Start at Poulton, on the A417 Cirencester to Fairford road. Go towards Fairford on the main road, but ahead where the main road goes sharply right, take the track – Ashbrook Lane – left a little further on, to a junction. Go over and follow the lane to Ampney St Mary. After the second block of houses to the left, a signed path leads across a field and along field edges to Ampney St Peter, emerging by the church which can be used as a guide. Go down past the church to the pub on the A417. Go over the main road to a lane that passes the treatment works. As Charlham Farm comes into view a signed path left is taken which obviously leads back to the A417 at Poulton.

BIRDLIP

Crickley Hillfort
Crickley Hill Country Park
☎ 01452 863170
Open: at all reasonable times.

CIRENCESTER

Brewery Arts
Brewery Court
☎ 01285 657181
Open: all year, Monday-Saturday
10am-5pm.

Cirencester Lock-Up
Trinity Road
☎ 01285 655611
Open: all year Monday-Friday during
office hours. The Lock-Up is administered by the Cotswold District
Council and the key can be obtained
from their offices (also in Trinity
Road).

Corinium Museum
Park Street
☎ 01285 655611
Open: April to October, daily 10am-
5pm, Sunday, 2-5pm; November to
March, Tuesday-Saturday 10am-5pm,
Sunday 2-5pm. Open all Bank
Holidays except 25-26 December.

**The Craftsman's Market & Cotswold
Craft Market**
Corn Hall
Open: March to December
Craftsman's Market: 1st and 3rd
Saturday in the month.
Cotswold Crafts: 2nd and 4th
Saturday in the month.
No market if there is a 5th Saturday.
Open for buying and commissioning
crafts.

GLOUCESTER

Tailor of Gloucester's House
9 College Court
☎ 01452 422856
Open: all year, Monday-Saturday
10am-5pm (4pm November to
March).

Blackfriars (English Heritage)
☎ 0117 975 0700
Open: April to September, Monday-
Friday 10am-3.30pm.

Cathedral
Westgate Street
☎ 01452 528095
Open: all year 8am-6pm (5pm from
October to March) subject to special
exhibitions and services.

City Eastgate
Brunswick Road
☎ 01452 524131
Open: May to September, Saturday
10am-4pm.

City Museum & Art Gallery
Brunswick Road
☎ 01452 524131
Open: all year, Monday-Saturday
10am-5pm. Also July to September
Sunday 10am-4pm. Open Bank
Holidays except Christmas, New Year
and Good Friday.

Folk Museum
Bishop Hooper's Lodgings
99-103 Westgate Street
☎ 01452 526467
Open: all year Monday-Saturday
10am-5pm. Also July to September
Sunday 10am-4pm. Open Bank
Holiday Mondays.

Gloucester Antiques Centre
Severn Road
☎ 01452 529716
Open: all year Monday-Saturday
10am-5pm, Sunday 1-5pm.

Jet Age Museum
☎ 01452 526467
Telephone for information on new
premises and opening times.

National Waterways Museum
Llanthony Warehouse
☎ 01452 318054
Open: all year daily 10am-5pm.
Closed Christmas Day.

Nature in Art
Wallsworth Hall
Twigworth
☎ 01452 731422
Open: all year Tuesday-Sunday and
Bank Holiday Mondays 10am-5pm.

Prison Museum
Old Gate Lodge
HM Prison Gloucester
☎ 01452 529551 Ext 425
Will re-open at Easter 2002.
Telephone, or ask at the Tourist
Information Office for details of
opening times.

Robinswood Hill Country Park
☎ 01452 303206
Open: all year.
Park: daily 8am-dusk; Visitor Centre:
daily 10am-5pm.
Ski Centre ☎ 01452 414300: open all
year, Monday-Friday 10am-10pm,
Saturday and Sunday 10am-6pm.

**Soldiers of Gloucestershire
Museum**
Gloucester Docks
☎ 01452 522682
Open: all year Tuesday-Sunday and
Bank Holiday Monday 10am-5pm.
Also Monday from June to Septem-
ber.

Transport Museum
Bearland
☎ 01452 526467
Open: visible from the road at all
times, otherwise by appointment
through the Folk Museum.

North Cerney
Cerney House Gardens
☎ 01285 831300 or 831205
Open: Easter to September, Tuesday,
Wednesday and Friday 10am-5pm.

SOUTH CERNEY

**Cotswold Water Park/ Keynes
Country Park**
☎ 01285 861459
Open: all year, but individual
facilities have different times. Ring
for details.

YANWORTH

**Chedworth Roman Villa
(National Trust)**
☎ 01242 890256
Open: May to September, Tuesday-
Sunday and Bank Holiday Monday
10am-5pm; March, April and October
to mid-November, Wednesday-
Sunday and Bank Holiday Mondays
11am-4pm

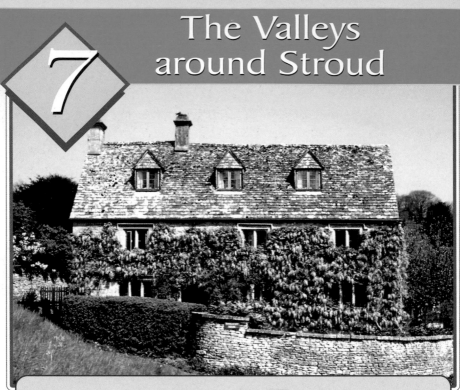

This section of the Cotswolds includes the Stroud Valley, the most heavily industrialised area in the region, and the wooded valleys on each side that drain into it. In earlier times the name Cotswold was applied only to that area of land around the headwaters of the Windrush, but gradually it was extended to more and more land to the south that was similar in geography and agriculture. By the latter part of the last century the name meant all land down to the Stroud Valley. More recently the area has been extended again to include the land south of Stroud. Geologically, the Cotswolds extend to Bath, but there is a change in geography, the wolds of the north being replaced by the lower wooded land of the south. Stroud represents the transitional region between the two.

The change is exemplified by the wooded escarpment around Birdlip, north of Painswick. Before seeking the woody seclusion, one should go along to Barrow Wake, a steep bare part of the escarpment on the A417, just a little south of the Air Balloon Inn on the junction of the road with the A436, where there is a fine viewpoint. To the right is the edge of

Opposite page:
Duntisbourne
Abbots

left: Painswick

right:
Prinknash
Abbey pottery

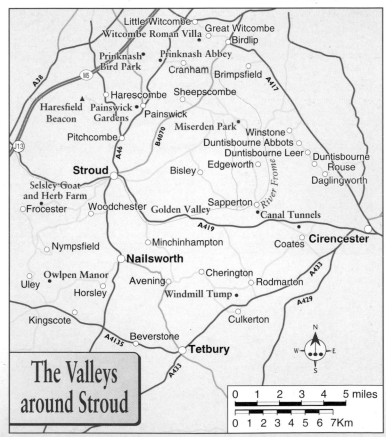

Little Witcombe
Witcombe Roman Villa
Great Witcombe
Birdlip
Prinknash
Bird Park
Prinknash Abbey
Cranham
Brimpsfield
A38
M5
A417
Harescombe
Sheepscombe
Haresfield
Beacon
Painswick
Gardens
Painswick
Miserden Park
Winstone
Duntisbourne Abbots
Pitchcombe
B4070
Duntisbourne Leer
Duntisbourne
Rouse
A46
Edgeworth
Daglingworth
J13
Stroud
Bisley
River Frome
Selsley Goat
and Herb Farm
Frocester
Woodchester
Golden Valley
Sapperton
Canal Tunnels
A419
Coates
Cirencester
Nympsfield
Minchinhampton
Nailsworth
A433
Owlpen Manor
Cherington
Uley
Avening
Rodmarton
Horsley
Windmill Tump
A429
Kingscote
Culkerton
Beverstone
A4135
Tetbury
A433

N
W E
S

The Valleys around Stroud

| 0 | 1 | 2 | 3 | 4 | 5 miles |
| 0 | 1 | 2 | 3 | 4 | 5 | 6 | 7Km |

Crickley Hill, with the clear escarpment outcrop. To the left is The Peak, the final promontory of Birdlip Hill, and beyond that, a section of wooded escarpment that forms the Witcombe Estate. Below are the villages of Great and Little Witcombe, and Gloucester cathedral beyond. Further on, the River Severn meanders its way around the Arlingham Bend in front of the Forest of Dean. At the northern end of the forest May Hill is seen, its summit distinctively topped with a crown of trees.

BRIDLIP AND PRINKNASH

Birdlip sits at the top of the escarpment, known here as Birdlip Hill. Those approaching the village from the Witcombe villages up the hill itself will see just how steep the escarpment can be. Beneath the wooded hill and the Peak are the remains of an Iron Age hillfort where excavations unearthed the finest collection of Iron Age jewellery so far discovered in Britain. It includes the **Birdlip Mirror**, a unique object, made around 50BC. It is a 6in diameter flat bronze disc with a 3in handle, made by the lost wax system, skillfully engraved and inlaid with red enamel. It can be seen in Gloucester Museum.

Witcombe Wood forms one of the best long wood walks in the Cotswolds. It follows a section of the Cotswold Way, from Birdlip to Cooper's Hill. A good return from here is to drop down the valley, and go between the reservoirs to Great Witcombe, although this involves a steep climb back to Birdlip.

Cheese Rolling

Cooper's Hill is famous for its cheese rolling competition which takes place annually at the Spring Holiday. Contestants chase large cheeses down the slope and anyone catching a cheese keeps it. The slope is sometimes fenced off to avoid erosion, but the healthy visitor can reach the maypole at the top by going through the trees at the side. Looking down it is easy to see why few people ever actually catch the cheese, and why minor injuries and concussions are frequent. Not long ago the event was cancelled because the injury list had become too long, but by popular demand it was begun again. The history of the event is lost in time, but most experts believe it was originally sun-based, the cheese (or any disc-shaped object) representing the sun, the contestants hoping to catch it and so persuade it to return the following day or the following spring. There are similar events, some involving the chasing of flaming discs, in other parts of the world. The maypole, another ancient symbol, would seem to confirm the event as pagan in origin, though the present pole is too close to the edge for dancing. A hundred years or so ago, in addition to the cheese rolling there were also wrestling contests, dancing and singing.

Near the cheese rolling slope is **Witcombe Roman Villa**. Though not in the class of Chedworth, nor containing anything to equal the Woodchester pavement, it is nonetheless interesting.

In the woods above the cheese rolling slope – known collectively as Cranham Woods, although that name is strictly only applicable to those near Cranham village, others being Brockworth Wood and Buckholt Wood – there are a number of nature trails with colour-coded, signposted ways and information boards that cross the **Cooper's Hill Nature Reserve.** Cranham village is, as one would expect, close to woodland, but on its southern side there is an area of common. The woodland around the village is one of the finest in Britain and is spectacular in autumn as the leaves change colour. Any walk from **Cranham** is worthwhile, and with Birdlip and Cooper's Hill only $2^1/_2$kms ($1^1/_2$ miles) east and west, and the pleasant hamlet of Sheepscombe also $2^1/_2$kms ($1^1/_2$ miles) away to the south, there is no shortage of excellent routes.

A little way from Cranham, on a pleasant site halfway down the escarpment, overlooking the Gloucester Vale, is **Prinknash Abbey.** The name is not pronounced as written, but as 'Prinage'. The abbey is not an ancient and historic building, but modern, looking in no way like an abbey. The visitor is immediately struck by the colour of the stone, but it is Cotswold. It was quarried in the Guiting Quarry not far from the Cotswold Farm Park, though it will need a few hundred years to mellow into the countryside. The visitor has limited access to the abbey itself, which is Benedictine, and can also visit the world-famous pottery where the monks, with lay craftsmen, throw, decorate and fire

their distinctive range of pottery.

The **Prinknash Bird Park**, set in about 10 acres of parkland that form part of the original Prinknash estate, houses a large number of birds, mainly geese and pheasants, free and free-flying in natural surroundings. There are also herds of muntjac and fallow deer.

PAINSWICK

Further south towards Stroud is **Painswick**, a gem of a village, almost a small town, with an interesting and long history. The visitor who braves the iron shots on the local golf course to reach the top of Painswick Beacon sees not only an expansive view, but also the ditches and ramparts of an ancient hillfort, which pre-dates the town by several centuries. The village had a lord in Norman times. A later lord was the infamous and callous Sir Anthony Kingston, who appears to have had a genius for cruelty.

Henry VIII came here with Anne Boleyn for a couple of happy days' holiday, but within twelve months the happiness had faded, and Anne Boleyn was led out by her jailer for execution; the jailer was Anthony Kingston's father.

Sir Anthony Kingston, one-time lord of Painswick, was a friend of King Henry, a friendship based, in part, on Kingston's willingness to carry out certain unpleasant tasks with enthusiasm. He put down a northern rebellion following the Dissolution of the monasteries with much enthusiasm, and later did the same in Bodmin. There he excelled himself by accepting the mayor's hospitality and then escorting him to a set of gallows rapidly constructed by the mayor's men at his command, but on Kingston's orders. 'Thinke you, Mister Maior, that they be strong inough' asked Kingston. 'Yea, sir, that they are' replied the Mayor, anxious to please. 'Well then get you even up unto them, for they are provided for you,' 'and so without respit or staie there was the maior hanged'.

Sir Anthony also officiated in Gloucester at the burning of Bishop Hooper. In the Painswick area he had a gallows erected and men paid to be ready to put it to instant use. Not surprisingly, he was hated in the town, to such an extent, that when the church was later damaged during the Civil War, the locals used it as a cover for their own vandalising of his elaborate tomb.

Painswick church makes a good start to a walk around the town. It is a fine building, but the churchyard is interesting too. The yews are steeped in legend. One version has it that they cannot be counted, while another says that there are ninety nine trees and that if a hundreth is planted, it dies. The churchyard paths below the yews thread through the very famous collection of table-top tombs: there are guides to tomb trails.

At the south end of the churchyard, just beyond the wall, are the town stocks and a set of leg-irons. To the side of these is the **Court House**, a superb early seventeenth-century house built for a clothier, but named from a later owner who was a lawyer. From here the walker passes, on the right, the vicarage, a delightful house. Further on through Friday Street is Bisley Street. On the right is a group of houses that date from the fourteenth century – the Chur, Little Fleece, and Wickstone. There is even an original arched packhorse doorway for deliveries to the rear of the buildings, parts of which were an inn.

Straight on from here and adding 20 minutes to the walk, is **Painswick House**, a fine house built in the eighteenth and nineteenth centuries in the Palladian style. The elegant interior includes a room with Chinese wallpaper. Although the house is not open, the Rococo Garden, the only complete survivor of this mid-eighteenth century style may be visited. The 6-acre garden is being painstakingly restored to the form shown in a painting of 1748. The coach house is now a licenced restaurant and coffee house. Left from The Chur is **New Street**, where there is a beautiful timbered house, now the post office. Foreign tourists regard such houses as essentially English, but in the Cotswolds they seem almost out of place. Further down the street is the Falcon Hotel, an eighteenth century inn, the scene of cock fights between Painswick and neighbouring towns.

Clipping the Yews

Each year on a Sunday in September the church is circled by the village children who sing hymns and dance. The service is called clipping and coincides with the clipping of the yews, but experts believe that this is a coincidence. They contend that the name derives from ycleping, the Saxon word for encircling and that the 'modern' service - which started in 1897 - was probably the reintroduction of a much older ceremony. The timing implies an agricultural rite and some believe the origins may even be pre-Christian.

Above left: The Rococo Garden at Painswick
Above right: A spring morning in Cranham Woods

Further down the Painswick valley is **Pitchcombe**, a tiny hamlet on the A4173, still almost secluded in spite of the road. It has a delightful manor house and a fine old mill house. Above Pitchcombe is Edge, another pretty hamlet with a name that is explicit in terms of its position, for the road that leads to Harescombe, in the vale below, seems to fall off the edge.

AROUND PAINSWICK

The valley floor from **Harescombe** to **Haresfield** has the distinction of being the only section of the Cotswolds AONB that lies at the foot of the western escarpment. The two villages retain a Cotswold appearance –Harescombe Grange is an elegant manor house with good views of the river – but lose something in being away from the wolds or out of a wooded, steep valley. In **Haresfield church** is a poignant epitaph by Dryden to an 11-year-old boy that ends with the couplet:

Knowing Heaven his home, to shun delay
He leap'd o'er age and took the shortest way.

To regain the Cotswolds from Haresfield the visitor must tackle the escarpment slope again, and it is long and steep. At the top is **Haresfield Beacon**, perhaps the finest viewpoint for the escarpment itself, and a good spot from which to see the Berkeley Vale, as the lower Severn Vale is known. The actual tip of the escarpment, which has a triangulation pillar, is reached by following the Cotswold Way from the top of the hill from Haresfield. The view takes in the sweep of Standish Wood, then Frocester Hill, the other side of the Stroud Valley, and Cam Long Down and Stinchcombe Hill (the most westerly point of the Cotswolds) above Dursley. In good weather one can glimpse the Severn Bridge.

The panorama is a little less expansive but better signed for the mapless, at the topograph a kilometre or so from the beacon. One can reach this by following the Cotswold Way again, reversing the outward route and continuing east. Beyond the topograph is Standish Wood, an excellent piece of woodland with numerous tracks. Beyond are Randwick and Whiteshill, villages on the side of the Stroud Valley.

East of Painswick the area is again characterised by steep-sided valleys each carrying a stream. The first of these is the Slad Valley, famous for its association with the late Laurie Lee's book *Cider with Rosie*. Many of the places mentioned in the book can be identified – Steanbridge, a modified Elizabethan house, is the squire's house.

The valley and road start above **Sheepscombe**, although this village is actually at the head of the Painswick valley. These two valleys were among the most important mill valleys in the Cotswolds at the height of the wool trade, as can be seen by the number of mills that line the tiny streams. Sheepscombe was too high to benefit from water power, but its name recalls the other element of a successful wool industry; the village was the site of Sir Anthony Kingston's gallows.

Above **Sheepscombe** the B4070 runs between the Painswick and Slad Valleys, dropping down into the latter below Bulls Cross, with a good view across to Painswick. It is a delightful road in these upper regions.

Further down, the valley closes in on each side.

BISLEY

The next valley to the east is the Toadsmoor, with a stream that flows down from **Bisley**. The village, high and unprotected, is a bleak place in winter, recalling the northern high wold villages. It has a very ancient six-sided memorial, with seats that cover what was elegantly called a bone hole where heaps of bones were dumped when old graves were broken open. It is said that around 600 years ago the priest fell into it one night and died. When the Pope was informed, he was so angry that he ordered, as punishment, that there should be no burials for two years. Instead the villagers trekked 24kms (15 miles) to Bibury to bury their dead in 'Bisley piece'. The route, known as Dead Man's Lane, can still in theory be followed past the Giant's Stone.

The Giant's Stone

The stone is all that remains of a long barrow, but has become woven into local legends. It is said that at the stone 'men have had the terrifying experience of seeing headless human beings which have now vanished'. Many other stones in the area also seem to be associated with similar legends. The name **Money Tump**, also said to have been haunted by headless men, suggests a treasure site, and another barrow nearer Oakridge, to the south, stands in **Golden Coffin Field**, so named from the belief that a golden coffin was buried here. The ghost stories were probably invented by field owners to keep strangers away while they searched for buried treasure.

All around Bisley there are delightful isolated, sheltered hamlets. Any of the minor roads from Bisley give rewarding walks and the valley stream can be followed to Eastcombe, the last village before the descent into the Stroud Valley.

THE FROME VALLEY

The Frome Valley actually becomes the Stroud Valley as the Frome flows on to the Severn. In its lower reaches, between Chalford and Stroud, it is called the Golden Valley. In its upper reaches the Frome is in a truly golden valley, particularly in autumn when the woodland that covers the steep sides turns copper-gold. The river rises at Brimpsfield, only a little south of Birdlip, where there are the remains of a castle built about 700 years ago by John Gifford, a descendant of one of William the Conqueror's captains. Unfortunately when Gifford opposed Edward II, his castle was slighted (that is partially demolished so as to be rendered useless as a fortress). The local people plundered the castle for building stone and so now only the foundations and ditches, or moats, survive. The portcullis grooves on stones near the entrance can just be discerned.

From **Brimpsfield** the descent to Caudle Green is steep, but there the motorist has to stop. The road is never continuous, darting occasionally down into the valley to cross it from the top of each valley side. Below Caudle Green is **Miserden**, with its park and well known gardens (the name of which is Misarden, rather than Miserden as for the village, a spelling which often creates confusion). The beautifully situated mansion is Elizabethan, but only the park is open to visitors. A visit is best made in the spring when the bulbs are out, but the rock gardens can be enjoyed all year round. Nearby Edgeworth has a fine manor house, seen particularly well from the road into the valley from Duntisbourne Leer.

At **Daneway**, 3kms (2 miles) further down river from Edgeworth, Daneway House (no longer open to the public) dates, in part, from around 1250. There have been numerous additions, and earlier this century it was used as a furniture and craft workshop by Sidney and Ernest Barnsley and Ernest Gimson.

Also at Daneway is an inn which stands near the entrance to **Sapperton Tunnel**, which formed part of the Thames and Severn Canal and was, at 3,817yd (3,491m), the longest ever built in Britain at the time of its completion in 1789. It was constructed by digging shafts from the surface to the correct depth and tunnelling outwards in each direction. The work was carried out by 'navvies' – the name for those who constructed 'navigations'. The tunnel is almost 5m (15ft) in diameter, bricked where needed, and the boats were pushed through by the boatmen lying on their backs and walking on the tunnel roof. Boat trips through the tunnel are available.

The tunnel is named from **Sapperton**, a larger village slightly closer to the canal tunnel entrance. It is a pretty village, once the home of poet John Masefield, well situated at the end of the Broad Ride from Cirencester Park on the side of the Frome Valley. It also stands at the crossroads between the old agricultural uplands and the industrial lowlands. The division is exemplified

Selected Walks

↑1 **Cooper's Hill to Painswick** *9 miles *Strenuous* 400ft and 300ft climbs*

Maps: OS Sheet 163 – Cheltenham & Cirencester area and
Sheet 162 – Gloucester & Forest of Dean area
Start at Cooper's Hill, below the cheese rolling slope. The route
follows the Cotswold Way from here, getting to the top of the slope
– awesome when viewed downwards – and traversing Brockworth
Wood to the A46 at Prinknash Corner (Prinknash Abbey, Pottery and
Bird Park are right from here). Go over and through Buckholt Wood
to Painswick Beacon, an impressive viewpoint. Beyond, the Way is
well marked past Catsbrain Quarry and into Painswick (Painswick
House and Rococo Gardens). To leave the village pass the town
stocks and bear right to the Weavers' Cottages. Go past the
Sheepscombe turn and take the next lane right, going over a stile,
right, after 50yd to a path that threads through a small wood to a
green track. Go right and pass Highgrove House. At a stream use a
stile to an obvious path bounded by the stream on the left, and trees
on the right, to a bridge at Damsell's Mill. Bear right here across
fields to the ruins of Oliver's Mill by a small copse. Here the path
goes right to Tocknell's Court and its drive. Go down the drive to a
lane that is followed leftwards and steeply up to the A46. Go right to
Prinknash Corner and reverse the outward route to Cooper's Hill.

↑2 **The Thames and Severn** *Canal 4 miles *Moderate* 400ft climb*

Map: OS Sheet 163 – Cheltenham & Cirencester area.
Start at Sapperton. Take the path beside St Kenelm's Church and
through sheep pens to a steep track to the river. Beyond, a path
rises through Dorvel Wood, curving leftwards to meet a broader
track that is followed to a road near Daneway House. Go over and
use a stile to reach a path that runs south-west to another road.
Cross this to a track in Siccaridge Wood. Continue to a crossroads
of tracks. Go left on the track that soon bends sharply left as it
drops down to reach a road and pub. Go right on the road and take a
signed path left that leads to the canal tunnel portal. Climb above
this and follow a rising path back to Sapperton.

↑3 **Frocester Hill to Uley** *5 miles *Moderate* 100ft climb*
Map: OS Sheet 162 – Gloucester & Forest of Dean area.
Start at the Coaley Peak Picnic Site (Nympsfield long barrow). This
route also follows a well-waymarked section of the Cotswold Way.
The route passes the Frocester Hill panorama dial and its excellent
viewpoint, before traversing Coaley Wood, behind Hetty Pegler's
Tump. At the wood end the way briefly touches the B4066, leaving it

for a signed path to the Uleybury hillfort. Go along the fort's northern edge, around its western end and back along its southern side to a cattle grid. Here go right, and down to a signed path to Uley church and the B4066 through the village. Go left and up to the green. Where the B4066 swings left go right along a lane for 250yd to a path on the left. Follow this across fields to a footbridge and take the path beyond that rises to trees and a lane. Go left, then right and towards Nympsfield. Just before the village, a path is reached over a stile on the left that leads back to Coaley Peak.

The Seven Vale and Cotswolds Edge from Frocester Hill

not only by the Sapperton Tunnel, but also by the tunnel that took the trains from Gloucester to Paddington – it was started down the valley from Sapperton, actually a little closer to the village of Frampton Mansell. From there it was driven about 1.7kms (just over a mile) towards the canal tunnel, at a gradient of 1 in 90 up and, later, 1 in 93 down. The railway passes over the canal tunnel about $2\frac{1}{2}$kms ($1\frac{1}{2}$ miles) west of Coates village.

THE DUNTISBOURNES

Leaving Sapperton and its tunnel, one can follow the Duntisbourne Valley which drains into the Churn at Cirencester. It is characterised not by the steeply wooded slopes of the Slad and the Frome but by a collection of fine villages. The first, **Winstone**, a hamlet of a few houses, straggles for almost $1\frac{1}{2}$kms (about a mile) along a minor road that links Caudle Green to Ermin Street, the A417.

From here quiet lanes lead past all the Duntisbourne villages to Daglingworth. **Duntisbourne Abbots** is the first. It is built down the valley side, but terraced so well that the visitor at the base of the slope can see all the houses and the church high above. The church has a most unusual, possibly unique, lych gate, with central pivot and folding brackets on which a coffin could be rested while waiting to enter the church. It is a place of considerable charm, a charm enhanced by the fact that between Duntisbourne Abbots and **Duntisbourne Leer** the road goes along the stream bed: or perhaps the stream goes over the road. The likely explanation for this is that carts and horses emerging from this section of the road might have clean wheels and hooves. Perhaps it was, in part, a cart dip, used to expand wooden wheels and spokes and so tighten the joints.

Duntisbourne Leer is, like so many other villages, named from the abbey that was awarded the manor in early medieval times. The difference is that the abbey was not in England at all, but at Lire, in Normandy. There are fords at Middle Duntisbourne and at **Duntisbourne Rouse**, but neither is as good as the Leer ford.

Rouse has a beautiful church, probably with considerable Saxon work, on the hill above the hamlet. In the churchyard there is a four-teenth century cross with a very long shaft.

The final village, **Daglingworth**, has a church that is an even finer piece of Saxon work. The interior includes three rare Saxon pre-con-quest sculptures, and the tomb of Giles Handcox which contains his 'dissection and distribution'. The in-scription states that the man wished the earth to have his remains, heaven his soul, his friends his love, and the local poor £5 for their 'best advan-tage and releefe'. Further down river from the church and main village is another section of the village, the Lower End. Here is the manor house, with a medieval circular dovecote and its rotating ladder that allowed access to the nesting sites. This dovecote has over 500 nest holes.

THE STROUD VALLEY

The Stroud or Golden Valley is a typical light industrial valley, but Stroud itself, at the opposite end from the Duntisbourne villages, is a pleasant town. There is a Sports and Leisure Centre at **Stratford Park**, with good park walks and a pleas-ant lake on the complex. The town museum has recently moved to the Park where it will be housed in an imposing mansion. When opened it will be a fascinating place with ex-hibits which include local archaeol-ogy as well as some surprising objects such as the world's first lawnmower. The subscription rooms, built in 1833, have a strik-ing façade, and are used for many different exhibitions, including artwork during the Stroud Festival. Another notable gallery for local artists and craftsmen is the **Rooksmoor Mills Gallery** housed in a nineteenth century mill on the Bath road going south from the town.

At the far end of the canal tunnel from Sapperton is **Coates**, a tiny straggling village that has not only the railway and the exit from the Sapperton Tunnel, but also the accepted source of the Thames within its parish boundary.

South-east from Coates is **Tarlton**, a hamlet with thatched cottages, then Rodmarton, a pleasant upland village with prehistoric and Roman sites in its surroundings. The long barrow on Windmill Tump is espe-cially good. The A433, which leaves the Foss Way for Culkerton at the quaintly named Jackaments Bottom, lies in a wooded valley below Rodmarton, and on the far side of the valley is Kemble airfield. This has the Foss Way running right through it.

Culkerton and nearby Ashley are exposed, but charming, hamlets. Ashley has a manor house that dates, in part, from the fifteenth century. West of Rodmarton, Cherington is at the head of another valley that flows down into the Stroud Valley. The village itself has dignified houses around a green on which is a drinking fountain inscribed 'let him that is athirst, come'. Next is Avening, a larger village that typifies more the industrialised Stroud Valley.

NAILSWORTH AND MINCHINHAMPTON

Beyond Avening is Nailsworth, a town rather than a village, built at the junction of two valleys. The town represents the transition from the old, wool-based industry to more modern manufacture and the buildings are mainly less than 200 years old. Despite that, it has considerable charm and is well worth a walk. The visitor will soon discover that many of the side streets are very steep. Steepest of all is the aptly named Nailsworth Ladder which is 1 in 2 or 1 in $2^1/_2$ – no one seems absolutely certain. The centre of the town is marked by a clock tower of 1951. Also the war memorial, and it is claimed to have been constructed in such a way that the sound of the chimes carried to the surrounding villages. The town church dedicated to St George is not inspiring, but inside it has a fine modern mural, colourful and full of lively portraits of the town such as the brass band and local views.

To the south of Nailsworth is Horsley, set on the side of the valley towards the town, with a fine collection of seventeenth century houses. Above Horsley, open wold land is reached again, on the far side of which is Kingscote, famous now not so much for its park and late Georgian house but for the excavations carried out at the extensive Roman settlement just the other side of the A4135.

To the north of Nailsworth is the land above the Stroud Valley, and the valley itself. Gatcombe Park (see p.161) is a late eighteenth century house, and close to its entrance is the Tingle Stone which has a central hole through which sick children were passed. Gatcombe is a little north of Avening, and west of it is Minchinhampton, a fine village with a golf course laid out on one of the largest areas of common land south of Cleeve Hill. The town boasts a very fine market hall dating from the late seventeenth century and supported by pillars, and a post office in a fine Queen Anne building. The town church is also worth a look, if only for its odd, truncated and pinnacled spire. The common also shows the remains of a rampart and ditch system called The Bulwarks. This is an apt name for an Iron Age hillfort that defends an area of over 600 acres. North of this, at Rodborough, is a further area of common.

The Avon flows into the Frome below Stroud, and between it and the escarpment is Woodchester, a tiny village which has seen not one but two monasteries, for Dominican and Franciscan monks. Above Woodchester the escarpment is rejoined at Selsley Common, an ideal picnic spot. Good views are to be found further south, from Frocester Hill, where there is a panorama dial.

The Orpheus Pavement

Surprisingly nothing is really visible at Woodchester of one of the most famous British Roman villas. Here was discovered the Orpheus pavement, over 200 sq m (2,210sq ft) containing 1½ million 1¼cm (½-inch) cubes, the largest mosaic in Britain and one of the finest outside Rome itself. The name derives from a representation of Orpheus playing a harp. The mosaic is not on permanent display. At one time it was revealed evry 10 years when the soil overlaying it - which protected it from the elements - was removed, but it has not been uncovered for many years and there are no plans for any future excavation. Occasionally an exhibition on the pavement and the Roman presence is put on at Woodchester Village Hall. In addition, a reconstruction of the complete pavement - the original has been damaged by grave diggers and unsupervised excavations - has been made and is regularly shown during the summer months at local venues. See the local press or ask at Tourist Information Offices for details.

THE COTSWOLD EDGE

Near the panorama dial is the Coaley Peak Picnic Site. It has numerous charts to help identify the local animal and plant life, together with the Nympsfield long barrow whose name derives from the village a little way from the edge, nestling in a fold of the hills. The Bristol and Gloucestershire Gliding Club is at the top of Frocester Hill. There are conventional gliders, hang gliders and radio-controlled model gliders flying from here. At Nympsfield itself, **Woodchester Mansion** can be visited. Started in 1856, but never completed, the house is now seen as a masterpiece of the period. The architect was Benjamin Bucknall, working for William Leigh who demanded that everything, including the bath and the drainpipes, be of stone. The work took fourteen years, but was never finished, money

or enthusiasm running out. Today what remains is a marvel, not least because all the original laddering and scaffolding is still in place.

The village of **Uley** sits underneath the Uleybury fort; below the village itself, in a valley to the east, is Owlpen, a tiny hamlet with perhaps the most delightful of all Cotswold manor houses. It is not an elaborate building. A straightforward three-gabled house, it does not have an architectural wholeness, parts dating from the fifteenth to the eighteenth centuries. But it possesses an elegance of line and a simple beauty, enhanced by the yew trees on the lawns in front of it, and by a simple church and dense woodland in the background. No single view so typifies the beauty of the Cotswolds better than **Owlpen** in spring when the daffodils are in full colour. The formal terraced garden is said to be the oldest complete garden in England.

The church of All Saints at
glass windows by William
Raphaelite artists including
Madox Brown and Rosetti.
movement claim that the
finest of all Morris's works

Selsley has stained
Morris and several pre-
Burne-Jones, Ford
Many experts on the
Creation window is the
in stained glass.

Places to Visit

The Valleys around Stroud

FROCESTER
Coaley Peak Picnic Site
Open: at all reasonable times.

GREAT WITCOMBE
**Witcombe Roman Villa
(English Heritage)**
Open: exterior at any reasonable
time. Guided tours to view the
mosaic interior are arranged each
year ☎ 01452 425674 for details.

MINCHINHAMPTON
Market House
☎ 01453 886904
Open: all year, Saturday, Sunday and
Bank Holidays 9am-5pm by appoint-
ment only.

NYMPSFIELD
Woodchester Mansion
Woodchester Park
☎ 01453 750455
Open: Times vary, telephone or see
local press for details. Tours start at
11pm and last about 21/2 hours.

PAINSWICK
Rococo Garden
Painswick House
☎ 01452 813204
Open: Mid-January to November
Wednesday-Sunday and Bank
Holidays 11am-5pm. Groups by
arrangement.

PRINKNASH
Abbey Church
☎ 01452 812066
Open: daily 5am-8pm.

Bird Park
Prinknash Abbey Park
☎ 01452 812727
Open: All year, daily 10am-5pm (4pm
October to April).

Abbey Pottery
☎ 01452 812066
Open: all year,
Pottery Shop daily except Christmas
Day, Boxing Day and Good Friday
9am-5.30pm. Pottery viewing gallery
daily 11am-4pm.

Places to Visit

The Valleys around Stroud

SAPPERTON
Sapperton Tunnel
Portals at Sapperton and Coates.
Tunnel, more than 3kms (2 miles)
long, on Thames & Severn Canal.
Trips through tunnel Sundays and
Bank Holidays, water levels permitting.
☎ 01666 502797

SLIMBRIDGE
Wildfowl Trust
☎ 01453 890333
Open: all year (except Christmas
Day), daily 9.30am-5pm (4pm
October to April).

STROUD
Miserdan Park Gardens
☎ 01285 821303
Open: April to September, Tuesday,
Wednesday and Thursday
9.30am-4.30pm.

Rooksmoor Mills
Bath Road
☎ 01453 872577
Open: all year Monday-Saturday
9am-5pm.

Stroud Subscription Rooms
George Street
☎ 01453 764999
Open: all year Monday-Saturday
9-10pm.

The Museum in the Park
(Stroud Town & District Museum)
Stratford Park
☎ 01453 763394
Open: May to September, Tuesday-
Friday 12am-5pm, Saturday and
Sunday 11am-4pm

ULEY
Hetty Pegler's Tump
(Uley Tumulus) (English Heritage)
Key for door available from Crawley
Barns, 800m south.

Owlpen Manor
Owlpen
☎ 01453 860261
Open: April to mid-October Tuesday-
Sunday and Bank Holiday Mondays
2-5pm.

In the vale below the edge there is also much that is worthy of note. At **Slimbridge** is Sir Peter Scott's Wildfowl Trust with flocks of wild geese and swans, together with numerous species of wildfowl from round the world. **Frampton-on-Severn** has the largest village green in England and a magnificent Georgian court. At Arlingham the Severn swings through 180° in two right-angled bends only a short distance apart giving the land around the village the feeling of being an island. The **Severn Bore** becomes noticeable here, although it is at Stonebench, a few kilometres further up-river, that it reaches its peak.

Hetty Pegler's Tump

H etty Pegler's Tump is the curious name given to Uley tumulus, a long barrow set away from the B4066 at the very edge of the escarpment. It is virtually intact and the visitor can only wonder at the dry stone walling of the 'horns' that protect the entrance. The art has changed little, if at all, in 4,000 years. The visitor is well rewarded, for although the doorway is low and the interior dark and wet, it is an unforgettable experience. The name is thought to derive from Hester Pegler, the wife of Henry Pegler who owned the field in which the barrow stands in the late seventeenth century, though quite why she was chosen is unclear. To complete a tour of the better historical monuments of the area, the visitor can then visit **Uleybury**, a large, well protected hillfort formed around a promontory of the escarpment. The fort encloses about 30 acres and it is probably the best in the Cotswolds.

Scenic Car Tours

1 Painswick and the Stroud Valley
From Painswick (House and Rococo Gardens) take the A46 northward passing Prinknash Abbey (Pottery and Bird Park) to the Brockworth roundabout. Go right on the A436. To the left here is Little Witcombe (Yew Tree Gallery) while to the right is Great Witcombe (Roman Villa). At the top of Air Balloon Hill go right at the roundabout on the A417 to Birdlip. Barrow Wake is to the right here. At Birdlip, where the main road goes left, go right on the B4070 and follow this for 2 miles to a pub beyond which a minor road bears left to Whiteway and on to Miserden (Miserden Park), Edgeworth and Daneway (Sapperton Tunnel). From Sapperton take the lane to Frampton Mansell and there go right to Oakridge and Bisley. From Bisley go north-west on a lane that narrows and falls steeply to the Slad Valley. Go right on the valley road, the B4070, to Bull's Cross and there go left back to Painswick.

2 The Severn Vale
From Minchinhampton (Market Hall, St George's Church) cross the Common (The Bulwarks) and drop down into Nailsworth. From there take the B4058 through Horsley and up onto the Wolds. Beyond the village take a lane right to Nympsfield and on to Frocester Hill (Coaley Peak Picnic Site). Go left along the B4066 and leave it sharply right and steeply downhill to Frocester (tithe barn) and on to the A38. Go left. Beyond Cambridge village (the Slimbridge Wildfowl Trust is right from here), take the A4135 to the left, through Cam to Dursley. Beyond Dursley's town centre go left on the B4066 to Uley. Just after the church go right to Owlpen (Owlpen Manor) on a narrow lane that then rises steeply to a T-junction. Go left, and at the crossroads go left again on the B4058 that returns to Horsley and Nailsworth.

The part of the Cotswolds that lies between the M4 and the A4135 is, correctly, termed the Southwolds, and in this area the change in character that was apparent in the villages above Stroud becomes much more distinct. To the east, towards Tetbury, there are still acres of wold land, but the countryside is now much softer with the distinctive feature being the 'Bottoms', as the valleys around Wotton-under-Edge are known.

TETBURY

Tetbury is the largest town in the area, and it maintains much of the delightful character of a Cotswold market town of the seventeenth and eighteenth centuries. Its actual history is much longer. In the Civil War between Stephen and Matilda in the mid-twelfth century, Malmesbury, the local and important abbey town, was besieged. The besieging army set up base at Tetbury, called a 'castle

only three miles distant'. The 'castle' may have been only a defensive earthwork, but Tetbury must have been of some note.

The town's position on, rather than beneath, the Wolds, prevented it being a great milling centre during the wool industry boom, but its central position allowed it to become a very prosperous market town. This had advantages when the woollen industry declined, for the small industries that grow up around markets helped to keep the town solvent. Its prosperity was also helped by being its own lord of the manor; the town bought the manor from Lord Berkeley, its last lord, in the early seventeenth century. It was then governed by a council of local yeomen, who were able to increase its prosperity by ploughing back any profits. The construction of the **Market Hall** in 1655 was an early expression of the place's prosperity.

To see the town it is best to walk, and there is a good starting point at the **church of St Mary**. This is a comparatively late church for the Cotswolds; there was no great wool-stapling family here. Built in a curious style, with huge windows that light up the interior, it has an interesting collection of large monuments including one to the Saunders family, but to which of its members?

In a vault underneath
lie several of the Saunderses
late of this parish; particulars
the Last Day will disclose

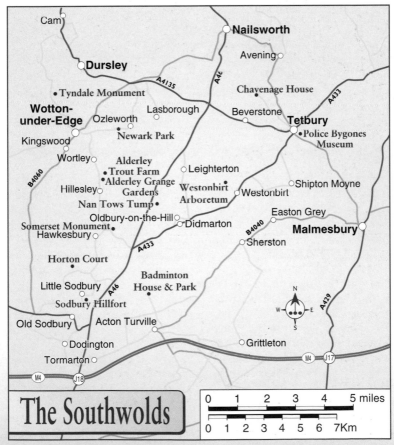

The Southwolds

In Newchurch Street there is St Saviour's Church, later than St Mary's. Apparently the parish church had few pews, and these were in the main bought by the town's rich merchants to the exclusion of the poor. This idea of buying, or endowing, pews was not unique to Tetbury, but the idea of building a second church to accommodate the poor certainly is unusual.

Walking from St Mary's down towards The Green one passes, at the far end to the right, **Barton Abbots**, a beautiful three-storeyed house. On the left is Silver Street and one then reaches the Market Place. To the right is the **Talbot Hotel** which is mainly seventeenth century, but with later additions. The Market Hall, as noted earlier, was built in 1655. Considered one of the finest buildings of its type in the Cotswolds, it was once even better for in 1817 it was 'renovated', being reduced by one storey and re-roofed; an end was filled to provide the town with a lock-up and to house the fire engine. The town's coat of arms is on the building.

Opposite the Market Hall is a seventeenth century building in Jacobean style, now called the **Snooty Fox**, formerly the White Hart Inn. The inn stands in the corner of Chipping Lane which leads to The Chipping. As mentioned previously, is the old word for a market; here the original market was held. From it the Chipping Steps, which are very old, lead down to Cirencester Road. Near them The Priory contains part of the old monastery buildings.

Those on foot can now return to the church by going along Church Street. The Close is a beautiful three-storeyed four-gabled house a little way up Long Street; or they can go along Long Street, then down Newchurch Street passing St Saviour's, and turning left into West Street. In Long Street at the Old Court House is a most unusual museum, the **Police Museum**, which houses a collection of articles on the history of the Gloucestershire Constabulary. There are uniforms, lights etc all housed in the old police cells.

The Woolsack Race

No visit to Tetbury would be complete without a look at Gunstool Hill, down and up which teams carry 65lb woolsacks during the famous woolsack races on Spring Bank Holiday Monday. The hill is occasionally as steep as 1 in 4; just the sight of it can make the visitor tired.

AROUND TETBURY

North-west from Tetbury, off the B4014 to Avening and Nailsworth, is **Chavenage House**. The house, largely of the mid-sixteenth century, is a fine example of the work of the period. The house has rooms called Cromwell's and Ireton's commemorating a stay by these two important Parliamentarians during a siege of nearby Beverstone Castle. There is also a fine collection of seventeenth century tapestries.

South from Tetbury the A433 runs past the **Highgrove estate**, the home of Prince Charles. The house, built in the last few years of the eighteenth century, had to be extensively restored a century later when it was gutted by fire. The lodge remains from the original construction.

Royal Gloucestershire

In the early 1980s the Cotswolds (or, more specifically, Gloucestershire) could claim to be a Royal area, the Queen's two eldest children living here. Highgrove, a house just to the south of Tetbury, was built in 1796, but burnt down in 1894. It was rebuilt and, almost a century later, was given to the Prince and Princess of Wales as a wedding present. The days when the Princess could be seen enjoying a shopping excursion in Tetbury are gone for ever, but Prince Charles still lives at Highgrove. It was here that he developed his ideas on organic farming. For the visitor, Highgrove is a disappointment, nothing being visible except the policeman stationed at the entrance to the parkland surrounding the house.

Gatcombe Park is occasionally more visible. The house was built in 1770 for Edward Sheppard, a rich clothier, and after modifications in 1820 has had no further remodelling. It was the home of Princess Anne and Lt (later Capt) Mark Phillips, and their family. Princess Anne, now the Princess Royal, still lives there with her new husband, though is less often in residence than before, and so infrequently seen out and about on her horse. Gatcombe Park is the scene of an important horse trials in early August. Visitors can then roam the parkland, though the house itself cannot be visited.

Further along the A433 is the hamlet of **Westonbirt**. Its famous school is housed in Westonbirt House, a mid-nineteenth century mansion set in parkland elegantly laid out with lawns and trees. The house itself is open to the public on one or two selected days each year, while the gardens are occasionally open under the **National Garden Scheme**. Opening times and dates for the house and gardens can be obtained from the Tetbury information centre.

The village has a famous arboretum covering over 600 acres with perhaps the finest collection of trees in the world, including the redwood. Although the specimen here does not approach the height of those in California, it does give some idea of the spectacular nature of those giants. The tree has a very strange bark, not hard as on most British trees but soft and fibrous, and a rich chestnut in colour. The arboretum, set up by Robert Holford whose alabaster effigy can be seen in the village church, is now managed by the Forestry Commission. Visitors in the autumn are assured of one of the most colourful sights in the Cotswolds, especially when the acers change colour, while those who come in the spring can see a spectacular show of rhododendrons and azaleas.

THE AVON VALLEY

To the south of Westonbirt, sandwiched between the A433 and the Foss Way, is a small area of the Cotswolds through which flows the River Avon. Here the Cotswold boundary is again the Foss Way, and the best way to explore these Avon villages is to follow the river and return along the Foss Way itself. But first is **Shipton Moyne**, a tiny village of grey stone, memorable for the three fourteenth century monuments in the church – two knights in armour, the third a lady, each in a canopied recess with elaborate decorations. Close to the village, the gardens of Hodges Barn, all that remains of a sixteenth-century manor house are open to the public.

The walk along the Avon (21kms - 13 miles - 5 hours) starts at Easton Grey and takes a path on the south bank to Sherston Parva and Sherston itself. From there the south bank is again followed towards Luckington. Then there is a lane towards Alderton and to the Foss Way at Foss Lodge. The Way can then be followed all the way back to the river near Easton Grey. This very long walk can be reduced by about 8kms (5 miles) by reaching the Foss Way directly from Sherston. This omits Luckington, a pretty village near the actual source of the Avon.

Sherston is a pleasant village, well situated and associated with the legend of John Rattlebones, who, with Edmund Ironsides, is said to have defeated the Danes near here in 1016. The church contains an effigy known as Rattlebones but as it is Norman, it is far more likely to be a saint than a Saxon general.

The last village, **Easton Grey**, is the best: there is a fine Georgian mansion and an arched bridge over the Avon. There are excellent views of the river from here. Beyond Easton Grey the Avon leaves the Cotswolds. The visitor to Malmesbury sees it again, and it reappears at Bath by which time it is a fine river on its way to the sea beyond Bristol.

Malmesbury lies to the east of the Foss Way and outside the AONB. It is also distinctly non-Cotswold, the Wiltshire market towns having their own atmosphere. It is worthy of a visit, however, to see the superb remains of the abbey.

Back on the A433 is **Didmarton**, near the source of the Avon. Like Tetbury, Didmarton also has two churches. Here the Victorians, who vandalised many Cotswold churches, decided that it was cheaper to build a new one. The lover of churches will be delighted, because the older building is unspoilt – with a fine triple-decker pulpit.

Oldbury-on-the-Hill is a group of cottages around a church dedicated to St Arild, a Saxon princess, but it has little as old as that. Much older is Nan Tow's Tump, which differs from all the barrows so far mentioned in being round rather than long. It is the finest example of its type in the area and is almost 3m (9ft) high in the centre. **Nan Tow** was the name of a local witch who, legend has it, was buried upright in the mound as a punishment for her wickedness. A supernatural aura surrounds the burial mound and the locals took handfuls of earth from it as a supposed cure for many illnesses.

BEVERSTONE AND LASBOROUGH

Beyond the Tump is **Leighterton**, a small village where six roads converge. The church here is a good example of the Victorian 'restoration' that has spoilt so many ancient churches. Here a beautiful hamlet church, dating from the thirteenth century, was restored almost beyond recognition 100 years ago.

Above left: Lace making at the Cotswold craft show in Tetbury
Above right: The Woolsack Race at Tetbury
Below: The Snooty Fox Inn, Tetbury

At **Beverstone**, a few kilometres west of Tetbury, is a castle that is still occupied. Although not open to the public, it is visible from the roadside. The castle was besieged in the Civil War in 1644 by Colonel Massey and his Parliamentarian soldiers. The castle was held for the king by Colonel Oglethorpe. Oglethorpe provided stout resistance, and a frontal attack, supported by guns, was beaten back. Massey settled down for a long siege and Oglethorpe, expecting a few quiet hours, if not days and weeks, slipped out to visit his mistress on a neighbouring farm, with just a few soldiers for protection. Acting on information received, as the saying goes, Massey visited the farm and Oglethorpe was captured.

Massey then offered safe transit to Malmesbury for the defenders of the castle, on condition they left behind their weapons, and Oglethorpe's deputy accepted. Ironically, as soon as Massey had taken control of Beverstone he marched on Malmesbury and captured it, taking prisoner all those who had been granted safe passage from the castle.

THE BOTTOMS

West of Beverstone, and west of the A46, is 'bottom' country, where deeply cut, wooded valleys split the wold right down through the escarpment. But before following a bottom down, one should stay on the wold a little longer. At **Lasborough** is a seventeenth century manor (not now open to the public) which contains many excellent fireplaces, as well as paintings and china.

A little south-west is another fine house, **Boxwell Court** (not open to the public), beautifully situated in the wooded upper folds of Ozleworth Bottom. Charles II came here after the Battle of Worcester, although it is not clear whether he stayed. One version of the story has it that he did, accompanied by Matthew Huntley, owner of the house. Another says that the king arrived without Huntley whose wife, fearful of his capture as the house had been searched several times in previous days, persuaded him to sleep in the barn of a nearby farm. In any case the king was grateful enough to Mrs Huntley to send her, from his hideout in France, a turquoise ring which is still in the family's possession.

Below Boxwell is **Ozleworth Bottom**. Its top is easy to locate for the British Telecom microwave transmitter above Ozleworth village is visible for some distance in all directions. The village is hardly a village at all, just a couple of farms around a park and a house of the eighteenth century. Within the private grounds of the house the visitor can reach the unusual church. A six-sided tower stands in the middle of the church, the only example in the Cotswolds and rare elsewhere: no sides are the same. The circular churchyard is also very unusual, and contains the grave of the last Englishman hanged for the crime of highway robbery.

Below the church the road falls steeply to a neat row of cottages – all that remains of a village which once housed 1,600 people. They lived here because the river, the Little Avon, that runs in the bottom was one of the strongest in the neighbourhood and was the source of power for many mills in the area. Indeed, when one looks at old maps of the area around Wotton it is astonishing just how many mills were working at the height of the woollen trade. A river such as this might have had more than two mills every three kilometres (about one mill per mile).

Beyond the cottages the river can be followed back up into the wooded valley, although the route is not easily found. An easier route of about ³/₄ hour is to follow the lane down towards Wortley, but walkers need to be met by car here to avoid having to retrace their steps, as the river bank is not a public right of way. The bottom is a delightful place, particularly in the upper reaches behind the cottages. In spring when the flowers are blooming and the birds are nesting, there are few places as quiet and more relaxing. There are no unusual varieties of flowers and the birds are common enough, but the setting adds a new beauty. The lucky visitor may also catch a glimpse of a pair of the famous Gloucestershire hares boxing in their madness. Near the exit from Ozleworth Bottom is **Newark Park**, a fine Elizabethan hunting lodge modified by James Wyatt in the eighteenth century to an interesting castellated house.

The Little Avon leaves the Cotswolds between Alderley and Wortley, small mill hamlets. **Alderley**, slightly the bigger, has a fine Elizabethan house which is now a boys' school. Alderley was the birthplace of Lord Chief Justice Matthew Hale who is buried in the churchyard. Alderley Grange, where Hale was born in 1609, is a beautiful house, the gardens of which are occasionally open for charity under the National Gardens scheme. **Wortley** is now little more than a couple of cottages and a memory of

past glories. Stephen Hopkins, who was born here, sailed on the Mayflower to the New World. Wortley is not, in fact, on the Little Avon, but on a tributary that flows in the quaintly named Nanny Farmer's Bottom.

WOTTON-UNDER-EDGE

North of Ozleworth is **Tyley Bottom** in which a stream, flowing down to **Wotton-under-Edge**, can be followed by a track above the town (3kms - 2 miles - 3/4 hour, return trip). Wotton is truly 'under-Edge', the escarpment looming above the northern and eastern sides of the town like a defensive wall. At the northern end it is called Wotton Hill, and a steep climb leads to a small enclosure of trees and a fine view of the town. In the town there is much of interest, and the walker will be well rewarded. In High Street is **The Tolsey** which has been a courthouse, a lock-up, and a few other things in its time. It has a large, interesting clock and a weathervane shaped like a dragon. From it, Market Street leads to **The Chipping**, another use of the old word, which contains some fine, restored timber-framed houses. So good was the restoration that the street has received an architectural award. In The Chipping, the **Wotton Heritage Centre** explores the town's history.

Further down High Street, **Berkeley House** had a room with green-painted pine panelling and Chinese wallpaper from the mid-eighteenth century; it was so fine that it was dismantled and moved complete to the Victoria and Albert Museum in London for permanent exhibition. Orchard Street contains the house in which Isaac Pitman lived while teaching in Wotton and where, it is believed, he first worked on his shorthand. At the bottom of High Street, on the left, is Long Street, where the **Perry Almshouses** can be visited. The seventeenth century façade gives way to a courtyard and a small, contemporary chapel – a quiet place. At the bottom of Long Street stood a grammar school founded in 1384 by Katherine, Lady Berkeley. Such a benefaction was remarkably early, and is commemorated in the name of the modern comprehensive school which stands outside the town.

Back in Long Street, a right turn takes the walker to the **Ram Inn**, a timbered house below road level, perhaps old enough to have been the actual one to house the masons who built the church, but it is no longer an inn. The church itself is an elegant building and has a very famous memorial brass to Thomas, Lord Berkeley, and his wife Margaret. Lifesized and very old, it is probably pre-1400. Lord Berkeley was a remarkable man. He fought the Scots for Richard II; under Henry IV he was admiral of the fleet that defeated the French allies of Owen Glendower at Milford Haven; later he fought with Henry V at Agincourt.

As was the custom of the time, his marriage to Lady Margaret was arranged very early in their lives. At the time of the wedding Thomas was probably 14 while Margaret was, at most, 7. She died at 30 having had one daughter. Thomas was grief-stricken, and never remarried for the remaining 25 years of his life. His lack of a male heir was the direct cause of the Battle of Nibley Green, the field of which can be seen a few

kilometres north of Wotton. Rubbings from exact resin replicas of the brass can be made with permission of the church.

AROUND WOTTON

A little way south-west of Wotton and just outside the AONB is the village of **Kingswood**: it was the site of a Norman abbey. The abbey was demolished following the Dissolution, but its fifteenth century gatehouse still remains, a fine old building which now houses the local council chamber – probably the oldest in Britain.

From Wotton the best way of continuing north is to follow a small section of the Cotswold Way through Westridge Wood above the town to the **Nibley Monument**, returning along any of the wood's many paths (6^1/$_2$kms - 4 miles - 2 hours). The wood itself, a delightful place, is criss-crossed with wide avenues, and so walking is easy. Within it there is an Iron Age hillfort known as **Brackenbury Ditches**. It is overgrown, however, and the ditches and ramparts are difficult to find. But a gateway can be made out, and the site has tremendous atmosphere.

Beyond the wood is the **Tyndale Monument**, erected in the last century to the memory of William Tyndale who was born near here, perhaps at Stinchcombe or Cam. Tyndale was, at one time, tutor at Little Sodbury Manor, further south, but he had left the area before translating the Bible into English, an achievement for which he was burned at the stake. The monument stands on Nibley Knoll, above North Nibley, which is a straggling place with a fine church; below this is

Selected Walks

1 Ozleworth Bottom *2 miles •Moderate• 100ft climb*
Map: OS Sheet 162 – Gloucester & Forest of Dean area.
Start from the road in Ozleworth Bottom. Go up the lane to where it turns sharp left. There go right and through a gate to the left, after passing cottages which are all that remain of a mill village that once had 1,600 inhabitants. Beyond the gate is a path to, and through, a short section of woodland. Where the path beyond goes sharply up and left go up with it, but right at the top to reach a bridge over the valley stream. Go over and right and follow the stream down to where a long step across can be made to the outward path. Now, however, go on with the track, where the outward journey would go left to regain the Bottom road.

2 Tetbury and Westonbirt *10 miles •Strenuous• 200ft climb*
Map: OS Sheet 162 – Gloucester & Forest of Dean area.
Start at Tetbury church. Go west along the A433, towards Bristol, and go right into Berrell's Road, then left into Long Furlong Lane. Go left again after 200yd where a signed path leads to fields. The path continues across fields using stiles at boundaries, squeezing its way between Highgrove House to the left and Elmstone House to the right, to reach the A433 again near a hotel. Go along the main road to the arboretum entrance and go along it to the visitor's centre and café (no entrance fee for the walker!) Beyond the centre is Waste Gate. Beyond that, in about 100yd, go sharply right on a path through woodland to reach a stone wall. Follow this, then cross grass to a road. Go right to a crossroads. Go over here following the lane sharply right near Nesley Farm and on to Hookshouse. There go left through a gate to a path that reaches a track for Beverstone. From there follow the A4135 to the right, back to Tetbury.

3 Kilcott to Hawkesbury Upton *4.5 miles •Moderate/Strenuous• 700ft climb*
Map: OS Sheet 172 – Bristol, Bath & surrounding area.
Start at Kilcott Mill. From the mill the walk follows the well-marked Cotswold Way – look for the painted arrow and dot – to the Somerset Monument and on to Hawkesbury Upton. The route is obvious south-west through Claypit Wood, beyond which the monument is a landmark for the walker. The path reaches a road where the route goes left, following the road past the monument and into Hawkesbury Upton to reach its excellent village pond. Turn left after the pond (the Cotswold Way goes right here) and follow the lane to a T-junction. Opposite, a gate leads to a path that falls and rises to a stile. Over this a path leads to Sticksey Wood and through it to a road. Go left to return to Kilcott Mill.

Nibley Green, the site of the last true battle fought between private armies on English soil.

The Battle of Nibley Green

The battle, fought on 20 March 1470, followed the death without a male heir of Lord Berkeley, whose memorial brass is at Wotton. Berkeley's daughter married the Earl of Warwick, but when the titles passed to his nephew, the succession was disputed by Warwick's children and eventually a great-grandson of Berkeley, Lord Lisle, challenged the new Lord Berkeley to a duel to decide the issue. This developed into a full scale battle between rival armies. Lord Lisle and several hundred others were killed, and his followers put to flight.

North Nibley sits at the head of Waterley Bottom which can be followed to the main road above Dursley, although there is no pathway. It is probably best to drive along a minor road to a point close to the top, and to walk down.

DURSLEY

Dursley has been modernised to such an extent that little remains of the original Cotswold town. The market house still stands at the centre of the town, with a recessed statue of Queen Anne gazing across at the church. This commemorates the Queen's grant of cash to assist in the repair of the church following the collapse of the spire in 1698. It seems that the spire was in poor shape and was patched up with a considerable quantity of lead and tiles. To celebrate completion of the work the bells were rung, and the vibration brought the spire down, killing several ringers.

In the past Dursley has produced gifted men, including Edward Fox, the Bishop of Hereford who introduced Cranmer to Henry VIII; and William King who has a stronger claim to having started the Sunday School movement than Robert Raikes in nearby Gloucester. Beyond Dursley is Cam, a small village with a still active flour mill, near a new housing estate. The village nestles below the hills of Peaked Down and Long Down, known locally as Cam Peak and Cam Long Down. The hills form a long ridged outlier of the Cotswold edge, and show its geological formation as rock has eroded back from the river. The peaks of harder, less easily weathered rock have been left behind. The two peaks can be climbed by following the Cotswold Way back from Home Farm (5kms - 3 miles - 2 hours).

From the summit of **Long Down** there is a good view along the edge towards Frocester Hill. Cam Peak offers views to Dursley itself, and down the Berkeley Vale. Beyond Dursley can be seen Stinchcombe Hill, the most westerly point of the escarpment. The hill can be readily explored as it is the site of a golf course. It is in the shape of the letter T, very narrow near the clubhouse, and several hundred yards wide Drakestone Point. Its shape allows the walker to see right back into Waterley Bottom, and there are also excellent views along the Cotswold edge, both north and south.

West of Dursley, closer to the river Severn, Berkeley is a town of considerable interest. **Berkeley Castle** has been held by the same family for over 800 years. It is a beautiful building both outside and inside, with a long and interesting history, being famous as the site of the murder of Edward II. In the town is a museum to Edward Jenner who pioneered vaccination against smallpox. Also west of Dursley, and near to Stinchcombe village, is the Blanchworth Cider Mill: it still has the original horse-drawn cider press, and is now a gallery for local artists. Further south, at Tortworth, is a 1,000-year-old chestnut tree which is over 18m (almost 60ft) round, next to the church.

THE COTSWOLD EDGE

Returning to the Cotswold edge, below Alderley is a string of villages along the spring-line, at the base of the escarpment. **Hillesley** is a pleasant little village near the Kilcott valley. The valley has a delightful narrow country lane with a stream flowing alongside it, and an old mill near a calm, timeless mill pond.

The next village, **Hawkesbury**, has a beautiful little church, with features from many centuries, well situated beneath the wooded escarpment. Above it is the Somerset, or Hawkesbury, Monument. The tower commemorates Lord Edward Somerset, a member of the Beaufort family from nearby Badminton. Lord Somerset served under Wellington at Waterloo with such gallantry that he received the official thanks of parliament. From the tower there is a wonderful view back along the edge, both the British

Telecom tower at Ozleworth, and the Tyndale monument at North Nibley being visible. The view southward is equally good, and on clear days the mountains of Wales can be seen.

The monument stands on the summit of the escarpment, and near to it is **Hawkesbury Upton**, the 'Upton' signifying its position. The most noticeable feature of the village is, perhaps, the pond, a large expanse of water with a good number of ducks. On the A46 just beyond the village are two small hamlets, Dunkirk and Petty France, whose names commemorate an important landmark in the development of the Cotswold woollen industry. In its earliest days the wool was exported raw to the continent, made into cloth and then imported here. This was obviously bad business, and an attempt was made to encourage Flemish weavers to come here. Crown agents were sent abroad to extol the virtues of England, its good beef, good living and 'good bedfellows!' The two names indicate their success.

Below Hawkesbury is **Horton**, a divided village; its church and court are nearly 800m from the cottages and post office. The court is interesting as part of it is an unfortified Norman hall (one of the very few known) dating from around 1150, though the roof is at least 200 years later. The hall contains a small museum of unrelated items including pewter and armour. The house itself was constructed around 1520 for Dr Knight, a chief secretary to Henry VIII, who negotiated with the Pope for the King's divorce from Catherine of Aragon. The Roman influence on Dr Knight can be seen in the loggia in the gardens which

Above left: *The Somerset Monument at Hawkesbury*
Above right: *Horton Court and Church*

has the heads of some Roman emperors.

Next along the escarpment is **Little Sodbury**, a tiny hamlet steeped in English religious history. The small church is dedicated to St Adeline, the only church in England with that dedication. The name may derive from a convent near the Normandy home of the first Norman lord, which was founded by St Adeline. Perhaps the dedication is another link with the imported Flemish weavers, however, as Adeline was their patron saint. The church originally stood next to the manor house, but was moved stone by stone to its present site when it fell into disrepair. William Tyndale must have preached regularly in the original church but little now remains of it. The pulpit has panels commemorating Tyndale and other contemporary martyrs.

Up the hill from the church is **Little Sodbury Manor** (not open to the public). It had a major restoration earlier this century, but retains the original fifteenth century great hall, one of the finest known. King Henry VIII and Anne Boleyn spent a night here as guests of Sir John Walsh, the king's champion at his coronation. It was Sir John who employed a locally-born chaplain and tutor, William Tyndale, in 1521. Tyndale stayed for two years, moving abroad when his desire to have an English Bible embarrassed Sir John. Tyndale was executed for heresy in 1536, only two years before Henry VIII decreed that every English church should have an English Bible.

On the hill above the manor is the very fine **Sodbury hillfort**. It is not as large as Uleybury, but it is clearer. The ditches and ramparts are still deep and high, despite erosion and infilling. Some idea of the massive undertaking can be gained by a walk around the ramparts. Its Iron Age builders constructed its defences so well that it continued to be used long after they had gone. There is evidence that the fort was occupied in Roman and Saxon times, and even as late as the fifteenth century by the

The Southwolds

BERKELEY

Berkeley Castle
☎ 01453 810332
Open: April and May Tuesday-Sunday
2-5pm; June and September,
Tuesday-Saturday 11am-5pm,
Sunday 2-5pm; July and August
Monday-Saturday 11am-5pm,
Sunday 2-5pm; October, Sunday 2-
4.30pm; Bank Holidays 11am-5pm.

Jenner Museum
The Chantry
Church Lane
☎ 01453 810631
Open: April to September, Tuesday-
Saturday 12.30-5.30pm, Sunday 1-
5.30pm; Bank Holiday Mondays
12.30-5pm; October Sunday 1-
5.30pm.

GREAT BADMINTON

Badminton House
Open: occasionally during the
summer months. Watch the local
press or ask at the Tourist Offices in
Tetbury or Bath. The House is also
open by appointment. Groups
preferred.

HORTON

Horton Court   (National Trust)
Open: April to October, Wednesday
and Saturday 2-6pm or sunset.
☎ 01249 730141

SHIPTON MOYNE

Hodges Barn Gardens
☎ 01666 880202
Open: Easter to mid-August Monday,
Tuesday and Friday 2-5pm. At other
times by apoointment.

TETBURY

Chavenage House
☎ 01453 502329
Open: May to September, Thursday,
Sunday and Bank Holidays, 2-5pm.
Also open Easter Sunday and
Monday, same times.

Police Museum
The Old Court House
63 Long Street
☎ 01666 504670
Open: All year, Monday-Friday 10am-
3pm.

**Westonbirt Arboretum
(Forestry Enterprises)**
Westonbirt
☎ 01666 880220
Open: all year, daily 10am-dusk.

Westonbirt House
Westonbirt School
☎ 01666 880242
Open: Check with local tourist
information office for details of
opening times, Parkland only is
open, with view of exterior of house.

WOTTON-UNDER-EDGE

Alderley Trout Farm
Alderley
☎ 01453 842540
Open: all year Monday-Saturday
9am-5pm.

Wotton Heritage Centre
The Chipping
☎ 01453 521541
Open: British Summer Time
Tuesday-Saturday 10am-1pm, 2-5pm;
British Winter Time Tuesday-Friday
10am-1pm, 2-4pm, Saturday 10am-
1pm. Also open occasional Sundays
in summer.

Places to Visit

**Kingswood Abbey Gatehouse
(English Heritage)**
Kingswood
☎ 0117 957 0700
Open: any reasonable time. Key for
interior available at nearby shop.

Newark Park (National Trust)
Ozleworth
☎ 01453 842644
Open: April to September Wednesday
and Thursday 2-5pm, by prior
appointment.

army of Edward IV before the battle of Tewkesbury.

Little Sodbury is the smallest of the three Sodbury villages. **Old Sodbury**, the next village along the edge, is the original. Chipping Sodbury, the newer market town, has a wide, airy main street.

South of Old Sodbury is **Dodington Park**, quite beautiful, a masterpiece of landscape gardening by Capability Brown who planted trees in 'natural' positions and dug lakes, made valleys and built hills – an astonishing achievement. Several nature trails are signposted through the parkland, enabling one to explore the landscaping and the natural beauty. The house itself, built for the Codrington family in the eighteenth century, is massively constructed, with an elaborate columned entrance, but the more delicate interior contains many fine pieces of work. It is not, however, open to the public.

Dodington village has little of great interest, but in the church is a memorial tablet to a member of the Codrington family, Sir Edward, who was captain of the Orion at the Battle of Trafalgar, and commander of the allied fleet at the Battle of Navarino. On the scarp top above Dodington is Tormarton, a small grey village with a church that has a memorial to Edward Topp, lord of the manor in the late seventeenth century. It is a relief sculpture of a mailed fist clutching a severed arm, all in full, gory colour.

To the north-east of Tormarton, the village of **Great Badminton** lies beside one of the most famous estates in Britain, the Beaufort. The name **Badminton** is famous throughout the world in two sports, the game named from the estate, and the three-day event, one of the world's foremost horse trials. The house is seventeenth century and a very fine example of this period. The interior is rich in decoration, some of it unique. The house stands in over 15,000 acres of park and estate land – the total estate being nearly 16kms (10 miles) around. The park is partly natural, partly the work of Capability Brown, and partly formal. One of the more formal aspects, the Great Avenue running down from Worcester Lodge and the A433 near Didmarton, is several kilometres long and contains thousands of trees. Within the park are deer herds and several excellent follies.

Badminton Horse Trials

The Three-Day Event for equestrian competitors was conceived to demonstrate the skills of a mounted cavalryman, his horse showing the ability to be calm and dignified on parade (dressage), while having the courage and stamina for long cross-country rides which included the need to jump fences. It is claimed that the inspiration for the Badminton event was the Duke of Beaufort watching the British team failing to win the gold medal at the London Olympics of 1948. So convinced was the Duke of the inherent superiority of the British rider and horse that he felt that only lack of practice had denied them the medal.

The first Badminton event was held in 1949 when John Sheddon won on Golden Willow. The prize was £150 which went to Mrs Home Kidston, the horse's owner. John Sheddon received nothing - apparently not even a rosette which, if true, is astonishing. The cross-country course, over which Golden Willow effectively won the competition, was unroped, the advantage to the competitors of being able to choose their own course between jumps being set against the need to beware of spectators strolling across the gallops.

Despite the Duke's efforts in providing practice, the British team was eliminated at the 1952 Helsinki Olympics. Since then however, it has become an established part of the world equestrian scene, its winners being a roll-call of the sports' masters. One notable absence from the list of winners is the Princess Royal whose highest placing was fourth in 1979.

Today the event is one of the highlights of the sporting calendar. It attracts around 250,000 spectators (only the Indianopolis 500 claims a larger crowd), many of them whiling away a few moments in the vast tented village housing upwards of 250 exhibitors. It is estimated that these exhibitiors do over half-a-million pound's worth of business. The standard buyer might still be in green wellies and a Barbour jacket but, as a scan of the crowd shows, the event now has a much broader appeal.

The church at Great Badminton, next to the house, has a number of monuments to the Beaufort family. One to the first Duke, by Grinling Gibbons, is $7^1/_2$m (25ft) high, so big that the church had to be enlarged to accommodate it.

A little way south of Badminton, at **Acton Turville**, is beauty of a much simpler form and no less striking for that. The village contains little that is architecturally unique, but the old well and its portcullis are delightful.

East from Acton Turville the AONB points towards Wiltshire, as far as Grittleton. It has a manor house, described as a hideous monstrosity the work of a committee, two architects and the owner, who seem to have spent most of the time at each others' throats.

H aving crossed into Wiltshire at the end of the previous chapter, this tour now stays in that county, moving south of the M4 motorway to visit the villages of the By Brook Valley. The brook rises near Burton, a small, neat village with a Georgian rectory that actually stands on the border between Wiltshire and Gloucestershire. The church tower is one of the best in Wiltshire. Indeed there is a group of five churches with distinctive towers, considered not only to be extremely fine but to form a 'Wiltshire group', because they are sufficiently different from anything else of their architectural period (the Perpendicular). The AONB includes three of these churches: Burton (although as a parish church this is shared by the village of Nettleton to the south), West Kington (a little way south of Nettleton) and Yatton Keynell, to the west of Castle Combe.

AROUND CASTLE COMBE

Nettleton, a scattered hamlet close to the Foss Way, has within its boundaries a collapsed long barrow with the loneliness that characterises these tombs, and the site of a Roman temple constructed among cliffs beside a stream flowing down to the By Brook. Both sites are visited by a 5 mile (2 hours) walk that links Nettleton and West Kington by path or lane.

West Kington lies on the same stream that passes the temple site, Broadmead Brook, which rises closer to the A46. Its church is set on a hill, its tower thus set off to perfection. Inside is a pulpit that was used by Hugh Latimer while he was rector here, before becoming Bishop of Worcester. Latimer was executed by burning with Nicholas Ridley, Bishop of London, at Oxford, when they refused to accept Catholicism after the accession of Queen Mary Tudor. Panels to these two martyrs are among those at Little Sodbury.

Further down the By Brook is the most famous of the valley villages, **Castle Combe**, one of the most picturesque in the Cotswolds. It is set in the valley, sheltered and secluded, and has been used as a film location for period dramas. The wealth of the village was based on sheep, as everywhere in the region, but Castle Combe had a charter to hold a fair, where sheep and wool changed hands, as well as other market goods. It was 'the most celebrated faire in North Wiltshire for sheep … whither sheep-masters doe come as far as from Northamptonshire'. To the north of the village there are the remains of the Norman castle built by one of the early lords of the manor.

A memorial to this lord, Walter de Dunstanville, is in the church, a fine tomb with an effigy of the knight in a full suit of chain mail. The rest of the church is good, though extensive late nineteenth century restoration was not entirely satisfactory. For such a wealthy village, the church is not automatically recognisable as a wool church although the tower, erected by local clothiers, is more elaborate than might be expected. The market cross stands at the village centre, covered by a roof on four pillars. To the west the restored Manor House, now a hotel, dates originally from the seventeenth century, as does Dower House to the north.

Dr Doolittle at Castle Combe

Despite being far from the sea when it was decided to film *Dr Dolittle* with Rex Harrison Castle Combe's picturesque qualities won out over villages with the clear headstart of being actually on the coast. By Brook and the cottages near it were therefore transformed into a port.

To the east of Castle Combe is **Yatton Keynell**. Keynell was added to the village's name by the lords of the manor who had the name. One of the earliest members of the family, Sir William, built the original church on this site: it was dedicated to St Margaret of Antioch as a gesture of thanks for his safe return from the Crusades.

South of Yatton Keynell is a final piece of wold and at its centre is **Biddestone**, the old village which is a reminder of the grey Cotswold stone in true Cotswold landscape. Two miles east of Biddestone is Sheldon Manor; 2 miles to the south is Corsham Court. The manor, one of the oldest houses in Wiltshire dating in part from the thirteenth century, has been continuously lived in for nearly 700 years. Its thirteenth century porch has been described as astounding. In addition to the house itself, the visitor can wander among the terraced gardens. Corsham Court is Elizabethan and houses the Bath Academy of Art: its fine collection of paintings is based on the Methuen collection. The gardens are another example of the work of Capability Brown and Humphrey Repton.

Returning to Castle Combe, the By Brook can be followed southwards to the point where it leaves the AONB at **Slaughterford**, probably given that name, as with the Slaughters to the north, to distinguish the ford near the sloes from the other ford, to the north. The village has a mill, not for cloth or grain but a paper mill.

MARSHFIELD AND DYRHAM

South of Slaughterford the AONB turns north, avoiding the RAF station at Colerne to meet the Foss Way at the pleasant Wraxall villages, North and Upper, set high above the By Brook. To the west is the village of **Marshfield**. The tower of the church, visible for miles around, is the dominant feature within the village, standing at the 'Little' end. Near to it Tolzey Hall, according to its inscription, was '. . . built by John Goslett, 1690. Was removed and rebuilt in 1793'.

At the far end of the delightful High Street are the almshouses, built in the early seventeenth century for eight village old folk. Between the church and almshouses are a number of very fine inns.

North-west of Marshfield is the village of **Dyrham**, of picture-postcard beauty, containing several interesting sites. To the north of the village is Hinton Hill, on which can still be seen the remains of the medieval field system known as strip lynchets. This method of terracing sloping ground eased the labour of working such land, and in addition assisted crop rotation and the division of land. The hill is also the site of one of the most decisive battles during the invasion of Britain by the Anglo-Saxons, and the ousting of the British into Wales in favour of the English. The Anglo-Saxon Chronicle says that in 577 the Saxon kings Cuthwine and Ceawlin fought the Britons at Dyrham, killing three kings and capturing Gloucester, Cirencester and Bath.

This simple, single-sentence entry conceals an event as significant as any in the history of Britain. The Saxons had been pushing westward across Britain for over a century, but their slow invasion had been halted, probably in Berkshire, by King Arthur at the battle of Badon around AD500. With his death, however, the Saxons advanced again. They cut the road from Gloucester and Cirencester to Bath, and encamped in the old hillfort at the summit of Hinton Hill. The three towns sent their armies to the site, where they attacked the well defended Saxon army and were annihilated on the slopes of the hill. Following the battle, the British retreated to Wales and Cornwall, leaving what is now England to the English. No memorial to the battle marks the hill, but it is as significant a battlefield as any in Britain.

Dyrham church contains a memorial brass considered to be of similar age to the Berkeley brass at Wotton-under-Edge, and even possibly by the same artist. This one is to Sir Maurice Russell and his wife. The Latin inscription starts

Entombed here, bereft of life
Behold a gentle knight!

which is very poetic, even if a little has been lost in the translation.

Immediately behind the church is **Dyrham Park**, a fine house and gardens, now in the hands of the National Trust. The original Tudor house was almost totally rebuilt about the end of the seventeenth century by William Blathwayt, a Secretary of State to William III. The house is open to the public and, in addition to its architectural and decorative interest, there are fine collections of paintings, particularly by contemporary Dutch artists, and china. There is also a large greenhouse, one of the earliest known examples. The park was laid out originally to include an extremely elaborate and very large water garden. Now, sadly, only the statue of Neptune in his fountain remains. The fountain has been dry for perhaps 200 years; the water garden fell into disrepair after only a relatively short time. The park, then landscaped by Repton, now contains

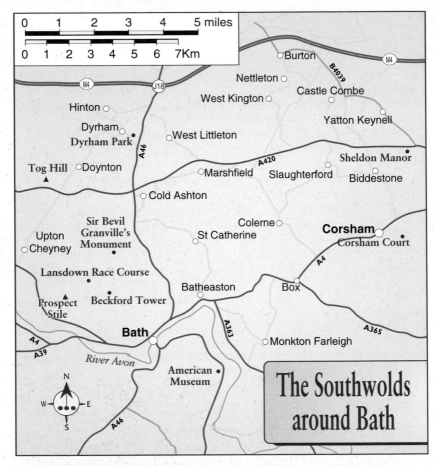

The Southwolds around Bath

Castle Combe

Above and below: Dyrham Park

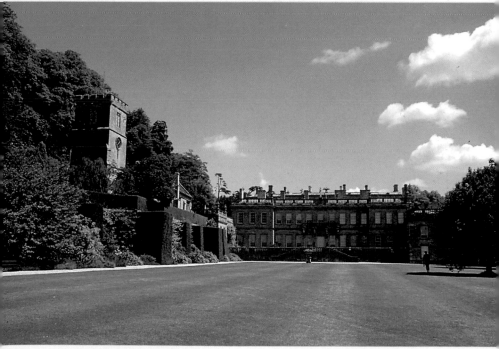

a herd of the unusual fallow deer.

A good walk of 3 miles (1 hour) that encompasses Hinton Hill, Dyrham Park and village can be made by following the Cotswold Way from the village to the hill.

DYRHAM TO BATH

To the south of Dyrham are **Doynton** – a pleasant village on the gentler bottom slopes of the escarpment, overlooking the outskirts of Bristol – and **Cold Ashton**. The latter is a quiet place with a church that was actually built by the rector, Thomas Key, in the early sixteenth century. The rector's mark, a T and a key interwined, can be seen in several places. The real mystery is how a humble country rector obtained enough money to build a church.

But it is not the only mystery in Cold Ashton. One afternoon in the late 1930s a portrait painter, Olive Snell, set out to visit a friend in the Mendips: losing her way in the dark, she stopped at a house in Cold Ashton to ask the way and was directed by a man whom she tipped half a crown, assuming he was the butler. Her Mendip host could not understand the story as the house she described was empty and boarded up; so the ladies returned to Cold Ashton. The house was found, and it was indeed locked and chained: on the front door-step was the half-crown.

The exact house of this true story is not known. But there are a number of houses old enough and grand enough to have ghosts, none more so than Cold Ashton Manor, a fine building from 1600 to which Sir Bevil Granville was brought. The word 'cold' was attached to the name to distinguish this village from

another Ashton near Bristol. Probably 'Cold' was used because it best describes the village in the winter for, situated at the head of the St Catherine's Valley, it can be a bleak place. But it has a fine view down the valley. The nearby picnic site at Tog Hill also offers fine views, in this case of the Bristol Channel and the Welsh Hills.

The valley itself is reminiscent of the wooded bottoms around Wotton-under-Edge. Here the sides are lower and shallower, and not as wooded, but it is still a fine valley. **St Catherine's church** dates, in part, from the thirteenth century, while the court, next door, is a much modified late fifteenth century Benedictine monastery. The court was sold very cheaply by Henry VIII to his tailor John Malte, an act of generosity – unusual for Henry – prompted by Malte's adoption and removal from the Royal Court of an illegitimate daughter of the king. The walk from below, back along the east side of the river, is waymarked through meadowland and affords fine views of the court itself.

The valley represents the southern tip of the Cotswolds, the AONB boundary being near Batheaston. To the west the boundary extends southwards to its western extremity at Upton Cheney, a village with a splendid name on the side of another Golden Valley, with the River Boyd flowing down one side of Bristol to reach the Avon. The AONB just includes **Hanging Hill**, a bleakly-named hill from the top of which there are views across Lansdown and to the Bevil Granville memorial. This stands near the top of the minor road that crosses Lansdown Hill, on its way from Bath to Wick. It is a massive structure, hardly elegant, but certainly imposing.

Sir Bevil was a Cornishman, deeply committed to the Royalist cause in the Civil War, who brought a small army of men from Cornwall to assist the king. In 1643 these men joined a large Royalist Army at nearby Chewton Mendip and marched on Bath, then held for Parliament by Sir William Waller. Waller was a clever soldier and he took up a position not in the town, but at this tip of Lansdown Hill. The Royalist advance was halted by his cannon fire and the day seemed lost until Sir Bevil led his Cornishmen in a desperate attack up the slope. In truly heroic fashion, Sir Bevil rode up and across the hill, shouting encouragement, and the cannons were taken. But at the very moment of victory, Sir Bevil was unseated and wounded: he was taken to Cold Ashton Manor where he died that night.

The battle for Bath continued, and when it was eventually taken, the Cornishmen had the honour of being the first troops to enter the city. The memorial was erected by a grandson who was ennobled and took the title Lansdown.

An interesting 4 mile (2 hours) walk from the racecourse on Lansdown Hill is to skirt it on its northern side, from the minor road or golfcourse, joining the Cotswold Way on the escarpment edge near the starting gates. From here it is a short walk to Prospect Stile, from which there are fine views to the Avon Valley and to Kelston Round Hill, a distinctive mound to the south, topped by a copse of trees. A return can be made on the southern side of the racecourse.

BATH

Though Bath does not actually lie within the Cotswolds it is impossible not to regard it as a Cotswold town, the Bath stone of the buildings being from the same bedrock as the villages of the northern Cotswolds.

Bath's origins are steeped in mystery. It is likely that earliest man knew of the existence of the hot springs, although as the surrounding area is likely to have been a salt marsh, he may not have had a home here. According to legend the town was built by Prince Bladud, descendent of refugees from Troy, and father of Shakespeare's King Lear. The poor prince contracted leprosy and was immediately banished from court to live out his days as a pig herder in the marshes. Inevitably one of the pigs also contracted leprosy but to Bladud's astonishment it was cured after taking a mud-bath near the hot springs. Bladud then tried the mud-bath himself and he, too, was cured, and allowed back to court. To commemorate this legendary founding of the city about 2,800 years ago, there are statues to Bladud at the baths.

The archaeological evidence of the founding of the city is more mundane. It is likely that the first town was Roman, Aquæ Sulis – the waters of the goddess Sulis – constructed in the first century AD. The Romans were undoubtedly tempted by the 250,000 gallons of water at 120°F that rushes to the surface daily, and constructed a town around the public baths. The baths themselves are a minor wonder, with central heating in all rooms, a sauna and, of course, the pool, all fed by the hot waters.

When the Romans left, the town

Royal Cresent, Bath

Above left: A view of Bath Abbey from the Roman Baths
Above right: Dining at the Pump Room, Bath Below: Pulteney Bridge, Bath

quickly decayed. The Saxon invaders, reaching here after the battle of Dyrham, could only wonder at the building. They were not great builders themselves and they believed the town was the work of giants, and haunted. Certainly the decaying buildings, the deep warm pools all overgrown, must have been ghostly. Gradually the site became holy, probably fired by superstition and legend, and King Offa founded an abbey here. This became an important site, and King Edgar was crowned here in 973. The abbot and the townspeople of medieval Bath knew of the hot waters and their medicinal purposes, for there are early references to people visiting the town to bathe in the waters. Indeed the visitors were a major source of income to the townspeople.

The bathers were subject to no regulations, however, and the baths became so unwholesome that people were reluctant to use them. In 1533 the chief bathers were those with 'lepre, pokkes, scabbes and great aches' and since there was no filtration or changing of the water it is hardly surprising that the baths were described as stinking. As with Cheltenham, Bath had to wait 200 years for the coming of a gentler age, when Richard (Beau) Nash regulated the bathing, stopped the sedan chair carriers from overcharging, erected theatres, assembly rooms and houses, and controlled the gambling that was at the heart of Bath's social position. The whole Georgian city is really a tribute to the energy of this one man, who died in 1761 at the great age of 88. His statue stands in the Pump Room, which dispenses warm salty water freely to visitors.

Continued on p.189

Jane Austen at Bath

Jane Austen

Jane Austen lived in Bath between 1801-6 at 25 Gay Street and gave detailed accounts of the city's streets in two of her novels, *Northanger Abbey* and *Persuasion*. To celebrate her connection with the city the **Jane Austen Centre** at 40 Gay Street looks at the Bath of her time, and of her life here. There is also a walking tour of Jane Austen's visiting sites which are featured in the books. Close to the Centre, the **Georgian Garden** (off Gravel Walk in Royal Victoria Park) has been restored to its original plan of 1760 using plants from a contemporary Webb's catalogue. It was in this garden that , in *Persuasion,* Captain Wentworth and Anne Elliot declared their love.

Short Cycle Rides

The Bottoms near Wotton-under-Edge make cycling hard work, and no really successful route can be made along the Cotswold escarpment without a considerable amount of doubling back, or a lot of switchback riding. To the east on the plateau there is one fine ride, however, making the most of the wolds and the valley of the River Avon.

1 Around Tetbury (20 miles)
Map: OS Sheet 173 – Swindon, Devizes & surrounding area. From Tetbury go southward on the A433 for about 1.5 miles to a turning, left, for Shipton Moyne – look for the sign at the Cat and Custard Pot Inn. From the far end of the village go right for Easton Grey, reached by going left at a T-junction, and straight across where the lane meets the B4040. Go through the village and on to a crossroads. There go right to Sherston, calling in to the village before continuing by lane to Luckington. From there go north on the lane through Sopworth to the A433 near Didmarton. Turn left, towards Didmarton, but go right almost immediately to Leighterton. There turn right on a narrow but excellent lane that runs north of the Westonbirt arboretum, and close to Bowldon Wood to a crossroads. Go over and follow the lane to the A4125. Go right to Tetbury.

2 Castle Combe (18 miles)
Map: OS Sheet 173 – Swindon, Devizes & surrounding area and Sheet 172 – Bristol, Bath & surrounding area.
From Castle Combe go north-east to join the B4039. Go left and follow it to Burton. As the village ends, go left on a lane that runs parallel to the M4 motorway all the way to the A46. Go left, and take the first left to West Littleton. Go through the village and on to a crossroads. Go left here and left again at a T-junction. The new lane goes almost due north: follow it over the Broadmead Brook then turn right for West Kington. At the far end of the village, just before another bridge over the Broadmead Brook, go right to West Kington then steeply down, then up to Wick. At the T-junction beyond go left. Go over at the crossroads and left at the signed road to Castle Combe.

Richard Nash was born on 18th October 1674 in Swansea, the son of a Welsh gentleman and a mother who was the niece of the Royalist Colonel killed defending Pembroke against Cromwell. Richard was educated at Carmarthen School and then went to Jesus College, Oxford. There, as Oliver Goldsmith put it, 'though much might be expected from his genius, nothing could be hoped from his industry'. Richard's problem was women or, rather, his extreme delight in their company. He became so infatuated with one Oxford girl of dubious reputation that his tutor sent him home when he heard that the 17 year old Nash had proposed marriage.

Richard next joined the army, apparently because he believed that the uniform was a sure way to a girl's heart, but left because the hours and discipline were not to his taste. He then joined the Temple as a student, living a life that seemed almost beyond his means, a life typified by the suggestion that he 'preferred a bow from a lord to a dinner from a commoner'. He was, by all accounts, well-mannered and friendly, and very compassionate. As an illustration of the latter, he once put in an expenses claim of £10 for 'making someone happy'. On being questioned, he said that he had been talking to a man who had said that £10 would make him happy and Nash had given him the money as an experiment. His employers, impressed, paid him the £10. Sadly, the result of the experiment is not known. In addition to these rather endearing habits, Richard also had an equally endearing farcical streak – for a bet he once rode a cow naked through a village.

It was probably the combination of being impressed with the upper-class and being eccentric in a way that would appeal to those same folk, that made Bath offer him the job of Master of Ceremonies (at first as the assistant to MC, Capt Webster, who was soon killed in a duel).

As MC, Richard – by now known as 'Beau' to everyone because of his manner of dress - cleaned and lit the pump rooms, brought in a band, drew up a list of rules of behaviour and scrupulously enforced them. These rules applied to both the nobility and the sedan chairmen, waitresses etc. One of the rules was 'That all whisperers of lies and scandal be taken for their authors'. Beau might have been a womaniser and a gambler, but he was also fair and honest. His compassion for the less fortunate remained too: he set up a hospital in the town for poor folk who received no help from doctors, too busy peddling their potions to the rich.

Under Beau Nash, Bath became the place, both to be and to be seen to be. His imagination helped the rich fill their time, his fairness and justice maintaining the city's reputation, and his wit keeping the place lively. Once when a (supposedly reformed) alcoholic came to dine with him (and others), the man drank too much wine and seemed intent on drinking much more. In response to Beau's aggravation, the man claimed that 'the company is so agreeable here that my resolution is quite gone'. Beau replied 'I ask your pardon sir, but I am sure that if your resolution is gone, it is time for you to go too'. Beau is also credited with the invention of the riposte that has seen frequent use since: in reply to the suggestion by James Quin, a retired actor, that he had been overcharged in a shop, Beau replied that the shopkeeper had been acting on truly Christian principles because 'you were a stranger and they took you in'. Interestingly, Quin is said to have responded with an even better line, claiming that had they really been Christians they would have clothed, rather than fleeced, him.

In 1750, at 76, Beau Nash seemed to age suddenly and became that worst of all things in society, a bore. People began to avoid him, though he nevertheless continued as Master of Ceremonies. By February 1760, in a wheelchair, with no teeth and most of his possessions sold to maintain his lifestyle (and very bitter about the fact) he was granted a 10 guineas per month pension by Bath Council. It was a very shabby way to treat the man who had brought prosperity to the town: in 56 years as MC, Nash had never received a day's pay, his income deriving from a percentage of gambling house profits (an income reduced by government legislation on the gaming house). Even this miserly pension was only paid for eleven months. On 12 February 1761 Beau, insisting he was fine but unable to stay awake, went to sleep. He never awoke. He was 86 and had lived through the reigns of 7 monarchs. His last mistress, Juliana Popjoy, was so distressed at his death that she left the house and lived out her days in a hollow tree, an eccentricity of which Beau Nash would doubtless have approved.

Scenic Car Tours

1 From Tetbury take the B4014 to Malmesbury. From there take the B4040 through Easton Grey and on to Sherston. Go left at the church, bearing left at a Y-junction to a T-junction. Go left and first right to a sharp right turn beyond Ladyswood Farm. This straight section of lane is the Foss Way, the Roman road, which is followed to Fosse Lodge. Why Fosse here is not Foss is a mystery. Go right at the Lodge to Alderton and through the village to the B4040. Go left and into Acton Turville. There go right for Badminton, going round the estate to the left through Little Badminton and on to the A46 at Dunkirk. Go left for 2 miles to a lane, right, for Horton. In the village go right to the church (Horton Court) and steeply up to a T-junction. Go left, passing the Somerset Monument, bearing right to Hillesley. There go left to Kingswood (Abbey Gatehouse) to the B4060 for Wotton-under-Edge. Leave Wotton on the lane for Alderley, but go left at Wortley into Ozleworth Bottom. Follow this, narow and steep but delightful, to the A4135. Go right to Tetbury.

2 Around Bath
From Bath take the A4 east for 1.5 miles beyond the traffic lights where the A46 joins the A4. There go left for St Catherine, up a single-tracked road with occasionally steep hills. At the top of the valley the lane joins the A46. Go right and take the lane, right, to Cold Ashton about half a mile further on. Go through the village to the A420. Go right, through Marshfield and on to a turning, left, for Castle Combe. Take this, through the village to the B4039. Go left to Burton, where you turn left for Nettleton. Go on to West Kington and westward from there towards Tormarton. At a T-junction go right, and at the next crossroads go left and down to the A46. Go over and down Hinton Hill and left into Dyrham. The entrance to Dyrham Park is on the main A46, not in the village. Go through Dyrham and up to the A46. Go right for half a mile, then right again on a lane to the Tog Hill Picnic Site. Beyond the site cross the A420 and take the lane that passes the Granville Monument to reach Lansdown. Continue past the Beckford Tower to Bath.

Across Orange Grove is the River Avon, crossed a little way north by **Pulteney Bridge**, a fine Georgian structure near the City Library and Art Gallery. Orange Grove is named after the Prince of Orange and at its centre is an obelisk raised by Beau Nash to commemorate the Prince's visit to the city. South of the abbey is North Parade Passage or Old Lilliput Alley where there are Bath's oldest houses, built around 1500. **Sally Lunn's**, named after a Georgian pastrycook, has a restored Georgian kitchen.

Architecturally and historically, Bath requires a guide book of its own. To see some, and by no means all, of the better buildings, the visitor can take a walk from the abbey. Highly recommended are the free walking tours led by very knowledgeable local volunteers who are understandably very proud of their fine city; they start from near the **Pump Room** and **Roman Baths**. By joining one of these tours you will learn much that might otherwise be missed: for instance the fact that the streets are built up above the land surface to allow coal to be discharged into tunnels that lead straight to the basements of the elegant houses.

Bath Abbey is a masterpiece; it was started about 1500 on the site of an older, Norman, church. Its construction followed a dream by Oliver King, Bishop of Bath and Wells, in which he saw angels climbing ladders to heaven and was told to rebuild the older church. The abbey's west front follows King's dream with angels actually climbing ladders on either side. The architects employed by King promised him that 'ther shal be noone so goodly in england nor in fraunce'. And who

would argue with the truth of that promise?

A statue of Bishop King can be seen inside. The walls inside the abbey are covered with numerous memorials to the rich who retired to Bath to take the waters in an attempt to improve their failing health. There are also memorials to Beau Nash and Sir William Waller's wife. Prior Birde's notable chantry is on the south side of the chancel. The stonework here is magnificent –so much so that the time spent by the masons on its construction bankrupted the benefactor. The Abbey Heritage Vaults house a collection of items illustrating the site's history.

In the courtyard (known as Abbey Churchyard) in front of the abbey are the Pump Room (built at the latter end of the eighteenth century) and the Roman Baths. The Roman Museum at the Pump Room houses many of the items found during excavations on the site and elsewhere in the city. Particularly noticeable are the head of Medusa, a stone carving from the Roman Temple, and a bronze head of Minerva. West of here are two of the original baths, the Cross Bath in Bath Street and the Hot Bath.

To the north is the **Theatre Royal**, part of which was once Beau Nash's house, and beyond is Queen Square. This is considered to be one of the best works in the city by John Wood the Elder, who with his son, John the Younger, formed the principal team of architects of the Georgian city that lies to the north of the baths. The obelisk is again a commemoration by Beau Nash, this time of Frederick, Prince of Wales. Running north from the Square is Gay Street built by the Woods. Josiah Wedgwood, the famous pottery manufacturer, lived here at No 30.

At the top of Gay Street is **The Circus**, a magnificent circular street lined with fine buildings by the Woods. Here lived, though not at the same time, William Pitt, Gainsborough and David Livingstone. Just off the Circus, in Bennett Street, the Museum of East Asian Art has a collection of over 500 items from China, Japan, Korea, Thailand and Indonesia. To the east are the Assembly Rooms by Wood the Younger. At the Assembly Rooms is the Museum of Costume, one of the world's largest displays, covering fashion back to medieval times and including exhibitions of jewellery. An extension of the museum that holds the library of books, magazines and photographs of fashion is at No 4 The Circus.

West from the Circus is Brock Street leading to the **Royal Crescent**, perhaps the best known and loved of all Bath's buildings. The Crescent is by John Wood the Younger and is superbly set off by the lawns and trees in front of it. Sir Isaac Pitman lived here, and from here Sheridan eloped with Elizabeth Linley. No. 1 Royal Crescent, owned by the Bath Preservation Trust, has been completely restored to show how an elegant Bath town house would look in the eighteenth century.

William Herschel, an organist, lived in New King Street south of the Royal Crescent: he made telescopes as a hobby and used one to discover the planet Uranus, later becoming Astronomer Royal. His house in New King Street – **Herschel House**, at No 19 – is now a museum of his music and astronomy. It is one of Bath's many museums.

In Manvers Street, near the railway station, a bookselling and binding shop has been extended to form the Book Museum where the history and considerable art of the craft of bookbinding are explained and displayed.

A fascinating addition to Bath's museums is the **Postal Museum** at 8 Broad Street. The city has very strong links with the postal service, and is grateful to it. Ralph Allen, a Cornishman, rented the postal service from the Government in the late seventeenth century and made it efficient and profitable. In the process he became rich, and his arrival in Bath around 1710 was the start of Bath's rise to fame. It was Allen who saw the potential of the hot springs and bought the Combe Down quarries that supplied the stone for his architect, John Wood the Elder, who designed Allen's own house near the abbey. All aspects of the postal service and the Royal Mail are covered in the museum.

The Royal Photographic Society has its **National Centre for Photography** in The Octagon, Milsom Street. It has both an exhibition centre and a museum of photography. In Sydney Place, at the far end of the Great Pulteney Street, is the **Holburne Museum of Art**, part of the University of Bath. This contains the collections of Sir Thomas Holburne: paintings including works by Gainsborough, Stubbs and Reynolds; silver, one of the finest collections in Britain; porcelain and glass; bronzes and enamels. In addition to the set collections, there are special exhibitions during the year, and a Craft Study Centre for modern craftwork in metal and glass. Outside, the gardens are also of interest.

At the other end of the street beyond Pulteney Bridge, the Victoria

Art Gallery houses, in addition to paintings, fine collections of glass and ceramics, and items of local interest. Many times during the year there are special exhibitions covering a range of subjects.

Finally within the city, the **Buildings of Bath Museum** at The Paragon deals with the architectural history of the city.

Away from the city centre there are three further museums. **The Bath Industrial Heritage Centre** (quaintly named Mr Bowler's Business) is at the Camden Works, Julian Street, to the north of the Assembly Rooms. There the visitor can get away from the social elegance of Georgian Bath to discover how the ordinary city dweller lived in the eighteenth and nineteenth centuries. The works themselves are an exact reconstruction of a Victorian brass foundry, with other exhibits illustrating different industries and lifestyles.

About $\frac{1}{2}$ mile north-east of the abbey on the southern bank of the Avon in Forester Road is the **Bath Boathouse**, a near perfect Victorian boathouse where punts can still be hired. For the less skilled there are also skiffs. There are no skills required to see Bath from the basket of a hot-air balloon; flights above the city are available from Heritage Balloons in Pierrepont Street.

The **American Museum** at Claverton Manor two miles east of the city centre, shows the history of North America from the time of the Pilgrim Fathers with period rooms containing fine examples of American furniture. Exhibits deal with the opening of the West and with the Indians, and in the gardens there are several exhibits including a covered wagon. From Beckford Tower, near Lansdown – it contains a museum to William Beckford – there are some outstanding views.

Finally, a bus or taxi is needed to visit Bath's most recently opened attraction, there being no parking at the National Trust's Prior Park.

The eighteenth century garden was landscaped by Capability Brown for Ralph Allen and has typical follies and a lake. The Park has been carefully restored and includes several miles of woodland walking. The views of Bath from the Park are breathtaking and are a fitting way to end this exploration of the Southwolds.

BATH

American Museum
Claverton Manor
Claverton
☎ 01225 460503
Open: Gardens Easter to October, Tuesday-Friday 1-6pm, Saturday and Sunday 2-5pm. Museum Easter to October, Tuesday-Sunday 2-5pm. Also open on Bank Holiday Mondays (11am-5pm) and all Mondays in August. Also open Saturdays and Sundays (1-4pm) from mid-November to early December.

Assembly Rooms and Costume Museum
Bennett Street
☎ 01225 477789
Open: all year, daily 10am-5pm.

Bath Abbey
☎ 01225 330289
Open: all year 9am-6pm but subject to Sunday services. The Heritage Vaults (☎ 01225 422462) are open all year Monday-Saturday 10am-4pm.

Bath Boating Station
Forester Road
☎ 01225 466407
Open: April to September, daily 10am-6pm.

Beckford Tower
Lansdown
☎ 01225 460705
Open: Easter to October, Saturday, Sunday and Bank Holidays 10.30am-5pm

Book Museum
Manvers Street
☎ 01225 466000
Open: all year, Monday-Friday 9am-1pm, 2-5pm, Saturday 9.30am-1pm.

Buildings of Bath Museum
Countess of Huntingdon's Chapel
The Vineyards, The Paragon
☎ 01225 333895
Open: Mid-February to November Tuesday-Sunday and Bank Holiday Mondays 10.30am-5pm.

Costume Fashion Research Centre
4 The Circus
☎ 01225 477752
Open: all year Monday-Friday 10am-12noon, 2-4.30pm. Closed on Bank Holidays.

Georgian Garden
Off Gravel Walk, Royal Victoria Park
☎ 01225 477752
Open: May to October, Monday-Friday 9am-4.30pm.

Guildhall
High Street
☎ 01225 477724
Open: all year, Monday-Friday 8.30am-5.30pm unless being used for a special function.

Herschel House & Museum
19 New King Street
☎ 01225 311342
Open: March to October, daily 2-5pm; November to February, Saturday and Sunday 2-5pm.

Holburne Museum of Art
Great Pulteney Street
☎ 01225 466669
Open: mid-February to mid-December, Monday-Saturday 11am-5pm, Sunday 2.30-5.30pm. Closed on Mondays from November to Easter.

Jane Austen Centre
40 Gay Street
☎ 01225 311342
Open: all year, daily 10am-5pm (opens at 10.30pm on Sundays).

**Mr Bowler's Business
(Museum of Bath at Work)**
Bath Industrial Heritage Centre
Camden Works
Julian Road
☎ 01225 318348
Open: Easter to October, daily 10am-
5pm; November to Easter, Saturday
and Sunday 10am-5pm.

Museum of East Asian Art
12 Bennett Street
☎ 01225 464640
Open: all year Tuesday-Saturday
10am-5pm, Sunday 12noon-5pm.
Also open on Bank Holiday Mondays.

No. 1 Royal Crescent
☎ 01225 428126
Open: Mid-February to October,
Tuesday-Sunday and Bank Holiday
Mondays 10.30am-5pm; November,
Tuesday-Sunday 10.30am-4pm.

Postal Museum
8 Broad Street
☎ 01225 460333
Open: all year, Monday-Saturday
11am-5pm, Sunday 2-5pm.

Prior Park (National Trust)
Ralph Allen Drive
☎ 01985 833422
Open: February to Good Friday,
Wednesday-Monday 12noon-5.30pm
or dusk; Easter Saturday to
Spetember Wednesday-Monday
11am-5.30pm; October and November Wednesday-Monday 12noon-
dusk; Decmber and January Friday-
Sunday 12noon-dusk.
Disabled visitors should ☎ 01225
833422 to reserve one of the three
disabled parking bays. There is no
parking for other visitors who must
arrive by bus or taxi.

Roman Baths & Museum
Pump Room
☎ 01225 477785
Open: April to September, daily 9am-
6pm; October to March, daily 9.30am-
5pm. Torchlight visits in August, daily
8-10pm.

**Royal Photographic Society
National Centre for Photography**
The Octagon
Milsom Street
☎ 01225 462841
Open: all year, daily 9.30am-5.30pm.

**Sally Lunn's House
and Kitchen Museum**
4 North Parade Passage
☎ 01225 461634
Open: all year Museum Monday-
Saturday 10am-6pm, Sunday 12noon-
6pm.Teashop Monday-Saturday 10am-
11pm, Sunday 12noon-11pm.

Victoria Art Gallery
Bridge Street
☎ 01225 477772
Open: all year, Tuesday-Friday 10am-
5.30pm, Saturday 10am-5pm, Sunday
2-5pm. Closed Bank Holidays.

BIDDESTONE

Sheldon Manor
☎ 01249 653120
Open: Easter Day to second Sunday of
October, Thursday, Sunday and Bank
Holidays, 12.30-6pm (House open
from 2pm).

Cold Ashton
Tog Hill Picnic Site
Open: at all reasonable times.

Dyrham Park (National Trust)
☎ 01179 372501
Open: Park all year, daily 12noon-
5.30pm or dusk. House Easter to
October, Friday-Tuesday 12noon-
5.30pm.

Fact File

The information given here and in the Places to Visit at the end of each chapter has been obtained from a number of sources. Admission charges have not been included as they are subject to revision.

ARCHAEOLOGICAL & HISTORICAL SITES

All sites listed below are open at any reasonable time, those with specified opening times are detailed in the Additional Information for the appropriate chapter.

Ablington Long Barrow
near Bibury

Bagendon Earthworks
near Cirencester

Belas Knap Long Barrow (English Heritage)
near Winchcombe

Brackenbury Ditches
near Wotton-under-Edge

The Bulwarks (National Trust)
Minchinhampton Common

Kiftsgate Stone
Above Chipping Campden

Nan Tow's Tump
near Hawkesbury Upton

Notgrove Long Barrow (English Heritage)
Notgrove

Nympsfield Long Barrow (English Heritage)
Coaley Peak Picnic Site

Rollright Stones
near Long Compton

Roman Amphitheatre & Town Wall
Cirencester

Sodbury Hillfort
Above Little Sodbury

Uleybury Hillfort
Above Uley
A large, well protected hillfort, probably the best in the Cotswolds

Uley Tumulus
See Hetty Pegler's Tump

Windmill Tump Long Barrow (English Heritage)
Rodmarton

Brass Rubbings

Many of the churches in the area will allow rubbings to be made (notably Northleach, Tormarton, and Wotton-under-Edge) but permission must be obtained before commencing work.

COTSWOLDS WARDEN SERVICE AND FARM OPEN DAYS

The Cotswold AONB has a Warden Service consisting of both full and part-time wardens. They offer a programme of guided walks and farm open days, and are also on hand at some places of interest mentioned above to offer help and information. They also assist in the up-keep of footpaths. Details of all warden services are available from:

Gloucestershire County Council
Planning Department
Shire Hall
Bearland
Gloucester GL1 2TH
☎ 01452 425500
SAE appreciated. Details of the
programme of open days are
also available in local libraries.

CRAFT & ART CENTRES

Many of the towns and villages of Shakespeare Country and the Cotswolds have thriving craft centres and art galleries. Details of the main ones are given in the Additional Information at the end of each chapter, but there are many other smaller ones which are worth visiting.

Bath
Bath has a very large number of excellent galleries covering all media and all periods. The local tourist office has details.

Chipping Campden
Guild of Handicrafts active at several places in the town.

Painswick
August, Annual Exhibition of Guild of Gloucester Craftsmen.
Sudeley Castle
The Cotswold Craft Show is held here annually in the summer.

NATURE RESERVES

There are many nature reserves within the Cotswolds area, some with associated nature trails. Other sites may be visited by permit. Full details are available from:

Gloucestershire Wildlife Trust
Dulverton Buildings,
Robinswood Hill Country Park,
Reservoir Road,
Gloucester
☎ 01452 383333

Wiltshire Trust for Nature Conservation
19 High Street, Devizes
☎ 01380 725670

Avon Wildlife Trust
32 Jacobs Wells Road, Bristol
☎ 0117 909 6693

OPENING TIMES

The details given in the Additional Information are correct at the time of publication, but are also subject to revision and should be checked beforehand if there is any doubt. This is particularly true for opening times at Bank Holidays. Most of the sites listed close at Christmas and New Year, but are open at Easter and all other Bank Holidays. This is not true of all sites, and there are changes from year to year.

SPORTS

Boating
Canal boats may be hired from points along the northern Avon, at Tewkesbury, Bredon and Stratford for example, to explore the river and the canal system around it. Boats may also be hired for outings on the Avon at Bath and other points along its length, and at Lechlade and nearby for the River Thames.

Cycling
Warwickshire and the Cotswolds makes an excellent centre for cycling and those who do not wish to bring their own cycles may hire them at many of the bigger towns. A full list of hire facilities for each season is available from tourist information centres.

Fishing
The rivers leading down to the Thames valley offer very good trout fishing, as do the reservoirs to the west of Bath. Elsewhere in the area there is good coarse fishing. All fishing is controlled by private owners or clubs, but permits can be arranged at some local hotels or by contacting club secretaries direct. Fishing is also available at the Cotswold Water Park, South Cerney, at several of the trout

farms, and at Aston Magna Pool near Moreton-in-Marsh (day-permits available from the Batsford Estate Office).

Gliding

Gliding courses are available from the Bristol and Gloucestershire Gliding Club at Frocester Hill, Nympsfield, near Stonehouse ☎ 01453 860342.

Golf

Bath Golf Club
Sham Castle
☎ 01225 425182/463834

Broadway Golf Course
Willersley Hill
☎ 01386 853683

Burford Golf Club
☎ 01993 822149

Chipping Sodbury Golf Club
Horton Road
☎ 01454 319042/315822

Cirencester Golf Course
Cheltenham Road,
Bagendon
☎ 01285 653939

Cleeve Hill Golf Course
Cleeve Hill
☎ 01242 672025

Cotswold Edge Golf Club
Wotton-under-Edge
☎ 01453 844167/843530/
844398/845120

Cotswold Hills Golf Course
Ullenwood
☎ 01242 515264/515263

Cotswold Water Park (9 hole)
☎ 01666 577995

Gloucester Golf Club
Matson Lane
☎ 01452 411331

Lansdown Golf Club
Lansdown
☎ 01225 422138/425007

Lilley Brook Golf Course
Charlton Kings
☎ 01242 526785

Minchinhampton Old Course
Minchinhampton
☎ 01453 832642

Minchinhampton New Course
Minchinhampton
☎ 01453 833866/837351/
837355

Naunton Downs Golf Course
Stow Road
Naunton
☎ 01451 850090

Painswick Golf Course
Painswick
☎ 01452 812180

Puckrup Hall
Nr Tewkesbury
☎ 01684 296200

Rodway Hill (9 hole)
Higham
Gloucester
☎ 01452 384222

Sherdons Golf Centre
Manor Farm, Tredington
Tewkesbury
☎ 01684 274782

Fact File

Shipton Golf Course (9 hole)
Northfield
Andoversford
☎ 01242 890237

Stinchcombe Hill Golf Course
Stinchcombe Hill
☎ 01453 542015

Streamleaze Golf Club (9 hole)
Canons Court Farm
Bradley Green, Wotton-under-
Edge
☎ 01453 843128

Tewkesbury Park Hotel
Lincoln Green Lane
☎ 01684 295405

Riding

Neither Warwickshire nor the Cotswolds is a centre for pony trek-king as there is only a limited amount of common land. There are, however, a number of excellent riding schools within the area.

Skiing

At Robinswood Hill, near Gloucester, is England's longest dry ski run. Courses are available at all levels. Experienced visitors can use the slope. Equipment available for hire, but gloves are essential. ☎ 01452 414300 open all year Monday-Friday 10am-10pm, Saturday and Sunday 10am-6pm.

Spectator Sports

Gloucester County Cricket Club play matches at Bristol, Cheltenham and Gloucester, with very occasional matches at Moreton-in-the-Marsh. Both Gloucester, Cheltenham and Bath have excellent Rugby teams.

There is horse racing at Warwick, Cheltenham – the Gold Cup meeting is in March – and at the Lansdown Race Course, Bath. There are also numerous point-to-point meetings in the area, most notably at Stow and Broadway in April, and Woodford near Dursley in May. Lovers of equestrian events will need little introduction to the Badminton Three-Day Event in April, and the polo matches at Cirencester Park on Sundays throughout the summer.

At Castle Combe the racing circuit is used about four times annually for car racing while the Prescott hill-climbs, near Cheltenham, are held about three times each year. The foremost Prescott meet is the vintage car event in August.
Motor cycle scramble meets are held at a variety of places through-out the year.

Swimming Pools

Bath
Beau Street
☎ 01225 425594

Bath Street
☎ 01225 425321

Bristol
Many within the city

Cheltenham
Sandford Park
☎ 01242 524430

Tommy Taylor's Lane
☎ 01242 528764

Cirencester
Outdoor at Cecily Hill
☎ 01285 653947

Indoor at Tetbury Road
☎ 01285 654057

Gloucester
The Leisure Centre
☎ 01452 306498

Stroud
Indoor and outdoor at the Leisure Centre
Stratford Park,
☎ 01453 766771

Tewkesbury
Ashchurch Road
☎ 01684 293953

Wotton-under-Edge
Symn Lane
☎ 01453 842086

Sports Centres

Bath
Sports and Leisure Centre
North Parade Road
☎ 01225 462563/462565

Bristol
Several in the city

Cheltenham
Several in the city

Cirencester
Tetbury Road
☎ 01285 654057

Gloucester
Several in the city

Stroud
Stratford Park
☎ 01453 766771

Tewkesbury
Ashchurch Road
☎ 01684 293953

Water Sports

Cotswold Water Park
South Cerney
near Cirencester
☎ 01285 861816

Country Park and Windsurfing
Club open all year.
Coarse Fishing: 16 June-17 March.
Children's Beach: June-September.
Day tickets are available for visitors who wish to bring their own craft rather than hire. There are extensive hire facilities for all kinds of craft.

TOURIST INFORMATION OFFICES

The majority of the Cotswolds falls within the area of the Heart of England Tourist Board, whose main office is at:

The Heart of England Tourist Board
Larkhill Road
Worcester WR5 2EW
☎ 01905 763436

Other offices which are open all year can be found at:

Bath
Abbey Chambers
Abbey Churchyard
Bath BA1 1LY
☎ 01225 4477101

Burford
The Brewery
Sheep Street
Burford OX18 4LP
☎ 01993 823558

Cheltenham
Municipal Offices
77 The Promenade
Cheltenham GL50 1PP
☎ 01242 522878

Cirencester
The Corn Hall
Market Place
Cirencester GL7 2NW
☎ 01285 654180

Gloucester
28 Southgate Street
Gloucester GL1 1PD
Kenilworth
☎ 01452 421188

The Library
11 Smalley Place
Kenilworth CV8 1QG
☎ 01926 852595

Stow-on-the-Wold
Hollis House
The Square
Stow-on-the-Wold GL54 1AF
☎ 01451 831082

Stratford-upon-Avon
Bridgefoot
Stratford-upon-Avon CV37 6GW
☎ 01789 293127

Stroud
Subscription Rooms
George Street
Stroud GL5 1AE
☎ 01453 765768

Tewkesbury
The Museum
64 Barton Street
Tewkesbury GL20 5PX
☎ 01684 295027

Warwick
The Court House
Jury Street
Warwick CV34 4EW
☎ 01926 492212

TRAVEL & ACCOMMODATION

With the M5 motorway in the Severn Vale to the west, and the M4 motorway cutting it in the south, together with major roads linking it to all the surrounding areas, the Cotswolds AONB is one of the easiest of tourist areas to reach. There are also good rail services to the larger towns.

Within the area the bus services are adequate, though typically country. Information on the services is available from the bus stations in the larger towns. The Cotswolds offers a wide variety of accommodation, hotels, guest houses, bed and breakfast, as well as camping and caravanning sites. A publication, Where to Stay in The Heart of England, is available from tourist information centres.

VIEWPOINTS & SHORT WALKS

Barrow Wake
Geological dial above Witcombe

Cleeve Common
near Cheltenham
Highest point of Cotswolds,
panorama dial

Dover's Hill
Above Chipping Campden,
panorama dial

Frocester Hill
Coaley Peak picnic site,
panorama dial

Haresfield Beacon
Above Haresfield
Topograph on nearby point (near Standish Wood).

Kilkenny Viewpoint
near Andoversford

Leckhampton Hill & Charlton Kings Common
Above Leckhampton

Penn Hill
Above Weston, near Bath

Prospect Stile
Lansdown Racecourse, near Bath

WALKING

In addition to the walks described in the book the visitor might like to join a walk organised by the Warden Service of the Cotswold AONB and led by one of their number. Details of the walks programme for each of the four areas of the Cotswold covered by the service (north, central, south and Avon valley) can be obtained from local libraries, or by sending a stamped addressed envelope to:

Gloucestershire County Council
Planning Department
Shire Hall
Bearland
Gloucester GL1 2TH
☎ 01452 425500

Within the area the towns of Gloucester, Cheltenham and Burford offer guided walks around the main sites of interest, and further towns are expected to follow their lead. The tourist information offices will supply details of the year's programmes.

There are three long-distance footpaths that have sections within the AONB:

The Cotswold Way is entirely within the area. It is 100 miles long and follows the escarpment closely from Chipping Campden to Bath.

The Heart of England Way is a 100 mile path linking Bourton-on-the-Water with Milford on the edge of Cannock Chase. The walk passes through Lower Slaughter, the Swells, Bourton-on-the-Hill and Chipping Campden.

The Oxfordshire Way is a 60-mile path linking Bourton-on-the-Water with the Chilterns.

FESTIVALS

There are numerous village and town festivals throughout the year, but the following are the most famous or unusual.

Bath
The Literature Festival is held in late February, and the International Music Festival in late May.

Bisley
The village's seven wells are dressed on Ascension Day.

Cheltenham
The Music Festival is held in July, the Literature Festival in October. There is now also a Jazz Festival which, it is hoped, will become an annual event in April. The National Hunt Festival (including the Gold Cup and Champion Hurdle) is held in March.

Cooper's Hill, near Painswick
On the evening of Spring Bank Holiday Monday, the famous cheese rolling event takes place here.

Dover's Hill, Chipping Campden
Robert Dover's Olympick Games are held on the hill on the Friday of the last weekend in May. On the Saturday the Scuttlebrook Wake fair is held in the village.

Marshfield
The village Mummers perform their outdoor play on Boxing Day.

Fact File

Painswick
In September the church is circled by the village children, linking hands in the famous 'clipping' ceremony.

Stratford-upon-Avon
The Shakespeare Procession is held on the bard's birthday (23 April). There is also a Mop fair in October. The origin of the fair's name is not understood, but is characteristic of fairs in Warwickshire and, strangely, in north Wiltshire.

Sudeley Castle, Winchcombe
The Cotswold Craft Fair is held here in the summer.

Tetbury
On Spring Bank Holiday Monday the 'World Championship' woolsack races are run between relay teams of four runners who carry a 30kg woolsack up and down the 1 in 4 Gumstool Hill. It is a moot point whether the downhill legs, where the runners tend to over-balance, are more or less difficult than the uphill legs. They are certainly more dangerous. The event is traditionally opened by the Norfolk Mountain Rescue 'A' Team (!) who race unicycles down the hill while carrying the same woolsacks. There is also a street fair.

Warwick
The Warwick and Leamington Music and Drama Festival is held in July, and the town's Mop Fair is held in October.

INDEX

Published in the UK by
Landmark Publishing Ltd,
Ashbourne Hall, Cokayne Ave, Ashbourne, Derbyshire DE6 1EJ England
Tel: (01335) 347349 Fax: (01335) 347303 e-mail: sales@landmarkpublishing.co.uk
website: www.landmarkpublishing.co.uk

3rd Edition 2004
ISBN: 1-84306-101-5

Print: Gutenberg Press Ltd, Malta
Design: Mark Titterton
Cartography: Mick Usher

Front cover: Castle Combe
Back cover, top: Awkward Hill, Bilbury
Back cover, bottom: Holy Trinity Chapel, Stratford